GREEN ORANGES ON LION MOUNTAIN

BY EMILY JOY

eye books

Challenging the way we see things

This Eye Classics edition first published in Great Britain in 2010, by:
Eye Books
7 Peacock Yard
Iliffe Street
London
SE17 3LH
www.eye-books.com

First published in Great Britain in 2004
Previously published as *What For Chop Today*

Cover design by Jim Shannon/Emily Atkins
Text layout by Helen Steer

British Library Cataloguing in Publication Data
A catalogue record for this book is available from the British Library

ISBN: 978-1-903070-73-4

*Some of the names in this book have been changed to protect some
individuals' identity.*

Karin, Zietje and Eelco Krijn

Father Felim McAllister

On 12th March 1994 Felim, Eelco, Karin and three year old Zietje were killed by rebels as they evacuated Panguma Hospital.

Dr. Eelco and his family were just coming to the end of their three year placement at Panguma and Father Felim had been Panguma's parish priest for over twenty-five years. They all loved Sierra Leone. This book is written in their memory and all the other unnamed souls who lost their lives in Sierra Leone's dreadful civil war.

ACKNOWLEDGEMENTS

My thanks to the people of Salone who were so welcoming and boosted my faith in human nature despite some appalling circumstances. I can't mention everyone, but I do have to thank Pa George, just for being himself. I met some of the best nurses in the world in Sierra Leone. In particular I'd like to thank Tiange and Alhusan (who taught me how to do surgery), Roberta (for her online real-time course in obstetric disasters), Sai Conteh (who kept my patients alive during the operations) and the marvellous Betty Sam for all her good sense, wisdom and kind heart. The Community Health Officers are now the lynchpin of medical care in Sierra Leone and Mohamed was a fantastic example of the enthusiasm and can-do attitude of this new breed of super-paramedic.

Voluntary Service Overseas gave me an amazing life experience but I would never have stuck it out without the support of my fellow volunteers, especially Alan O'Connor and Paul Weinberger. Thanks must also go to the Sisters and Fathers, in particular to Margaret Brennan and Pete Queally for their kindness and Hilary Lyons for her inspiration. Richard, Nick and Gladys in the VSO field office did their best to keep us safe and sane in difficult circumstances, despite all our complaints!

For my recent trips I'd like to thank Richard Kerr-Wilson from the Kambia Appeal for making it possible for me (and my family!) to keep my promise to return to Salone, and to Moses and Charles for looking after us so well when we got there.

Back in Serabu, I have to thank Fathers John Sandi and Sylvester Swaray for their hospitality and tireless work to rebuild the hospital and community. Royalties from this book are to try and help Serabu and Kambia in a small way.

None of it would have been possible without Terry's advice support and patience. He also gets 10/10 for agreeing to our six weeks in Salone en famille in 2008, and 11/10 for looking after the troops so I could go again in 2009. On the writing front, my biological Pa George rescued me from the worst of my grammatical faux pas. Finally I'd like to thank Dan and Helen at Eye Books for giving me another bite of the banana.

And of course big kisses to Craig, Paul and Kristin. They were such troopers in Salone.

CONTENTS

MAP OF SIERRA LEONE

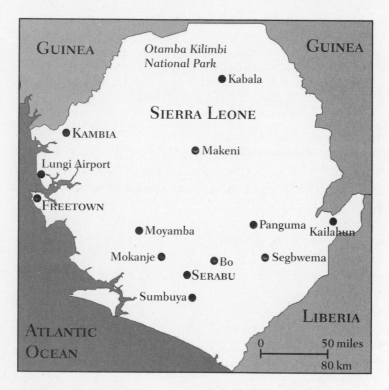

Sierra Leone 1990
Population: 4 million
Life expectancy: 42
Under-five mortality: 20%
Literacy: 17%
HIV infection rate: 3%
UN Human Development
Index: bottom

Sierra Leone 2009
Population: 6.2 million
Life expectancy: 41.8
Under-five mortality: 20%
Literacy: 35%
HIV infection rate: 7%
UN Human Development
Index: 3rd from bottom

PROLOGUE – 2008

"Are we nearly there yet?"

"Ella! Shh!" echoed the boys, their faces shiny red and orange after eight hours of dust and sunshine pouring through the windows. My family definitely had more right to be cross at their mother than vice versa.

"Yes," I said, suddenly feeling quite choked. "We're nearly there."

"There it is! Serabu!" yelped Frankie, pointing at a sign saying Southern Eye Clinic, Serabu. I frowned a little. This didn't look like the Junction – no shacks, or traders, or people. The sign made no mention of the hospital.

We turned down a road, so overgrown and furrowed that it was hard to believe that anyone travelled here anymore. Art, our eleven year-old official trip photographer, took shots of palm and banana trees and the occasional burnt out building that dotted the route down the hill onto the main street.

"Is this it, Mum?" asked Frankie.

"I... think so..." I looked out of the Landrover window at the rebuilt houses, the shiny new Eye Clinic and the street-side stalls. The stalls seemed more numerous than before, and had added mobile phone scratch cards, dresses and flip flops to the more usual wares of little piles of chillies, rice and Maggi cubes. But where were the customers? At least I recognized the church. Jesus was extending his arms in welcome, with yellow flowers at his feet. The rebels hadn't touched Jesus – the first sign that they had known any limits at all.

"This is your dream come true, isn't it Mummy?" said Ella. Gosh, what a strange thing for a six year old to say. Had I said that? Fairy-tale terminology for a fantasy promise that you never really expected to become reality.

A new school, painted bright yellow and blue, had appeared in the patch of land between the church and the hospital. Beyond the school were the concrete walls that now surrounded the New Serabu Hospital. I didn't like the walls.

Father Jabati met us at the gates. "Dr. Em, Mr-Dr-Em and the children! Welcome home!"

Surgery for Non-Surgeons

"And the Golden Rule, Dr. Joy?"

"Where there's pus, let it out."

"Exactly. So if you learn nothing else…" Mr. Lord stared down at the cat's cradle of sutures imprisoning my stubby fingers.

"Remember never, EVER, sew up an infected wound. Especially in a hot climate. The rest is in here – twenty years of African experience." He thumped a tome the size of the Glasgow yellow pages. "Maurice King's *Primary Surgery*. Everything you need to know from lancing boils to amputating legs."

What? Surely no one would seriously expect me to amputate a leg? Fortunately the phone rang, rescuing us from further insights into the alarming contents of the DIY surgery book.

"Lord."

"Mr. Lord, this is really too much" shrieked an irate female voice, "There's been a delivery to Casualty. From your butcher!"

Mr. Lord held the handset at arm's length. "Indeed?"

"It's dribbling something unspeakable all over my desk!"

"We'll be right there. So, class," He grinned. "Time for our practical."

Mr. Lord marched briskly down the corridor, his moccasins making no noise on the shiny white tiles. My friend Morag (slim, pretty, crisply ironed, compassionate, steady, able, hardworking, serene, professional and if that wasn't bad enough, ever so nice too) glided beside him. I trudged behind, wondering if Voluntary Service Overseas actually believed we could be turned into surgeons in a week?

"I believe you have something for me?" Mr. Lord beamed at the middle-aged receptionist. She thrust a Marks and Spencer's carrier bag over the counter.

"Much obliged." He turned back to us. "Let's practice our bowel anastomoses."

Morag and I exchanged horrified glances. Mr. Lord was talking about major abdominal surgery.

"This way." He held open the swing door opposite. "The plaster room appears to be free."

"Mr. Lord." The receptionist peered over her glasses.

"Yes?"

"You're dripping."

Once inside, Mr. Lord released a tangle of sheep's bowels, letting them slither onto a metal tray. "My butcher is always most cooperative."

We gaped. "Come, come, no time to lose. Trouble with your gloves, Dr. Joy?"

Mr. Lord handed me ten feet of clammy intestines just as I was trying to free my middle finger from the index finger-hole. His slimy offering sloshed faecal fluid across my newly laundered white coat.

"Hold the ends up, woman. Are you trying to give your patient peritonitis?"

Gulping back my nausea, I set to work on the sheep's innards while Mr. Lord paced behind us. "Let us pretend that the middle foot is dead bowel that you have just released from a strangulated hernia. Smooth away the bowel contents back to healthy tissue. Good. Double clamp either end…"

What would VSO say if I wimped out now? Even worse, what would Morag say? It would mean she would have to go to Zambia on her own, but really, I wasn't up to this.

"Dr. Joy, are you concentrating?"

"What? Yes, of course Mr. Lord."

Ten minutes later, I knotted off my final stitch. Morag's intestines were already neatly arranged on the tray.

"So. The moment of truth is upon us." Mr. Lord declared with relish. "Have you saved your patient's life? Will your anastomoses allow the bowel contents to pass freely without leakage? Undo your clamps!"

We gingerly released the clamps that had held back the intestinal juices from our newly stitched anastomoses.

"Hold up your intestines to test the join. Good, Dr. MacDonald, absolutely watertight, excellent… Oh dear, Dr. Joy."

Faecal fluid oozed between my stitches and dripped onto the table.

I couldn't do it. Well honestly, even with Morag holding my hand, how was I ever going survive two years running a hospital in the back of beyond?

So while Morag packed her bags for Zambia, I returned to verrucas, colds, bad backs and enough marital misery to convince me that being single was probably a blessing. In fact I turned out to be quite a good doctor, but I couldn't stop dreaming of the world beyond my cosy backstreet surgery. One day, after hearing about Mrs Jones' twenty-two separate symptoms, followed by a drug addict calling me a fucking cow for not replacing his methadone script that had allegedly been eaten by his dog, I finally decided I had had enough. I picked up the phone to the VSO Postings Officer. Surprisingly, prior cowardice was no barrier to future employment.

"Excellent, we need a Doc in Sierra Leone."

South America, how exotic! My atlas index sent me to page 36 – Africa? And sure enough, there it was – Sierra Leone, a country the size of Ireland on Africa's western bulge, sandwiched between Liberia and Guinea. I had heard of Liberia, thanks to an unpleasant sounding civil war a couple of months back. Hmmm, civil war a hundred miles from my new home didn't sound too good. Still, there'd been no recent media attention and no news was hopefully good news.

The details of Serabu Catholic Mission Hospital fell through my letter box the next morning along with a four-page resume of Sierra Leone. The name came from an intrepid Portuguese seafarer, Pedra da Cinta, who had spotted the mountainous Freetown peninsula jutting out into the Atlantic Ocean in 1460 and called it Serra Lyoa – lion mountain.

Over the next few hundred years various Europeans passed through, largely to pick up ivory or slaves until some spoilsport banned slavery in 1807. However the British government couldn't allow ex-slaves to mix with polite white society, so decided to ship them all 'home', although virtually none had originated from Sierra Leone. These British slaves were destined for the euphemistically named Freetown (the Americans had a similar idea and called Sierra Leone's neighbour, Liberia). Most of the early shipments died – those that disease spared were killed off by the indigenous Africans.

Undeterred, the British Government tried to mould the survivors who had no common language or culture into a homogenous Christian community – the Freetown Krios. The rest of the country was labelled a 'Protectorate'. I think that meant that the gold, diamonds, rutile (used for white paint and the coverings of space ships), aluminium bauxite, palm oil (used in making the original Palmolive soap) and piassava (used for the bristles in sweeping brushes) were protected for the exploitation of the British, but history is rarely the strong point of we scientific types. Admittedly railways, power stations, hospitals and telephone lines were built in exchange for removing the aforesaid goods (or in order to remove them more efficiently). We British even set up black Africa's first institute of higher learning, Fourah Bay College, to turn the Krios into teachers and missionaries.

By 1961, the British were washing their hands of the colonies and handed Sierra Leone over to Sir Milton Margai, a former doctor (should have been a good bloke then). Unfortunately the reins of power were soon seized by one Siaka Stevens.

Siaka Stevens and his Swiss bank account did very nicely. So nicely that there was not a single railway line, power station or up-country telephone remaining when he retired thirty years later. Nor was there any opposition (opposition having been conveniently outlawed, murdered or executed) to his handpicked successor, Major General Momoh, commander of the armed forces.

Momoh made his own fortune from the British, the Lebanese and various others with rich pale skins, by coming to an agreement whereby they could help themselves to the gold, and the diamonds and the rutile and the bauxite, without having to worry too much about little inconveniences like tax. Meanwhile the sixteen tribes that made up the four million strong population of Sierra Leone continued to scrape an existence off the land.

Sierra Leone's only claim to fame seemed to be that Graham

Greene had once stayed in Freetown and written *The Heart of the Matter* about the British colonial days, when Sierra Leone was known as 'White Man's Grave' – largely due to the particularly lethal falciparum malaria.

White Man's Grave rather missed the point if you looked at the statistics for the indigenous population. With a life expectancy of 42 and an under-five-mortality of 20% (the world's second worst), the black men, women and particularly children were filling graves much faster than their expatriate counterparts but who cared about them?

That was where I came in. I would care. I would make a difference. I would change those statistics....

Five months later, I was sitting on the toilet at Gatwick Airport opening a bag of Maltesers. I popped a couple in my mouth and leaned against the cistern to stare at The Pregnancy Advisory Service number. Not that I was ever likely to need their services. 'Finding a man' was on my list of goals – after saving the world, saving lives and saving my soul. And losing weight. Four more Maltesers followed their siblings.

Hiding in the Ladies to avoid check-in didn't say much for the state of my soul and with only two blokes in our group (a little Cockney mechanic and a married man pushing fifty with a wooden leg) finding a man had to be easier in Dunblane.

That left saving the world (always a bit unrealistic) and saving lives (not likely after the Surgery for Non-Surgeons course). I stuffed a handful of Maltesers in and crunched. Although I wore a mantle of sunny optimism, my robust exterior and endless jollity belied my lack of self-confidence but then, of course, all extroverts claim to be shy. People my size, with the voice to match, are not allowed to be vulnerable.

My voice. Ughh, now there was a thing. Too loud and too English. How I longed for a soft Scottish burr like Morag's. I had spent six years at Dunblane High School and six years at Edinburgh University, declaring that I was a real Scot. It wasn't my fault that I had spent my pre-school years as an Air Force daughter (until my father crashed his plane into a water buffalo which inconsiderately ambled across the runway). With this hereditary tendency for embarrassing disasters, why was I setting myself up for more?

"OK, Em. You don't have to go." I was right, I didn't. I hadn't checked in and could easily sneak off before my VSO compatriots even knew I'd arrived. There were other ways of achieving my goals. I could go on a diet, for instance. Hell's bells, I could even start going to church!

I rummaged around in the bottom of the bag of Maltesers to find only a single osteoporotic crumb of honeycomb. Pathetic. I crumpled the bag and was about to sling it on the floor when my middle-class upbringing got the better of me. I was not a mere smoker who indulged her habit in the toilets and threw her butts in the pan. I was a chocolate eater and we were surely a better breed of addict. I put the wrapper in the sanitary disposal unit and sighed. Time to make a move.

I kicked my rucksacks, crammed with Tampax, rubber gloves and of course *Primary Surgery*, out of the cubicle. The choice between the rubber gloves and a pile of rubbishy best-sellers had been a difficult one, but AIDS mania filled the tabloid and medical press at that time, and Africa's figures were alarming. Catching HIV from a patient during surgery seemed a cruel reward for attempting to save the world. Another good reason for staying at home.

Turning the cold tap full on, I washed my face under the washbasin mirror. My usually warm brown eyes frowned back accusingly, puckering my neat nose and cupid's bow mouth. Perhaps the straight dark bob with Cleopatra fringe didn't flatter my square face and perhaps if I ever tried a little makeup? Still, I looked quite young for twenty-seven – a sturdy example of a female Homo Sapiens, built to withstand the rigours of Africa. Nice teeth too, I was told. I smiled to reveal my best feature. All the better for eating with.

"Hi, Emily, you're here!" I jumped. Lindsey dropped her bags next to mine and threw her arms round me. "The others are all checking in. They thought you'd wimped out!"

"No way!" I laughed. "Not me!"

"That's what I said," Lindsey giggled in a lovely Scottish lilt that I would have killed for. It was hard to imagine a more unlikely librarian. "Wait for me, would you? This is the fourth time I've been. I'm so excited!"

I watched Lindsey's svelte figure slip into my cubicle then cursed at the mirror.

Positive thinking. That was the trick. Visualise yourself as you want to be and it will be so. I closed my eyes to imagine my metamorphosis, two years hence.

There I was, slim and glamorous, an accomplished surgeon, stepping off the plane on the arm of a handsome diplomat, my friends gaping at the swan before them....

"Dream on." I stuck my tongue out at my reflection "Just try to survive two years without killing too many patients or sticking yourself with an AIDS-infected needle."

At least there was still time to buy another bag of Maltesers.

We exited the Ladies, arms linked, and spotted our fellow VSOs standing in line at the Freetown check-in desk, each accompanied by matching bulging rucksacks.

"Kushe everyone!" I waved over-enthusiastically.

"Hey, it's the Doc! Told you she'd show up eventually." Klaus waved back. Good Lord! What had happened to his hair? People called Klaus really shouldn't have a skin-head.

Klaus was the Cockney mechanic, despite the name bequeathed by a German father. He was a thirty-year-old ex-rigger, who had worked in Saudi and the North Sea, before adding Sierra Leone to his rather dubious list of workplaces. Half the size of my idea of a rigger, he seemed even shorter with no hair.

"Klaus! Love the hairdo!" I rubbed his shorn head. Neo-Nazi or Buddhist monk, it would undoubtedly prove cooler than my bob.

"So, Doc!" Mike with the wooden leg appeared and put his arm around me. "You didn't abandon us?"

"Would I do that?"

"Course not, we need you to tend to all our ailments," winked Mike. "Glad you're here too, mate." Mike thumped Klaus on the back. "Rescue me from all these women, eh?" Mike's much younger wife smiled indulgently beside him.

"Pity we're posted miles away from the delectable Lindsey." Klaus nudged Lindsey's shoulder. Lindsey tucked a wayward brown curl under the twist of multicoloured material holding her fringe off her forehead, and stuck up two fingers.

"Good odds though, Klaus. Seven to two!"

"Six to one," corrected his wife.

"Of course darling."

"Six to one, and take a look at the one!" I thought, eyeing Klaus unkindly before adding out loud. "So tell me, Mike, what's with all this extra luggage?" I looked down at his two large rucksacks, plus a three-foot oblong box.

"My spare leg."

"Of course."

"In case this one gets eaten by termites."

"A hazard of wooden legs, I suppose."

"Not with my high-tensile graphite number. Look." Mike hoisted his trouser leg and unstrapped his leg as the queue shuffled forwards around us. "No termites are likely to get this boy."

"It's so light!"

"Shhh! I claimed an extra twenty kilos," Mike whispered. "And since good old VSO is too PC to quibble with poor disabled me, there's lots of extra books and sweeties for us!"

"You are defrauding VSO of valuable funds," a high-pitched Home Counties voice cut in. Susan was a medical secretary who would be teaching typing to Salonean college girls. Unlike the rest of us who all wore light cotton trousers and a T-shirt, she was dressed thirty years out of her time, in a brown corduroy skirt, brown jersey and high-necked lacy blouse, set off by delicate pearl earrings nestling in short blonde curls. "Funds that could be better spent on the Africans we are trying to help."

"Oh Susan," Lindsey sighed. Mike just laughed and strapped his leg back on.

"So, girls." Lindsey changed the subject. "How did you fit two years' Tampax into your bags?"

"Left everything else at home."

"Won't it be the rainy season when we arrive?"

"Ye-es?" Lindsey furrowed her brow. "Why so concerned, Susan?"

"What will happen to all the Tampax if our rucksacks get wet?"

We collapsed in giggles at Susan's face and the vision of hundreds of expanding tampons bursting out of our bags.

Keen to thwart any potential VSO uprising, the customs men pulled

Susan aside and started rummaging through all her Tampax. They obviously didn't believe anyone could look so innocent. Whilst Susan blushed, the Neo-Nazi mechanic popped his bag onto the conveyor, where it slid unobserved past the TV monitor displaying spanners, monkey-wrenches and all manner of other lethal weapons.

"What have you got in there?" I asked as Klaus swung his bag off the conveyor belt as easily as if it contained a mere change of underwear.

"Tools of the trade. Haven't you brought a set of surgical instruments or something?"

"Only rubber gloves. I can't equip an entire hospital in twenty-five kilos."

"What happens if I need my appendix out, then?"

"I'll use your monkey wrench."

"Ouch," Klaus winced. "So, two years in White Man's Grave, eh?"

"Have you been reading *The Heart of the Matter*?"

"Yeah, what was VSO thinking, putting Graham Greene on the reading list? Let's call it Lion Mountain instead."

"Lion Mountains," Klaus corrected. "Serra Lyoa is plural."

"Smartarse."

"But I agree, Lion Mountain is more romantic."

I smiled. Perhaps Klaus was all right, small, but perfectly formed, and after all, hair grows.

I had done it now. I was actually on my way to Sierra Leone. I needed a chocolate fix so pulled the family size bag of Maltesers from the sick-bag holder and tugged it open. The bag split and Maltesers danced away under the seats.

"Oh no," I wailed, watching the chocolate marbles roll down the gangway of the climbing aircraft.

"Never mind, Doc," said Klaus. "You can have one of my Minstrels once we've finished our ascent."

"That long!"

"Ingrate!"

"I suppose I'll manage ten more minutes." I gripped the armrests instead.

"A big strong girl like you scared of flying?"

"No. Scared of two years alone in the wilderness."

"You'll be fine. A big…"

"Strong girl like me?" I glared at him.

"Yeah. At least we've got a fortnight's Krio lessons before they dispatch us to fend for ourselves up-country. Look." Klaus nudged me. "Drinks already. Fancy a beer?"

"No thanks! I don't like beer. I'll have Drambuie."

"Yugh!"

"It'll go well with those Minstrels…"

"Okay, okay." Klaus pulled his rucksack from under the seat in front.

"Thanks." I reached over to pluck a Minstrel from his bag and spilled my Drambuie over his leg.

"Sorry, sorry!" I frantically rubbed Klaus' sticky thigh with my sleeve, but only succeeded in knocking his beer into his lap. He adjusted himself a little in his seat. "Oh, no. I'm sorry. I'll…"

"Leave it," he sighed. "I hear beer is a good mosquito repellent."

"But mosquitoes probably love Drambuie. Sorry."

"I won't smell so sweet for a long time. Stop saying sorry."

"Sorry."

"For heavens sake, have another Minstrel."

"You've only got one left." I looked pleadingly at him.

"Eat it. It looks like your need is greater than mine. Besides, I've got another packet. In fact, why don't you take that too?"

"Really?" Klaus shot up in my estimation.

"Really, but only if you promise to save them for Serabu."

And he gave me his very last bit of chocolate for two years. I instantly forgave him his haircut and all comments about big strong girls.

ARRIVAL ON LION MOUNTAIN

The VSO office sat huddled in concrete, two floors above the Red Cross, just off Siaka Stevens' Street in the throbbing heart of Freetown. Not a place to linger.

The British High Commissioner certainly didn't hang around, keeping his pep talk focused on the perils of having relationships with or, God forbid, marrying the locals. He wasted no time in asking about our jobs, destinations or worries, as obviously British High Commissioners have much better things to do. After a curt goodbye, he tippety-tapped down the staircase, past the Red Cross office and pushed his way through a crowd of Liberian refugees to head straight for his shiny, air-conditioned car. There were no windows in the VSO office, but we watched him through the latticed brickwork that allowed a little air to circulate.

Mike found it all very amusing, but then he was a seasoned Aid Worker who had already spent a number of years overseas. Wooden leg or not, he was unlikely to have problems. Mike told us the two main reasons for volunteers being med-evacced were motorcycle accidents (not a problem for me, I wasn't going on any motorbike) or psycho-vaccs. Well, nervous breakdowns weren't my style either. After all I was a stable sort of character, wasn't I?

Of course anybody could be stable when they'd had an easy life like mine: never abused or raped, no major bereavements, no ghastly relationship breakdowns, and even my parents were still married to each other. A spoilt only child with a cushy, middle class upbringing; that was me. I had no excuse to be anything but an optimist. And now it was payback time. Help!

"He's totally ignoring all those refugees," Susan sniffed as the British High Commissioner's chauffeur shut him into his cool oasis, closing the passenger door on the smelly, noisy humidity of downtown Freetown.

"What can he do, Susan?" asked Mike.

"He's the High Commissioner, he should help them."

"How, Susan?" pressed Klaus, ever the realist. "He's not responsible for Liberia, and besides he's only in Salone for decoration. The Foreign Office is hardly likely to send its leading lights here."

"Apparently he's been relocated from Outer Mongolia," whispered Lindsey.

"I rest my case," said Klaus. "At least he's invited all we lowly VSO subjects to his Christmas Party."

Only three months till Christmas. I tried to forget about the bit in-between.

"Did everyone see that bit in *The Guardian* about Doe?" continued Klaus.

"Who's Doe?" I asked.

"Liberia's president. Don't you docs pay *any* attention to current affairs?" groaned Lindsey.

"No, we leave that to smartarse librarians."

"Well he's an ex-president now," laughed Mike. "Got himself knocked off by the rebels last week."

"And good riddance by the sound of him," added Lindsey.

"Oh dear," said Susan. "Will that bring peace to Liberia?"

"I must say, civil war does sound worrying."

"How does it worry you, Doc, when you obviously don't know a thing about it?" teased Mike.

"Actually, Liberia came up at a family planning lecture last month."

"What?" spluttered Lindsey.

"Liberia was one of the main producers of rubber for the condom industry. The civil war's caused a bit of a supply crisis, especially with AIDS causing such a surge in demand."

"So is that all we care about the dreadful things that are happening in Liberia?" Susan howled. "Our condom supply?"

"Well the Saloneans sound a pretty laid back lot. Sixteen tribes and no wars," mused Klaus. "Sound safe enough for you, Doc?"

"That's the only reason I agreed to come."

It's hard to feel chipper when you are emotionally and physically exhausted. The two-hour introductory tour of the Capital, on top of a six-hour flight, four hours at Lungi airport, five hours waiting for the Freetown ferry, an hour on the ferry, and only four hours in bed (or rather on the Field Officer's settee), had assaulted all our senses, leaving "Oh my God, what have we done?" hanging unspoken in a big black cloud above us all. With the exception of Mike of course, who had done it all before.

Once the British High Commissioner had beaten his retreat, our rather weary, sad-eyed Field Director repeated, verbatim, the potted history of Sierra Leone that VSO had sent us in our introductory packs.

An overhead fan limped in time to the Field Director's monotone voice and my attention wandered to the one beacon on the horizon of my two year sentence – Nick.

Nick was our Dutch-Indonesian Field Officer, all multicultural designer cool and immaculate grooming. Despite this, he treated us as comrades, rather than naughty school children as already seemed to be the Field Director's wont. Admittedly the Field Director did manage a smile or two for me, which I put down to my dazzling personality, but Klaus said he had no choice – it would not do to alienate even the most dubious of doctors when you lived in White Man's Grave.

The Field Director paused to point out the large map of Sierra Leone, sellotaped onto a cork notice-board which hung on the yellowing walls of the VSO office. Fifty red pins protruded, scattered around the country, each representing a volunteer. Most were in clusters, like the eight pins in Freetown itself, and four in Moyamba, where Klaus was headed, but there were a few singles, including me in the Southeast.

"The lonely onlies. Look at this poor person." I pointed to a pin, way out East. "Miles from anyone."

"That's Panguma Hospital." said Nick. "But another doctor has just arrived this month."

"Great. So I won't have to deal with all VSO ailments myself?"

"No," said Nick. "Your pals will be relieved that they can see Morag instead."

"Morag…?"

"Yes, here she is." The Field Officer pushed another pin in his map. "Dr. Morag MacDonald, Medical Officer at Panguma Hospital."

"Morag?" I couldn't believe it. "Morag's here! What happened to Zambia?"

"Somebody left her in the lurch, so it fell through." Whoops, I thought, but kept quiet. "But Panguma's delighted," Nick continued. "We suggested she wait to come over with you lot, but she was desperate to get to work."

"Typical Morag!"

"She left you a letter." Nick waved toward the alphabetical pigeonholes at the front of the office.

Predictably the letter was full of enthusiasm for her job and her colleagues and said I was going to love Salone. Somehow I wasn't comforted. It sounded like bloody hard work, and I was singularly unimpressed so far.

"I'm in heaven," said Klaus, lying between Lindsey and me on soft yellow sand. "A beach that stretches forever, sun on my skin and two beautiful semi-naked women by my side."

Beautiful? Me? I shivered with pleasure. "Better than Club Med," I sighed.

The moment we had seen Freetown's idyllic beaches, we had forgotten all about poverty and suffering. After all, how could it coexist in a world that had beauty such as this?

"You've never resorted to Club Med, Doc!" There he went again, implying that I was a desirable woman surrounded by suitors. I bristled with satisfaction. Klaus was right, I had avoided Club Med holidays, but not through tasteful superiority. It was those brochures featuring page after page of skinny blonde women draped over rugby-muscled men that scared me off. I wouldn't stand a chance.

"This is awful," said Lindsey, turning over on her towel. "Did you know they filmed the Bounty Bar advert here? How can I write home about the lush palm trees and the blue sea lapping at my feet without losing all credibility?"

"Yep, it's a problem," agreed Klaus. "Not nearly enough suffering to report."

"Kushe, kushe." Mike's hefty body loomed over our little ménage à trois. His wife stood by his side with a tray of drinks. "How di body?"

"Kushe. We're just fine."

"How di body is the singular form of how are you. We're plural." Klaus chastised.

"Swot!" I grumbled. Klaus had come top in the Krio test – imagine being beaten by a mechanic!

"So what is the plural of how di body, Herr Top-of-The-Class?" Lindsey asked.

"I have absolutely no idea." Klaus cat-stretched to his full five foot five, then sat up, cross-legged on the sand. "Do I see beers?"

"Here you are mate." Mike distributed drinks from his wife's tray. "And a double price G and T for the Doc."

"Sorry," I said. "But I really don't like beer."

"Time you learnt." Klaus offered me his bottle. "There'll be no pink gins up-country."

"I doubt there'll be any beer either."

The Venue was the first place we'd found with the luxury of a fridge. It was an enormous raffia basket that housed a beach bar run by members of the enterprising Lebanese contingent. Despite the flimsy walls that had to be rebuilt at the end of each rainy season, trade roared. There were always plenty of thirsty volunteers, eager for a beach break from their up-country postings: fifty VSOs, a hundred American Peace Corps, numerous priests, nuns and other assorted missionaries, plus various outfits with names like CARE and CONCERN. Whatever the organisation, the Venue was the place to be.

"Here's to our first week on Lion Mountain." Klaus raised his bottle.

"Serra Lyoa," agreed Lindsey, and we all clinked glass.

"Isn't Susan joining us?" Klaus nodded towards the small figure huddled over a book in the corner out of the sun.

"Doesn't drink," said Mike.

"What's she reading?" asked Lindsey.

"Jane Austen," I said. "She was reading it in class. Poor girl can't bear Krio's bastardisation of the Queen's English."

"Krio's great," enthused Klaus. "So descriptive."

"A German Cockney's bound to love Krio." teased Lindsey. "You can't quibble with Susan's taste though."

"Huh?"

"Sense and Sensibility. It's great fun."

"Great fun?" I mouthed in amazement. Now Susan was bound to love such books, but real people like Lindsey? Well just wait; even I fully intended to spend my spare time in the wilderness expanding my reading repertoire. The one book I had not sacrificed for more rubber gloves was an exceedingly small-print edition of *Tess of the d'Urbervilles*. I was proud that it had triumphed over other options such as Jilly Cooper. Hopefully at the end of my two years I too could announce in front of my literary friends that I adored Jane Austen and Thomas Hardy. All part of saving my soul.

"Anyway," Lindsey continued. "Reading tastes aside, I don't think Susan approves of me."

"Or any of us."

"Oh, no. She thinks you're fantastic, Em; you're a doctor, you're here to save lives!"

"Hmmph."

"In fact, you've got quite a fan club already. Did I tell you about my granny?"

"Your granny?"

"She saw your picture in the *Stirling Observer*: Dunblane Doctor Goes to Africa."

"Oh yes?"

"Isn't it marvellous, that young lady doctor going to Africa?" mimicked Lindsey. "I pointed out that I was going to Africa too, but that didn't seem to count. After all, *I'm* only a librarian."

"Sorry," I mumbled. I would have to perform well now, so as not to disappoint Susan *and* Lindsey's granny.

"Never mind, Lindsey," laughed Klaus. "Em's hardly heroic doctor material."

"Hoi, what do you mean?" Heroic doctor definitely fitted my goals and, although I couldn't quite see it myself, I rather wanted everybody else to think I was wonderful. Especially Klaus, although I couldn't imagine why I should care what *he* thought.

"You're not pompous enough, that's all." He punched my arm.

"Hmmph," I grunted. Now, as if the expectations of Susan and Lindsey's granny weren't enough, I'd have to prove myself to Klaus too.

"Come on, Doc," Klaus jumped up. "Race you to the sea."

And we ran laughing across the expansive sands, two white bodies, little and large, hurdling over the waves to plunge into the turquoise Atlantic.

The second week flew past. We were let loose on the vibrant markets of Freetown to practice our newly acquired Krio. The market women draped from head to toe in tie-dyed primary colours, tried to sell us piles of dried fish, rice and chillis from their stalls, or tempt us with strange coloured fruits and weird vegetables from the baskets balanced on their heads. I accidentally bought a bag of dried fish, thinking *bonga* too pretty a name to be applied to five-year-old reject sardines that never made it to a cosy oiled can. Klaus, of course, only went for the mouth-watering options like mangoes and pineapples. Smartarse, I thought, as we walked companionably back for our afternoon Krio lesson.

Two days before the end of our orientation fortnight, Serabu Hospital radioed to say that I was needed ASAP and that they'd collect me that afternoon. Susan nodded approvingly – no time to waste when there are lives to be saved. My brief surge of self importance was rapidly replaced by panic. I didn't want to be dragged away from the security of our little group. It would be three months before we would be reunited at the VSO Christmas Conference. Three months of work and God knows what else, and three months before I would see Klaus again.

Whoa! Why was that suddenly a problem?

"Hard luck, Doc," said Mike.

"You'll do fine," said Klaus.

"See you at the Christmas Conference," smiled Lindsey. "Don't work too hard."

"I'll write." Klaus gave me a hug. "Tell me all about your first op."

"Okay." I shrugged. He said he would write!

As I climbed into the front seat of the Serabu Hospital Landrover the driver nodded a silent 'hello' and the Field Director handed me a plastic bag stuffed full of money.

"What's all this?"

"Your monthly allowance."

"Good Lord. It looks like I've robbed a bank!"

"Eighty pounds," said the Field Director. "That's Salonean inflation."

"Don't spend it all on gin and chocolate," teased Klaus. His words were lost in a roll of thunder, followed by a curtain of rain swooshing onto the roof of the Landrover like a celestial car wash. I tried not to think of it as an omen and smiled weakly at Klaus. He gave a little wave, then dashed for cover with the others.

The big strong girl was on her own now.

STAND BACK, I'M AN ADMINISTRATOR

The rain had stopped as suddenly as it had started, leaving an eerie silence. After seven hours imprisoned in the suspensionless Landrover rattling over the most dreadful pot holed roads, I was suddenly reluctant to get out.

Eight hours ago I had been surrounded by friends, my hair damp from the sea and my face flushed and salty. Now Moses, the hospital driver, had bypassed the Promised Land and delivered me straight to the Gates of Hell. My posting.

Well I couldn't stay in the damned Landrover forever, so I opened the passenger door and jumped straight into a puddle.

"I am Sister Ignatius," announced an austere voice. "Welcome to Serabu Catholic Mission Hospital." I looked up. She was dressed in a white polyester veil and habit. The kerosene lamp that she held, à la Florence Nightingale, illuminated thin, blue-veined skin stretched over an angular face. Shadowy buildings loomed behind her, shrouded in hot damp mist.

I straightened to my full five foot six – physically half a foot taller and some four stones heavier than Sister Ignatius, so why did I feel so small?

"Er, thank you." I held out my hand. "Emily Joy."

"You are late, Dr. Joy. We were expecting you in daylight."

"Sorry," I muttered, unsure as to why I was apologising for my long uncomfortable journey. Perhaps the pull of my subconscious had slowed the vehicle down, so strong was my desire to remain in Freetown with Klaus and my friends on the beach. Unlike Morag, I certainly hadn't been in any hurry to come to this black concentration camp run by the

Ghost of Christmas Future. My future for the next two years.

"Come with me, Dr. Joy. You will need food."

For the first time in my life, I just didn't feel hungry.

Sister Ignatius sat across the convent table and watched me eat dry bread and sardines. Finally she spoke.

"Are you a surgeon, Dr. Joy?"

"Sorry. I'm afraid not."

"I see."

"I'm willing to learn," I offered. Willing, yes – but able? Ignatius fell silent again, so I took another bite of my bread and tried not to slurp my tea.

"You are here to replace Dr. Pat. Patients travelled from all over Salone to benefit from Pat's surgical skills." Ignatius looked me up and down, no doubt wondering why VSO had sent such an inexperienced girl.

Why indeed? I swallowed my bread and felt the hard lump scrape its way down my oesophagus. "I'm sorry," was all I could say. I *was* sorry. I was sorry for Serabu Hospital, I was sorry for Ignatius, and I was very sorry for myself. Why hadn't I trusted my instincts in the Ladies at Gatwick, or even earlier, when I pulled out of Zambia? I wasn't a selfless hard worker like Morag, or a surgeon like this Dr. Pat, or an idealist like Susan, or even a confident cynic like Mike. I was a spoilt only child who liked gin and chocolate and running round a squash court. What was I doing here?

"Well, we have to make do with what is available." Sister Ignatius stood up.

"I'll… er… I promise to do my best," I stuttered. For heaven's sake, this wasn't a Brownie badge; it was two years' responsibility for hundreds of lives.

"Very well. Mass is at six-thirty every morning, if you wish to attend."

I cast my eyes down, unable to find the courage to tell her that to compound my inadequacies, I wasn't a Catholic. Brought up rigidly agnostic, I hadn't even been baptised. Forget my soul, would somebody please save me?

God granted me a brief respite in the form of a pot-bellied, bearded redhead. My angel of mercy burst into the room, dressed in a traditional Salonean suit of pink and blue tie-dyed material with a fancy embroidered yoke which did nothing for his shiny, sunburnt, bald pate, but somehow I couldn't imagine him dressed in anything else. He was a thirty-something Santa on holiday, beaming 'welcome' across his freckled face.

"Ah, now, would I be seeing our brand-new doctor?"

Irish! Look, Ignatius, this is how the Irish are supposed to be. While I was considering throwing my arms round him in relief, I found myself already enveloped in an enormous bear hug. "Welcome to Serabu, Dr. Emily!"

"Good evening, Nathaniel," Ignatius interrupted. "Please take Dr. Joy to her house."

"Good evening, Sister." He gave her a curt nod as she left, then bowed to me. "Nat O'Connor, Assistant Hospital Administrator of Serabu Hospital."

"I'm Emily. Em. Hi." I squeezed his soft pale hand tightly in mine.

"It's mighty to have you here."

"She didn't think so."

"Don't be worrying about Ignatius," Nat reassured me. "The staff are all a-buzz over the new lady doctor."

"Oh no," I whispered, my fears flooding back. I could talk to Nat. "I'm not sure I'm up to this job. Sister Ignatius has just been telling me about Dr. Pat. I think…"

"You'll be grand." He thumped me on the shoulder. "Come for a beer."

"I don't really like beer." I knew I sounded churlish, but I was exhausted, I still hadn't seen my house, and I really *didn't* like beer.

"Rubbish. The night is young," Nat continued unperturbed. "After meeting MT, you'll be needing a few beers."

"MT?"

"Maggie Thatcher. The staff call her MT."

I laughed despite myself. "How do they know about the Iron Lady?"

"The World Service. Everybody knows Maggie."

"And I came to escape her!"

Five bottles of Star beer later, Nat took me on a midnight tour.

All I wanted to do was crawl into bed, but I was too tired and too drunk to argue.

The hospital looked grim, each ward more unwelcoming than the last, all housed in concrete with kerosene lamps illuminating rows of windows along the sides.

"You'd better know up front that Serabu Hospital, like the whole country, is in dire financial straits." Nat offered me a cigarette.

"No thanks." How could he smoke in this heat? "Yes, we've been told all about inflation – the VSO Field Director gave me a bag of money that would have warmed the hearts of Bonnie and Clyde," I giggled. Oh dear. That beer was strong.

"I'm afraid it's not funny." Nat turned serious. "The people have no money, so they don't come to us until it's too late. It's disastrous – for our patients and for our hospital. Our income depends on attendance."

"But surely you don't charge!"

"Of course we do. The Catholic Mission isn't made of money. Things are so bad now that unless our finances improve, they'll withdraw their funding in July and that'll be the end of Serabu Hospital."

VSO had made no mention of the fact that my hospital might close before my first year was up. "That's awful!" I exclaimed loudly, attempting to cover the shameful thought that I might not be committed to two years after all. So much for saving the world.

"It's fearful, but everybody's mighty excited that you've come. Enthusiastic new doctors are always good for business."

"Oh God!" Never mind saving the world – was I was expected to save Serabu? Nat took one look at my face and laughed.

"Are you sure you're not wanting that cigarette?"

"I almost wish I did!"

"Well you didn't drink beer three hours ago," he teased. "Enough gloom. On with the tour. This is Medical Ward and up here is the Administration block that backs onto Outpatients' department. There's also a small lab for simple tests…"

But I had stopped listening – there was a body slumped against the wall. Its head lolled forward with its arms akimbo, palms open to the black sky. Shit! I supposed I ought to do something.

Nat puffed on his cigarette, waiting, no doubt, for the new doctor to spring into action. Shit, shit, shit. "Nat." I tugged at his cropped sleeve. "I… I can't." And I couldn't. Nat took a long drag, making his cigarette end glow hot orange in the dark. Ashamed, I looked away and focused on a raindrop clinging to the guttering of Medical Ward. Slowly it stretched until it could cling no more, then dropped onto the woolly bonnet that covered the Body's head. Nat puffed again. "Nat," I coughed. "We can't just leave it… him… there."

"Ah, no indeed." Nat stamped on his cigarette. "Stand back, doctor. This is a job for an Administrator."

"Huh?"

"Shhh!" Nat crept up to the Body and lifted its woolly bonnet to expose an ear. "EMERGENCY!"

"Aaah!" The Body sprang to its feet.

"Aaah!" I echoed, jumping back into a puddle.

"Kushe, kushe." Nat draped his arm round the wiry figure's shoulders. "Is Serabu Hospital's laziest night-watchman sleeping on duty again?"

"I notto sleep, Mr. Nat," replied the Body.

"Sweet dreams, I hope, Almamy?" Nat pulled a box of matches from his pocket and lit another cigarette. I hung back in the shadows.

"No, Mr. Nat, I notto dream."

"Well if I find you asleep one more time, Almamy, it will be nightmares. Understand? Bad, bad dreams."

"No, no. I notto sleep, Mr. Nat." Almamy shook his head until his woolly bonnet fell off.

"Of course not." Nat picked up the bonnet and brushed it down. "Your hat, Almamy. Better have you looking your best for Dr. Emily." Nat pulled me forward.

"Dr. Em!" Almamy sandwiched my pale hand in his black vice and crushed it with delight. "Kushe, kushe, Dr. Em!"

"Aaaah, kushe, Almamy," I gasped. "How di body?" At least I could remember 'Hello, how are you?'

Almamy replied by dropping his trousers to reveal a large scrotal hernia.

"Almamy has been saving his hernia," whispered Nat. "For the new lady doctor."

"I'm sorry," I spluttered, catching my giggle with my hand. "I'm not a surgeon." Unimpressed, Almamy tugged up his trousers, pulled his woolly bonnet back over his eyes and made himself comfortable against the wall.

"I wouldn't be staying awake either, for £10 a month."

"And I was complaining about £80! How can he live on £10?"

"And half a sack of rice."

"Wow."

"But I don't want you thinking Almamy is typical. Our staff are mighty, you'll see."

"I'm more worried about what they think of me." I slurped behind my new friend along the muddy path that led to my house. "So far I've met Almamy, who'll be telling everyone I can't even fix a simple hernia, and Ignatius. I bet you never realised those two had anything in common."

"Bejasus! Such talk. We'll be turning you into a surgeon within the week."

"I doubt it," I grunted, side-stepping a small pond.

The path was cut through long wet grass that brushed against my legs, soaking my dress and plastering it to my thighs. Muddy water splashed my shins and trickled back down to my leather sandals, which were now so soft that my feet slid off the soles and chafed against the straps.

There was a damp sweet perfume in the thick air that reminded me of Klaus soaked in Drambuie. I was already missing the little mechanic.

"Don't you have a torch?" I asked Nat.

"No batteries. I hoped you'd bring supplies from the land of electricity."

"I've two spare sets and a torch at the bottom of my rucksack, wherever that is."

"Don't worry, Moses' taken everything to your house. But always hang onto your torch. You don't want to be standing on any snakes or driver ants." Nat certainly knew how to cheer a girl up. "Now then, here we are. Chez Dr. Em."

We stood outside a big dark bungalow, the last building on the compound some five hundred metres from the wards. The moon picked out silhouettes of three tall palm trees standing behind my house, casting their shadows protectively over the corrugated iron roof. My personal guards.

"Is that all for me?" Where was the mud hut? This was bigger than my own York semi – currently overrun by lodgers. Oh dear. A sudden vision of my cosy living-room redecorated with purple flowery wallpaper popped into my head. Stop it. There was enough to worry about right here.

"The volunteer doctors often have families."

"I'm young, free and single, I'm afraid."

"Lucky you. The biggest and best house on the compound – all for our new doctor." Nat slapped me on my back.

"Only me and my two rucksacks to fill it."

"Your keys, doctor."

I fumbled with the lock, opened my door and vainly flipped the light switch.

"Forgotten that electricity bill again!" Nat smacked his wrist. I peered inside and could just make out two easy chairs, a sofa and a table lurking in the shadows.

"Your bedroom's second door after the toilet." He pointed into the darkness. "Sleep tight. Don't let the mosquitoes bite. Pa George, our cook, will be up to see you in the morning."

"We have a cook?"

"Of course."

"I haven't come to expand the British Empire. I can cook for myself."

"You'll be too busy saving lives."

"I don't want a servant," I persisted.

"So you're good at cooking rice and mashed cassava over a three-stone fire?"

"I can learn."

"Concentrate on learning your surgery," Nat retorted. "Besides, Pa George will be delighted to work for a doctor again. Pat's departure left him stuck with me, a mere administrator."

"Hmmph."

"Good night." Nat kissed me, scraping my cheek with his beard. "God bless." And he ambled back down my path singing *Danny Boy* in a surprisingly angelic voice. I stood alone in a strange, pitch black house. My new home.

WHAT FOR CHOP TODAY?

A machine-gun knocking at my door catapulted me into morning from the haven of my bed. Pa George stood barefoot in the doorway, arms folded. He looked me up and down. With my British reserve still intact, I tried to observe him a little more surreptitiously.

"What for chop today?"

Neither of us were aesthetic examples of our race. He had a ploughed field for a face, his head driven forward on a stringy neck, led by a big nose and protruding bottom lip. A gargoyle carved in charcoal, I thought unkindly. However, judging by his expression, Pa George was thinking equally unflattering thoughts about me. What did he make of my podgy body, still clad in the same mud-splattered sundress I had fallen asleep in some five hours earlier? And what about my bloodshot eyes and breath, heavy with the fumes of Nat's hospitality? All I wanted to do was collapse back into bed. Pa George's sinewy frame looked ready for anything.

"What for chop today?" he barked again. I assumed he was asking me what I wanted for lunch.

"Er... er," I stammered. Pa George pursed his lips and his black eyes challenged mine from deep weather-beaten sockets. Sweat popped out in globules over my forehead. Come on, Em, remember your Krio, think of a dish. There's no Klaus to help you now.

"Um... plassas?" I hoped plassas was good.

"Bonga forty leones." He thrust out his hand. "Rice ten leones, cassava leaf eight leones, pepper four leones, onion twenty leones, palm oil thirty leones." It took me a minute to realise that this was the shopping list.

"Uh... okay. I'll just go and find my money." I'd put it all in one of my bags. Now there was a point. Where were they?

According to Nat, my rucksacks would be here. However, like most doctors, I did not trust administrators – especially not Irish ones with a wicked sense of humour who dressed in pink and blue tie-dyed pyjamas.

Feeling Pa George's eyes on my back, I turned to search my new abode for my elusive possessions. The sparse furnishings left little hiding place. Flimsy cotton curtains tried to soften the window bars and rusting mosquito mesh but they were no match for the stream of sunlight that was further fading an unsavoury looking mustard velour sofa. At the other end of the living-room, a large table was covered with tie-dyed material that looked remarkably similar to Nat's suit.

Before I could ponder further on Nat's taste in clothing, I spotted my two muddy rucksacks through the open door to the kitchen. Moses had propped them against a chest-high, black and red oil drum that sat by the door. A thick black crack cut the concrete floor in half. Oh dear, I hoped the rest of the house was structurally sound. I was about to step over the crack when it moved. I recoiled. Good Lord! Ants!

My pulse gradually slowed down allowing my mother's biology teacher gene to kick in. Such big ants and *so* many! I bent down for closer inspection. Each one made of large and small glossy black beads, all in perfect formation; their mission, to stop me getting to my money. Well I wasn't going to be beaten by a few formicidae.

Taking a deep breath, I reached over and carefully lifted up the smaller backpack. I pulled out the plastic bag stuffed with money and something fell to the floor. It was the last of Klaus' Minstrels. The ants were delighted. They congregated around the Minstrel, and started to rock it from side to side. Once enough of them had taken up position, they hoisted their massive prize aloft and bore it away. I watched, helplessly mourning the loss of my only remaining bit of chocolate.

Pa George had finally moved from the doorway and was now standing, hands on hips, in the living-room. Neither the ants nor my Minstrel were of any concern to him.

"Here we are." I tried to sound efficient. "Your money for the shopping." He plucked the proffered one hundred and twenty leones from my hand and started to count.

"Onion twenty leones." Pa George's huge callused hands thumped one twenty leone note on the table.

"Bonga forty leone." He counted one twenty on top of another. Bonga? Surely he wasn't planning on feeding me that awful dried fish?

"Rice ten leone…" He paused and straightened up.

"What's wrong?"

Pa George shoved the money back across the table and refolded his arms firmly over the corrugations of his chest. Bewildered, I picked up the grubby notes and turned each one over in my hands before grasping Pa George's problem. These were all twenties and rice was *ten* leones. Fishing in my plastic 'purse', I found a ten leone note, handed it over and counted out the rest of the money into separate piles to the exact value of each remaining item. Pa George seemed satisfied. He took the money, grunted and slammed the door behind him. What was that Nat had said about Pa George being delighted to work for me? We hadn't even said hello.

I stepped outside and my pupils constricted painfully in the morning sun. The cloudless blue sky bore no hint of the rain that had pummelled the Landrover last night. I stood and watched Pa George march bandy-legged off to market through steaming knee high grass. The rubber plants and palm trees, lush and abundant at the end of the rainy season, obscured my view of the wards, but I could hear a distant bustle of activity. It wasn't comforting to think I was going to become part of that action.

Before I could do anything, I had to empty my bladder – Pa George's arrival had left no time for such things. I wandered into the bathroom, disturbing a couple of cockroaches that scuttled behind the toilet, and sat gingerly on the plastic seat.

Once relieved, I pulled the chain but nothing happened. I pulled again. Nothing but a dry clatter. I tried the tap but again nothing. I looked around. There was no bath, only a large bucket of water, a jug and a plug hole set into the floor. Fair enough, I'd have a bucket bath and change my filthy dress. The toilet would just have to wait.

Washed and wearing a crumpled but clean dress, my body now craved rehydration. I went into the kitchen in search of drinking water. The tap in the kitchen was no more use than the one in the bathroom, so the water was probably in the oil drum. I lifted the wooden lid. Yep. Water. Pity about the flecks of rust and dead flies floating unappetisingly on the surface. Turning round, I spotted a two foot water filter in the corner. I opened its little tap and filled a glass tumbler. Thankfully it looked quite clear, so I drank long and deep. Next to the water filter was a plastic bag containing two bread rolls, a banana, two processed cheese triangles and a note: *Bon appetite, Nat xxx*.

I smiled, glugged down another two glasses of water, then returned to the living-room, taking big bites out of my breakfast.

"You must watch out for the ants." A six-foot beanpole arose from my sofa.

"What?" I jumped.

"Je m'excuse, but the ants, they will like this too much." The beanpole pointed to the trail of bread crumbs I'd left on the floor.

"Yes. You're right. I've already met the ants." I thought of my precious Minstrel. "But who are you?"

"Dr. Philippe at your service."

"You're Philippe?" I tried, belatedly, to hide my surprise. *This* was the Medical Superintendent of Serabu Hospital? He looked no older than me, his boyish face split by a beaming smile and topped by a mop of straw. His shirt lay open at a rather scrawny, unshaven neck and its tails hung out of baggy shorts that sagged to bony knees. Beneath, two hairy stilts ended in prehensile toes poked into yellow flip-flops.

"Bonjour, bonjour." He stretched out a long arm to shake my hand.

"Hi. Bonjour. I'm Emily."

"Welcome, Dr. Emily. Sister Ignatius told me that you have arrived."

"What else did she say?" I asked anxiously.

"Rien du tout. I make not big conversations wiz the sister."

Philippe grinned and I giggled with relief. "And you have met already Pa George?"

"I think that's who it was."

"Ah yes, Pa George also makes no big conversations. So you have taken your breakfast, yes?"

"Mmm," I confirmed, swallowing my last mouthful of banana.

"And the 'angover, it is a little better?"

"Yes, yes, I'm fine," I nodded, rather alarmed that my new boss thought that I looked as bad as I felt.

"So we make our ward rounds?"

"Yes of course, but... um... what do I do about flushing the toilet?"

"I am sorry but the 'ospital water pumps do not work for one month now. You must pour inside the dirty water from your bucket bath."

"Oh. Okay."

"On y va?"

"Yes. Let's go." I tried to sound keen.

The sun blazing down on Serabu Hospital did its best with the six whitewashed concrete blocks roofed with corrugated iron and windowed with a series of metal bars and mosquito mesh. A prisoner-of-war camp.

"Where's Sister Ignatius?" I half expected her to be shouting out orders in the middle of the compound.

"Generalement, MT comes not to the wards. She stays up in Admin." Philippe pointed to a larger block, with an open-fronted waiting area, set slightly up a hill.

"The 'ospital has been here since thirty years," Philippe explained as we walked between the buildings. "First it was a clinic only. Then one year Sister Hilary built a ward and the next year anozzer then anozzer. Now there are one hundred ten beds, the outpatients and the nursing school."

"Sister Hilary?"

"You have not heard of Hilary Lyons? The Irish Sister Doctor?"

"Sister Ignatius told me about the wonderful Dr. Pat," I ventured.

"Ah yes, Pat was very good, but for six months only, and there were many doctors before Pat. No, Sister Hilary was Administrator, Surgeon, Doctor and Politician at Serabu for thirty years. She is a big legend."

"So Serabu is Hilary Lyon's Mountain on Lion Mountain. Did she go back to Ireland?"

"No, she still lives in Bo, running Primary Health Care for the whole of Southern Region."

"Oh." All these wonderful people. I couldn't cope.

Philippe told me more about the hospital and its history, but I gave him only half my attention. Nurses dressed in crisp white uniforms bustled past and patients meandered to and fro. Strings of bedsheets, patched to rival Joseph's Technicolor coat, hung drying outside one of the wards and a family were making use of the sheets' shade to have their breakfast. They sat cross-legged on the rough-cut grass and dipped their hands into a communal food bowl as three goats grazed nearby.

"They are so poor now that the women, they buy the onions one quarter at a time," Philippe was saying, his eyes joining mine on the family eating their meal. "Salone has diamonds, gold, rutile and bauxite mines, but the people, they have nothing."

"So where does all the money go?"

"To the Lebanese dealers, to the mining companies and corrupt government ministers. Did Nat tell you that Serabu has not enough money?"

"Yes, he said that people can't afford the fees and Serabu may close."

"C'est vrai. The hospital has had the big struggle since Hilary left. Admissions went up when Pat came, but she returned to America." He shrugged. "Serabu is too far from any place. Even the locals call it Serabush."

"Serabush!" I laughed. "So why didn't they build it closer to Bo?"

"Serabu is the Archbishop's home village."

"I see."

"When there were roads and railways it mattered not, but now, ha!" Philippe shrugged. "Now the Archbishop never visits and, probably, the 'ospital will shut after the review next July. Ce n'est pas juste!"

"Oh," I said and we crossed the compound in silence. We stopped outside a shelter made out of sheets of corrugated iron held up by wooden poles. Underneath, seven women tended big black pots that bubbled on top of open fires, whilst children scampered perilously between the flames.

"Voila the kitchen!" It didn't look much like a kitchen to me. "Here the women make meals for their sick relatives."

"Kushe kushe, Dr. Fleep," called the cooks.

"Una kushe." He waved. "Dis na Dr. Emily."

"Kushe, Dr. Em," the women chorused.

"Kushe," I replied with a smile. A pot-bellied child with swollen limbs ran up to Philippe from behind the twists of wood-smoke.

"Bua, Dr. Fleep." The little boy held his arms out to Philippe.

"Bua, Fatoma." Philippe bent down and swung Fatoma up to sit on his hip. "Fatoma's twin died of measles last week."

"Oh no," I sighed. "Kushe, Fatoma." The child caught my eye and buried his head into Philippe's stubble.

"But Fatoma is better now." Philippe smiled. "Bi gahujena, Fatoma?"

"Kayingoma," answered the little voice, muffled by his protector's bony shoulder.

"Is that Krio?"

"No, Serabush is Mende-land. Mende is a language too difficile for the poomuis."

"Poomuis?"

"White people."

"Well this poomui can't even get to grips with Krio," I said. "And Krio is just English with no grammar."

"Ah non." Philippe wagged his finger. "Krio is a tongue wiz her own history…" Three goats sauntered across the compound to explore the bins outside the latrines. "Allez-vous en!" he bellowed. The goats scampered off and Fatoma, still clinging to Philippe's neck, burst into tears.

"Pardon, Fatoma. Osh osh." Philippe bounced the boy up and down and soon brought the smile back to his face. "Eh bien. To Surgical Ward?"

I stood on the chipped brown tiles that partially covered the floor and looked at the yellowing paint peeling from the walls of Surgical Ward. Twenty rusty metal-framed beds were lined up on either side of me, their occupants lying directly on patched and taped brown rubber mattresses. Where were the sheets?

A thin cotton screen failed to conceal a nurse giving an enema to a curled up victim. She scooped up a jugful of soapy water from a bucket, poured it into a large plastic funnel connected to her patient's rear by three feet of half-inch plastic tubing, then held the funnel aloft like the Olympic torch. My buttocks clenched in sympathy.

On the neighbouring bed an old woman fed her sick husband from a tin cup and spoon whilst a child slept on the floor beneath the bedsprings, curled up alongside a blackened cooking pot. Another nurse dished out pills from rows of identical little bottles sitting on a rickety trolley. She made her entries on the paper charts that hung on the bedposts, oblivious of the patients who lay moaning on their sheetless beds.

At least the ward was clean. An old man, holding a bundle of twigs that served as a brush, was bent double, sweeping under the large wooden cross that hung over a crack in the wall at the end of the room.

"Eh bien, here comes Dauda, charge nurse on Surgical," Philippe announced, waving his long arm at a rather chubby nurse who appeared pushing a trolley piled with foul-smelling bandages.

"Dauda, this is Dr. Emily."

"Kushe, Dr. Fleep. Kushe, Dr. Em. Welcome."

"Thank you," I replied, hesitating to shake Dauda's extended hand, which was covered with the unsavoury evidence of his toils.

"Oh, sorry-oh," Dauda chuckled, revealing a broken front tooth, the only harsh angle in his plump round face. He removed his rubber glove. I smiled and shook.

"Can you do small small surgery, Dr. Em?"

"No," I sighed. "But I can learn."

"Ah." On hearing my unsatisfactory reply, Dauda turned his attention back to Philippe. Crushed, I studied the broken tile by my sandal, feeling almost as demeaned as that poor patient having the enema. And if that wasn't enough, I was as hot as a Dulux dog locked in a car on a summer's day. Wiping the sweat that clung to my eyebrows and upper lip, I squinted through the condensation collecting under the face of my watch. Nine-thirty. Was that all? I had scarcely survived an hour. "We are quiet today, Dr. Fleep, no big big problems," Dauda continued. "You can make your round this afternoon."

"Fine, Dauda. On y va, Emily?" Philippe touched my shoulder. "I will show you theatre next."

I was pleasantly surprised by the operating theatre, which was old-fashioned of course, but in good repair. There were clean white tiles, a proper overhead operating light, and best of all, an air conditioner. I positioned myself to get the maximum benefit and luxuriated in the stream of cool air blowing up my skirt.

"Tiange, here is our new doctor, Dr. Emily." Philippe introduced me to the scrub nurse, a small woman in a thin blue cotton theatre dress. Her uniform was topped with a little green theatre hat, tied on with frayed tape, which failed to cover a cluster of braided hair that poked out of the back. Nature had not blemished her smooth black skin, but man had scoured symmetrical sets of three one-inch scars at the corner of each eye, like parallel crow's feet. Tiange was unlikely to acquire crow's feet the normal way – that woman had surely never smiled in her life.

"Kushe, Dr. Em. Can you do surgery?" Oh no, not again.

"No, but I can learn," I repeated. This was not the answer Tiange wanted to hear. She went back to cutting up gauze.

"Pat said Tiange was the best theatre nurse she had ever worked with," Philippe told me.

"Well Tiange didn't think much of me. Nobody does." I said miserably. "They all want a surgeon, someone who will boost attendances and save the hospital." Someone like Sister Hilary or Dr. Pat, I thought bitterly.

"Ah yes," Philippe agreed. "They believe the scalpel can cut out devils."

"Well I'm not going to be any use, am I?" I snapped.

"Doucement. I also could not do surgery when I came. You will learn."

"But I can't! Maybe I should go home now and stop wasting everybody's time."

"No, no. Please stay," begged Philippe. "I need your help. It is six months since Pat left."

"What? Six months?" No wonder he looked so thin.

"Listen well." Philippe clasped my shoulders. "Two per cent only need surgery. You can help ninety eight per cent, even if you never go inside the operating theatre. Do you know why Sister Hilary left?" I shook my head. "Enfin, she believed the Community Health Team do more good than clever doctors, by vaccinating the children and teaching the mothers to boil their water." Philippe paused to take breath. "You are a woman. The pregnant ladies will come to antenatal clinic to see a woman."

"Good." I was glad I might be good for something.

"Yes," Philippe mused. "Perhaps now we will see the difficult cases before they have laboured for three days and have already a dead baby."

Philippe's cynical words horrified me, but I was soon to realise that he was only stating harsh facts. A student nurse, with hair braided in elaborate fingerprint swirls and whorls against her scalp, ran up to us. "Dr. Fleep, Dr. Fleep, you get for come to Maternity. We get one woman with afterbirth that no want come out."

"A retained placenta?" I asked. This was quite a common problem, even in Britain. If the afterbirth wasn't removed, the mother wouldn't stop bleeding.

"Yes," agreed Philippe. "Okay Theresa, we de go?"

We followed Theresa into the cramped labour, squeezing past a large fibre glass contraption. "What's this …thing?" It was if somebody had hoisted one of those old roll-top baths onto a podium.

"Ah, yes. This is the birthing chair. It was a donation from America. No woman has ever used it. It will not work without the electricity and it is too big too move."

Instead, the midwife tied the mother's legs up to wooden poles so that Philippe could do his examination. A fly landed on the mother's knee as she lay naked on the bare rubber mattress with her legs suspended in the air. No one flicked it away. She stared silently at the wall as blood poured between her legs. Her baby lay dead in a metal tray on the floor.

I let out a little cry and backed into the corner of the room. I wasn't prepared for a stillbirth – Theresa had obviously not thought it a relevant detail. My whole gaze focused on the little purple hand that hung over the edge of the tray. I could see its fingernails. Perfectly formed miniature fingernails.

Theresa was chatting away to the midwife in a blur around my head. I could hear Philippe shout, "She is bleeding too much," and the snap of rubber gloves. I just couldn't take my eyes off those tiny fingernails.

"We have to get this afterbirth out quick quick." Philippe's voice again. The midwife kicked the tray with the baby under the bed to make space for Philippe.

"Oh, no. Don't," I sobbed, but nobody was listening to me. The midwife forced the mother's knees apart and Philippe thrust his hand inside the young woman's womb to grab the placenta. Thinking that I would be sick, I covered my mouth and looked around for the door, but the midwife had yanked a trolley out of Philippe's way and it was blocking my escape. I shot a guilty glance at the patient, but her head was still turned to the wall. There was no escape for her either.

"What about the anaesthetic?" I gasped, appalled.

"We're running out... have to save it... can... usually... do these... without... Voila!"

Philippe pulled out the ragged afterbirth, a pound of liver grasped between yellow rubber fingers. The midwife rubbed the mother's lower abdomen releasing a final gush of blood that trickled onto the floor.

"Bon. Now she will be okay." Philippe dropped the placenta into a bucket then gently lowered the mother's legs. He picked up a bloodstained length of material from the floor. This was the lappa that she had worn around her waist to walk to the hospital, which Philippe now used as a sheet. He squeezed his patient's hand and smiled reassurance, but the young woman's gaze never left the wall.

"We go to C Ward, yes?"

All I wanted to do was go home, but could find no words to argue. I nodded my assent with my hand still over my mouth. Then, turning my back on the mother and her dead baby, I stumbled out of Maternity Ward behind Philippe.

Children's Ward was full of toddlers with malnutrition. Malnutrition with or without various other diseases. Philippe let children who had tummies so swollen that they looked pregnant clamber all over him. Watching him, so at home with his young patients, helped me to compose myself. After a few minutes, I felt able to begin conversation again.

"You're very good with children."

"Myself, I have two pickins." Philippe was tickling a little girl's tummy as he examined her. "When we are finished, you will meet Nicole and les enfants."

"Thank you. I'd like that." I smiled, thankful that there might be a haven of normality somewhere in this dreadful place.

"Would you like to make examination of this little girl with malaria?"

"Of course. Kushe." I smiled at the frightened yellow eyes in front of me, then bent over to examine her abdomen. She let out a shriek, rolled off the bed and scuttled underneath.

"Oh dear."

"Oh, Dr. Em," laughed Aisha, the nurse. "The pickin is scared of poomuis."

"Isn't Philippe a poomui?"

"Dr. Fleep a black man now." Aisha gave Philippe a hug. He blushed.

"Don't worry Emily." Philippe dropped to his knees and started to play peek-a-boo with the toddler under the bed. She started to giggle. "Probably MT is the only other white woman these pickins have seen."

"I see." I was not consoled by the comparison. "But doesn't your wife ever come to the wards? Didn't you say she was a nurse?"

"Nicole goes to the villages wiz the Community Health Team. She is mother to two babies. She likes not to come to C Ward."

Before I could comment, he looked at his watch. "Ah. We must go to theatre before they close the generator."

"So when do we have electricity?" At least the electricity supply was a non-emotive topic.

"If there is diesel then we have electricity from eight o'clock until midday, then from six until ten, evening-time."

"What about emergencies?"

"Then we must turn the generator back on. MT likes it not. Diesel is too expensive. But we look forward to the emergency operations."

"Why?" I was struggling to think of how emergency surgery could be a treat for anyone.

"Cold water."

"Cold water?"

"Eight hours of electricity will not keep our fridges cold, but extra generator time gives beautiful cold drinking water." Philippe licked his lips as though dreaming of a five course slap-up meal.

Lansana had limped ten miles to the hospital with a huge festering wound in his buttock. I couldn't see how he had managed to walk across the room, never mind make his way unassisted from his village. He told Philippe he had shot himself a week ago.

"How can you shoot yourself in the backside?" I asked as we scrubbed up.

"Lansana was shooting monkeys and fell on his gun."

"Some sport." My sympathy ebbed.

"It is no sport. They shoot monkeys for food. But yes, c'est vraiment difficile to get such a wound by yourself. Dauda thinks he was, how you say, shooting where he was not allowed?"

"Poaching?"

"Yes. Dauda says that probablement he was shot and had too much fear to come to the hospital."

"Why?"

"In case the chief's men found him."

"How much more can they punish him? Surely he won't survive?"

Tiange and Philippe rasped their scalpel and curettes against bone, dolloping rotten tissue and chinking bits of shotgun pellet into a metal dish. My stomach churned as the operating theatre filled with the stench of rotting meat. I didn't strain to watch.

An hour later Philippe picked out the last splinter of bone, leaving a cavity big enough to hide three oranges. "We can give Lansana antibiotics, but Mozzer Nature, she will be the one to heal this hole."

Mother Nature would have to come up with some sort of miracle to close that crater, but since I had no better suggestions, I made no comment.

"Now I go for lunch," Philippe announced. Squeamishness obviously wasn't the cause of Philippe's skinny frame. "Pa George, he is cooking for you?"

"I think so." I assumed that making lunch had been Pa George's intention.

"Good. Then we meet on TB ward at three?" Philippe held the theatre door open for me to step outside.

The oppressive midday heat was only small relief from the odours within. It was autumn back home, my favourite season. Oh! to fill my lungs with clean frosty air and jump into a pile of crunchy golden leaves, watching my laughter condense into little puffs.

"The TB patients will be very happy wiz a new lady doctor" added Philippe.

That made two things I was good for.

OH LORD, GIVE THIS PATIENT WELL BODY

"And we hope that Dr. Em able give this patient well body. Tenki-ya. Amen." Earnest, the nurse anaesthetist, cast his eyes in my direction as he finished his supplication to the Almighty. Sheepishly I laid my scalpel down – a naughty child reaching too eagerly for her knife and fork before grace.

Lunch had been interrupted by my first-ever surgical patient. She had a twisted ovarian cyst, which Philippe said would be a nice easy one for me to start with. I wasn't so sure. My patient was numbed from waist to toes with a spinal anaesthetic, leaving her able to hear every word of the prayer. Still she looked trustingly up at me. A droplet of sweat trickled down the inside of my spectacles. I was scrubbed so couldn't wipe it away

"This is a Catholic hospital." Philippe's eyes smiled reassurance above his faded surgical mask. "Earnest prayed before Sister Hilary's cases too."

I nodded and smoothed the rubber gloves over my trembling, stumpy fingers, but no magical pair of rubber gloves was going to transform them into a surgeon's lithe hands.

Tiange slapped a scalpel into my palm. I swallowed, nodded, and made my first incision. The blade barely broke the skin. I tried again. This time I snaked off to the left, tried to pull the knife back on course and nicked a blood vessel that spurted over my glove.

Tiange clamped the bleeder with one hand and prised the scalpel from my fingers with the other. Sent off in the first minute, I could only watch from the sidelines as Philippe sliced cleanly through the abdominal wall so that he and Tiange could remove the off-purple melon that had once been our patient's ovary. Tiange reluctantly allowed me back on in the closing minutes to sew together the last layer of skin with a needle and thread that my grandmother would have refused to darn socks with. I still managed to snap it.

"This is last needle." Tiange stated as she pulled it away. "I will finish the work."

She sutured the ten-inch wound together in under a minute. My eyes were transfixed on the premier division embroiderer's nimble fingers, partly with admiration, but mostly to avoid catching the eye of Philippe, or the patient. My only achievement was to hold back the sobs long enough to escape from the operating room.

Nat lay draped across my sofa, Star beer in hand. Today he was wearing a green and yellow tie-dyed suit that clashed horribly with the mustard velour.

"I need a gin."

"Star beer?"

"I don't like beer." I blew my nose.

"Bejasus. Last night you were after drinking five bottles." Nat pulled himself up.

"I thought it rude to refuse. Oh God…" I dropped my head in my hands.

"The first day is always the hardest. Have a Star."

I took the warm bottle, flipped off the gold star lid, then moved the blue and gold paper label aside to check for creatures within. "Earnest actually prayed in front of a fully conscious patient," I complained, wiping a smear of glue from my hand. "Talk about inspiring confidence."

"We all need prayers," came a voice from the corner.

"Oh, hello," I said to the gaunt, shivering, yellow-eyed stranger in my sitting-room.

"Hi. I'm Tom." He held out a clammy hand, which I shook ever so carefully. "Malaria, I'm afraid."

"Tom teaches at our nursing school."

"Are you alright, Tom?"

"Much better, thank you, Dr. Emily," he said, although the evidence pointed to the contrary. "Are you enjoying Serabu?"

"No! I wanted to save lives and be a better person and I'm just useless," I howled. "I'm no Sister Hilary."

Tom looked a little alarmed but Nat just made a face. "Stop being such a pessimist and drink your beer, doctor."

"People are starving! How can I drink beer?"

"And stop wallowing in Catholic guilt. Guilt is self-indulgent and destructive."

And yesterday I had thought of Nat as my angel of mercy? "I take it you're not one of these religious types yourself?" I glowered.

"Me? I'm going to be a priest."

Nat looked rather satisfied at my horrified expression and took a deep swig of his beer. Tom excused himself and staggered back to bed.

"Vegetarian," sniffed Nat. "He'd rather get malaria than swat a mosquito. He forgoes the healing properties of Star beer too. Drink up."

There was nothing else for it. I finished the bottle, just as Pa George thundered in from outside and dumped two soot-blackened pots on the table. He piled our plates with mounds of soggy rice followed by green gunge.

"What's that?" I exclaimed, my eyes fixed on the bright orange oil that was seeping under the rice and heading for the edge of the chipped plate.

"Plassas," said Pa George. "I de go." And he went. I looked in dismay at the steaming cowpat before me. Nat burst out laughing.

How was I ever going to survive two years of this? At least I might lose some weight!

"Dr. Em, you got body," said the first patient on TB ward.

"Yes, Dr. Em really get body," agreed a skeletal man in the bed opposite. Twenty male heads nodded their approval.

"What are they saying, Philippe?"

"They say that you have the woman's curves. Notto so, Mr. Kpukoma?" Philippe turned to the Charge Nurse, a kind-eyed man with scattered curls of grey hair who scarcely reached Philippe's shoulder.

"Yes, yes, Dr. Fleep. Dr. Em is fat," Patrick Kpukoma agreed enthusiastically. My jaw dropped, accentuating my double chin.

"This is a very big compliment in Africa," Philippe reassured me.

"Hmmph!" I straightened up, lengthened my neck and sucked in my tummy.

"Dr. Em get fine body," Mr. Kpukoma grinned.

"A big 'ealthy woman is a big prize for a Salonean man. Especially for these patients wiz dry cof."

"Dry cough?"

"Tuberculosis," explained Philippe.

"Yes, but *dry* cough?" Back home a dry cough was an annoying tickle without any gratifying phlegm. But here? The first patient coughed up his soul to half fill a tin cup with guacamole-green sputum, then proudly displayed his efforts. I balked. "Philippe, how can you call that *dry* cough?"

"Ah. Dry means thin."

"Dr. Fleep dry." Mr. Kpukoma held up Philippe's scrawny arm. "And Dr. Em get body!" He squeezed the soft flesh above my elbow.

"Fat," I snapped. Twenty men with concentration camp physiques, looked at me accusingly. "Skinny cough," I mused. "What a good name for TB."

Perhaps it was time for the big strong girl to revel in her plentiful coverings.

I spent my second day making myself as inconspicuous as possible in the hope that Philippe wouldn't suggest I actually lay hands on a patient. Thankfully, he let me observe quietly, content with throwing me little titbits of advice and information. Philippe's caring manner really impressed me, as he did what had to be done within the confines of Serabu's meagre resources. But his clinical abilities did nothing to boost my confidence. I had been a good GP, although that was easy, with a hospital full of consultants only ten minutes down the road. Why hadn't I stuck with my strengths?

The next patient arrived, ushered in by his four wives. I smiled at the old Pa. He had a lump the size of an orange where his right testicle should have been.

"Tumour," said Philippe, palpating the normal testicle dwarfed by its malignant neighbour. "But I think it spreads not, we need only remove the bad one."

"Can we do that?"

"Bien sur. It is not difficult." Philippe turned to his patient. "I very sorry Pa, but we get for pull your ball."

It cannot be easy for a man to hear he will have to lose a testicle.

I waited for the anguished howl.

"No problem, Dr. Fleep," came the cheery reply. "Pull all two. I get nineteen pickin."

"Nineteen children!" I spluttered once our patient had left to arrange his admission. "Don't you have *any* family planning?"

"This is a Catholic hospital!" Philippe sounded affronted. "En tout cas, this makes only five children for each wife."

"Of course." I bit my tongue. Had those VSO courses taught me no tolerance? "Sorry."

Philippe's eyebrow raised a fraction. "Fais-voir, Dr. Emily." He unlocked his top drawer.

"Condoms!" There were enough to service the whole population of Serabu twice over.

"We smuggle them from Freetown. MT sees not the women weak from ten, fifteen, twenty pregnancies with no food for the children they have already. Twenty percent of the pickins die before they reach five." Philippe shook his head as he continued. "The women get desperate and go to the, how you call, 'quacks,' for abortion. Then they come, bleeding and infected." Philippe sucked in his breath. "Go home and unpack. Then come to meet Nicole at six."

"Okay," I replied, although I didn't want to unpack. That would imply that I was staying.

Glad as I was to leave the wards, my house gave no comfort. It was not, and would surely never be, home. This oppressive heat was sapping my energies and it was too hot to lie down without a fan. More air could circulate if you stood upright. I fiddled with the dial on my compact short-wave radio and found the World Service, that faithful companion of displaced souls like myself, but all it had to offer was a programme on tapestry. What I really wanted was a big television showing *Eastenders*, or even *Neighbours*, and a large box of Thornton's chocolates.

What was I going to do? *Tess of the d'Urbervilles* was about as inspiring as tapestry and the nearest phone was in Freetown, one hundred and seventy miles away. I could write some letters. Of course, I would write to Klaus.

In minutes, three sheets of paper were filled with doctor's scrawl. Pausing to flex my cramped fingers, I skimmed through my efforts. Oh dear. The long list of complaints wouldn't enhance that heroic doctor image. I couldn't have Klaus knowing how pathetic I was being, so scrunched the sheets into a ball and threw it into the bin. Morag? No – her letter from Panguma had been so enthusiastic. I was interrupted by Nat pulling faces behind the mosquito mesh.

"Lunchtime, Dr. Em!"

"Already? My tummy's not rumbling." Nevertheless, Pa George clattered in and slammed a pot on the table.

"What's for chop today then?" I sighed.

"Potato leaf plassas," snapped Pa George and stomped out of the room.

"Look at that oil," I whispered, eyeing the soggy green mash with the bright orange palm oil floating a centimetre thick on top. No wonder my hunger signals had gone on strike.

"We're poomuis," Nat explained. "Extra oil for the rich white man."

"I'll ask him to cut down."

"What? And insult him?"

"Hmmph." Nat was right. After our inauspicious start, I couldn't afford to get on the wrong side of Pa George. "Anyway, this looks just like yesterday's."

"Yesterday cassava leaf. Today potato leaf." Pa George returned with the plates; his grasp of English clearly better than I'd assumed.

"What for chop tomorra?" he barked.

"Er…" I backed away. "What do you suggest, Pa George?"

"Crin-crin."

"Okay. Crin-crin."

"Crin-crin eight leone, onion twenty leone, pepper four leone…" Nat was sniggering again.

"Okay, so what's crin-crin?" I asked as soon as Pa George had gone.

"Oh, it's like cassava leaf, only slightly greener."

Nicole, cradling eight-month baby Simone at her breast, handed me a glass of freshly squeezed orange juice. She wore only a sleeveless white blouse, tie-dyed shorts and flip-flops but still managed to look coolly elegant, despite unevenly cropped blonde hair (presumably Philippe's work), and unshaven legs covered with mosquito bites.

"Philippe says you are doing well," she smiled.

"Huh?" I spluttered on my orange juice. I had taken Philippe for an honest man.

"It eez very hard at first. Philippe also could not do the surgery when we came. Please. Have some more orange."

"Thank you." I waved the flies from the mouth of the jug and refilled my glass. We sat outside their house as the sun set behind a palm tree and watched Philippe playing football with two-year-old Pierre and four Salonean children.

Pierre, ghostly white next to the shiny healthy black skins of his team-mates, was splodged with gentian violet dabbed across an assortment of spots and scabs. He bent over to pick up the ball, revealing a two-centimetre boil on his bottom.

"Viens, Pierre. Qu'est que c'est, mon petit?" Nicole handed me Simone and gave the boil a gentle squeeze. "Tiens, c'est la Tumbu."

"Tumbu fly?" Baby Simone and I peered at poor Pierre's bottom.

"Let me show you how to treat Tumbu. Un moment."

Nicole returned, holding a pot of Vaseline.

"Vaseline?"

"Fais voir." Nicole smeared it over Pierre's gobstopper boil.

"Ne bouge pas, mon petit. Vaseline cuts off the maggot's oxygen, then we wait."

"Huh?"

"The Tumbu must come for air. Regarde."

The boil erupted and a juicy prawn wriggled out.

"Yugh!"

"Voila, Pierre." Nicole flicked the larva on the floor and squashed it under her flip-flop. Pierre ran off to continue his game and Simone started to scream.

"Madame Tumbu likes very much to lay her eggs in the seams of underpants," Nicole explained, taking Simone back and fixing her onto her breast. "Pa George must iron your underwear to kill the eggs."

"Pa George isn't ironing my knickers!"

"Eh, bien. If you know how to use a charcoal iron…"

"So, Nicole, how long have you been here?" I asked, changing the subject away from my smalls.

"Two years. Since Pierre was a baby."

"What about Simone, you surely didn't have her in Serabu?" I gasped, but Nicole's attention had been diverted by delighted squeals. Her husband was trotting round the grass like a tame giraffe, giving the children rides on his shoulders.

"He is 'appy that you have come, Emily. Look. He laughs again!"

I was about to thank her for her kind words, but something in her change of manner made me hesitate. "Dr. Pat left six months ago, and from then, Philippe has had no day off…"

"Six months is an awfully long time," I agreed. Two days had been a long time.

"He is very tired, yes?" Nicole leaned toward me and I gulped, realising where this conversation was going. "Philippe very much needs a break." I nodded dumb agreement. "We have been waiting for you so we can go on 'oliday for one week." Nicole hesitated. "Emily, I want to ask you… I… We…"

"Nicole, not yet." Philippe appeared at his wife's side, with Pierre still perched on his shoulders.

"Mais oui, Philippe." Nicole placed a hand on his arm. "You are getting ill. You need to sleep, you must rest."

"But it is too soon."

My head turned from Nicole to Philippe and back again.

"And we must think of Pierre… We would like to go next week," she blurted out

"Next week," I repeated dully.

"I know it will be difficult, but Pierre…" She looked at her little boy scratching the angry prickly heat on his tummy. "The sea breezes will make his skin better."

"Yes, of course." I attempted a nonchalant smile.

"No, Emily. It is too much," Philippe protested feebly.

"It's okay. I'll manage," I announced without thinking. Never one to say no, how could I refuse? Philippe was exhausted – six months alone, and that poor little boy. But how could I agree? Good God. A whole week alone. Next week?

I'm Not Old, I'm Just Ugly

"What for chop today?"

Roast beef, pink in the middle, horseradish sauce, crispy roast potatoes, lashings of gravy, mange tout peas and perhaps a smooth dark chocolate mousse for afters.

"Plassas please, Pa George," I sighed. A full week and I was still here! The trouble was I couldn't bring myself to abandon Philippe before his break. And then there was Klaus, and Lindsey's granny. What would they think if I wimped out within a week?

"Cassava leaf, eight leones, rice, ten leones, onion ten leones." I cringed at the thought of more mashed green leaves spiked with bonga, smothered in bright orange oil. If God would deliver me some chocolate, then my soul was his forever. "Palm oil ten leones, bonga twenty leones. What's your name?"

"Er, Emily. Emily Joy," I replied, trying to keep a straight face. "And yours?"

"George Williams."

Pa George was called George *Williams*?! "Pleased to meet you, Mr. Williams." We shook hands solemnly. Conversation! This was progress. "Do you have family?"

"I get one wife an one girl-pickin."

"How old is your little girl?"

"Two rainy seasons."

"And what's her name?"

"Dr-Pat."

"Doctor Pat?"

"Dr. Pat fine doctor," he stated.

"Yes. Yes. Of course."

"Do you get pickins?" he asked.

"Er no. I have no children."

"Do you get man?"

"No. I have no husband."

"Is that why they sent you here?"

Great, just great. Incompetent, undesirable and barren. Well Dr-Marvellous-Pat might well have boosted their attendances and saved their hospital from closure, but not me. I was evidently not their knight with a shining stethoscope. My paranoia was symptomatic of a more general misery: prickly heat and mosquito bites battled for possession of every inch of my body, fungus grew in the moist hiding place beneath my breasts and the armpits of my clothes were turning yellow as palm oil literally seeped from my pores. Tom had told me that palm oil is sometimes called tree lard, containing more cholesterol than virtually anything, so to add to the insult of having to eat the stuff (in double, poomui-doctor quantities) my arteries were hardening by the minute without a single piece of chocolate passing my lips. It just wasn't fair! AND Philippe was going on holiday tomorrow. Bloody Hell!

Perhaps I could give my prickly heat its medical title, *milia rubrae* (Latin for little red spots), and pretend it was a serious tropical disease that required an immediate med-evac. Who could argue with the only doctor?

MT, that's who. After twenty years in Sierra Leone, even an administrator could no doubt spot prickly heat from 200 yards, regardless of fancy names. With Philippe away, MT was never going to allow her hospital's only remaining doctor to leave, no matter how low her opinion of me.

I wasn't exactly homesick. Returning home so soon without a very good excuse seemed rather pathetic and besides, as Pa George had so succinctly pointed out, what was there for me at home? No husband and no children. Perhaps I should just become a nun. At least then no one would expect me to find a man.

It was ten o'clock on Saturday morning and Philippe had given me the day off to calm myself before the storm. Relaxing was out of the question, so I rubbed the mould off my leather sandals, strapped them on and headed down to Nat's. He answered the door in a gara dressing gown, fag in hand.

"Not dressed yet, Mr. Administrator? It's gone ten!"

"Jaysus, that early? What do you want at this unearthly hour?"

"I thought you might fancy a walk."

"Is the girl mad?"

"Come on, I'm getting cabin fever."

"Cabin fever? You've only been here a week!"

"I know, I know. Please, Nat, I need you to cheer me up."

"I'll put on my shorts."

I followed Nat's frighteningly pale legs down the path that ran alongside the hospital compound. Pa George passed us, carrying water up from the village.

"Kushe, Pa George." He nodded in reply, but not enough to spill a drop from the bucket on his head. "He's already brought me my two buckets this morning," I whispered. "Is he moonlighting?"

"No, that's his house." Nat pointed to one of the mud houses with corrugated iron roofs, set amongst the ubiquitous rubber plants and palm trees.

"Really? I thought the women carried the water."

"Pa George always carries the water for his wife. Serabu's first new man!"

"Wow! Pa George!!!"

The path led onto Serabu's main street, a red laterite road dotted with puddles. A goat stopped to take a drink, then sauntered off between the houses made of the same job lot of concrete, rusting roofs and rotting wooden shutters as the hospital. The children called "poomui, poomui", then ran to hide behind trees or toothless grannies. White man, white man. I smiled and waved.

"Spot the newcomer," teased Nat and, right enough, by the time we reached the market square my jaw was aching with smiling so much and I was beginning to understand why the queen always looks so glum.

Serabush's market was nothing like the jostling hub of Freetown. Seven ramshackle stalls displayed meagre piles of rice, bonga, cassava leaf, quartered onions, green oranges and rotten looking black bananas – nothing I was tempted to buy. We just smiled and said kushe to the disappointed vendors.

Beyond the market the road ran alongside a stream where naked children splashed happily in the shade of the lush greenery.

"Oh, let's jump in!"

"No! What would they think of Serabu's new doctor cavorting with the Assistant Administrator in her birthday suit?"

"I was going to keep my clothes on, but anyway who cares?"

"And you don't care about schistosomiasis, giardiasis, amoebic dysentery or larvae migrans either?"

"Smartarse," I sniffed. "Why don't *you* fill in for Philippe this week?"

"I faint at the sight of blood."

A little further upstream, three women were washing their clothes against the stones with bars of soap.

"Have you met Sesay?" enquired Nat.

"Oh yes, the maintenance man."

"Meet his wives."

"What? All of them?"

"Only three!"

"Hmmph." I snorted. "Although they do seem to get on very well," I added, watching the women laugh together as they spread their lappas out to dry on the bank.

"Like sisters."

Hmm. I'd always wanted a sister. "How does anything dry in this humidity?" I added out loud.

"The same way things get washed in the dry season when there's no stream left."

"But our nurses are so crisp and white. Is there a hospital laundry?"

"You're joking! With our fancy electric water pumps broken for six weeks? The nurses are responsible for their own uniforms, and the patients bring their own sheets. Fortunately you and I have Pa George."

"Okay, okay, so you were right about him too."

Three miles uphill we reached the Junction, where the road met the main road to Bo.

There were several people milling around with trays of fruit, groundnuts and little plastic bags of homemade ginger beer on their heads. Nat suggested we buy oranges from Musu, a painfully thin lady whose eight-month pregnancy was grotesquely exaggerated against her six-stone frame.

"But Nat, those oranges are green," I whispered. Sorry though I was for Musu, who told us she was trying to make a few leones after the recent death of her husband and before her baby came, I didn't want bellyache from eating unripe fruit.

"Never judge a fruit by its colour. Try one."

Musu sliced the top off an orange for us to squeeze straight into our mouths. Nat was right. Green oranges gave sweet orange juice.

"Why all these vendors?" I asked Nat. "I can only see two houses."

"They're waiting for the poda poda."

"Poda-poda?"

"The local bus. It means slowly-slowly. You'll see."

And slowly, slowly, right on cue, a poda-poda creaked down the road. It was a rusty truck, sardine packed with people peering out from the metal grills that ran along the sides, and a roof that was piled high with more people, firewood, sacks of sweet potatoes, the occasional goat and bits of old furniture. It all looked very precarious.

The poda-poda lurched round the side of a pothole, then wobbled to a halt. A couple of people jumped down from the roof and helped an old lady out of the back. Four other people squeezed themselves into her place. Musu passed her oranges through the grill, and the passengers passed out their money. It was a race against both time and the other sellers to sell as many oranges as she could before the poda-poda pulled away. The truck creaked off to Bo and we set off back to the village.

Nat took me home through the back courtyards of the village where the concrete buildings that fronted onto the main street gave way to houses of mud and stone. Children scampered barefoot in torn knickers whilst a woman cooked. She was a classical Mende beauty, with high cheekbones, slim line nose and a dimple-faced baby strapped to her back. I gaped with horrified admiration as she lifted a rice pot directly from the fire with her bare hands. Turning she gave us a beautiful smile with her full friendly mouth. She looked awfully familiar.

"Kushe Dr. Em, kushe Nat."

I blushed. Serabu's matron was dressed only in a black stripy bra and green lappa, whilst we stood, uninvited, in her kitchen.

"Kushe, Mariama, kushe Hindolu." Nat tickled the baby's toes. "How were you ever managing to lift that off the fire without gloves?" He pointed to the pot filled with bubbling plassas.

"Training. If I cried when I touched the hot pot, my mother hit my hands with a stick."

"That's awful," I cried.

The child torturer in question turned out to be an elderly woman who was pounding a five-foot pestle into a giant mortar.

"Kushe," I nodded curtly at Mariama's mother, who nodded back. "What's she doing?"

"She must pound the cassava leaves for one hour to get the cyanide out."

"Cyanide!"

"But you don't need Pa George, do you Dr. Em?

"Shut up, Nat."

"Mariama spent a year at the Liverpool School of Tropical Medicine." Nat led me back through to the main street. "She knows, unlike most Saloneans, what a cold and lonely sort of paradise the affluent West can be. Not that she'd be saying anything bad about your homeland, but we're mighty glad she hated it and came home."

"She's super with the staff and patients. Even MT's civil to her."

"MT knows that Serabu's fortunes slumped as much because of Mariama's year out as Pat's departure, so she can forgive a bit of premarital baby-making. In fact our MT's quite gaga over Hindolu."

"You're joking."

I left my friend to stagger back to his own house muttering that he'd be up for lunch when he'd recovered, and continued home. A young lad intercepted me.

"Kushe, Dr. Em. You want bananas?" The boy, no more than ten years old, pointed to the bunch of bananas on the tray perched on his head.

"No. Look at all these bananas!" I had already bought four bunches as a penance for false allegations of selling rotten fruit, but how many did he think I could eat?

"You want groundnuts?" he persisted, determined to make a sale.

"Oh, okay. How much?" He took his tray down to show me his wares. The peanuts were fresh and almost juicy looking. "Twenty leones." He made a little paper funnel and poured in a tomato puree tin measure of nuts.

"What's your name?"

"Nurse."

"Nurse?" I raised an eyebrow.

"Nurse Sankoh." He handed me my parcelled groundnuts.

"Twenty leones."

"Well thank you, Nurse."

He put the tray back onto his head, and put my twenty leones into his sandshoe. He was the first child I'd seen with shoes; selling groundnuts must be good business. I pocketed the nuts and returned to my house.

I went straight to my water filter and downed three glasses. Taking a fourth, I flopped on my sofa and listened to Pa George clattering around outside. I knew I should be grateful for him but the smell of plassas was making me nauseous. Aw fo do, I can probably survive on bananas and groundnuts. Just a minute. This looks a bit familiar. I stared at the wrapping round the groundnuts.

The paper was covered in my own scrawl – it was my discarded letter to Klaus!

"And what is our Dr. Emily studying so intently. A letter?"

I jumped. "Nat! I didn't hear you."

"A love letter!"

"Hoi!" I clutched the letter to my chest.

"Let me see, let me see."

"It's not a love letter," I protested. "It's just an unfinished letter I threw out. That boy, Nurse, has wrapped my groundnuts in one of my own letters!"

"So why did you throw it out? Scared it might be too slushy?" Nat fluttered his hand against his heart.

"It was full of moans, I don't want him to think I'm a whinger."

"Who?"

"None of your business."

"Well it's half of Serabu's business now!"

"Oh no, I've complained about everyone." I groaned. My popularity ratings were low enough already. "I just can't believe they rake through our rubbish."

"Of course they do, we poomuis are terribly wasteful. Never mind, literacy is less than 17% and your writing is illegible."

"I hate you."

"Of course you do. Now then, I think we've earned our Stars today." Nat produced two bottles from behind his back. "I'll make the toast. Hilary and Pat, eat your hearts out, there's a new doc in town. Slainte!"

"I still hate you. I have nightmares about those two. Did you know that Pa George even called his daughter after Dr. Pat? Literally Dr-Pat?"

"Oh don't you worry, Pa George'll be singing your praises soon enough."

"I doubt it," I snorted. "But don't you think he looks old to have a two-year-old?"

The door burst open and Pa George stomped in with the rice pot.

"I'm not old. I'm just ugly!"

LOCKED OUT

Lansana, the gunshot man, presented Philippe with a chicken as a thank you for the miraculous healing of his buttocks.

"I have no need for a chicken at the beach." Philippe handed the flapping bird straight over to me and jumped in his truck. "Bon appetite, Emily, et bon chance."

Well, if Lansana had survived, perhaps there was hope for us all. But this thought didn't stop the hand of doom grip my gullet as I watched Philippe's family vanish out of the compound. It gave an extra little squeeze when Tiange thrust the Theatre keys under my nose.

"You no get for lose those keys, Dr. Em. Other keys are not there."

"Can't you cut more? Ouch!" The chicken clawed my leg.

"Hold that fowl by the legs." Tiange hung the bird upside down and continued.

"If we take those keys to make other set, we get for leave theatre open. MT say the thiefmen go thief everything."

"Who would steal theatre equipment?"

"The quacks able look like real doctors, the drapes make fine sheets and they melt scalpels and forceps to make cooking pots."

"You're joking!"

But Tiange didn't joke. "We go see back."

I christened the chicken 'Tikka' in eager anticipation of something other than plassas on the menu. First she needed fattening, so I left her in the kitchen with some rice. It was only seven pm, so I had three hours of electricity to read *Tess*.

Munching a banana in a vain attempt to assuage my chocolate craving, I flopped onto my sofa, but after ten minutes the big words in tiny print blurred in front of me. Oh why hadn't I brought a glossy best-seller, and why oh WHY had I agreed to be the sole doctor for a whole week? Seven-thirty. I paced round the living room, sat down, picked up my pen to begin a letter home, chewed the end, stood up and fiddled with my dial to find the World Service. The eight o'clock classical concert might have been enjoyable if my radio had been any bigger than a pack of cards and if the rain hadn't suddenly started battering my corrugated iron roof with a noise like a million marbles bouncing directly off my brain. The rain was spraying through my mosquito mesh so I shut my windows, sat down again and doodled a couple of smiley faces on an envelope. I gave my faces bodies, then gave one a motorbike and a monkey wrench and embellished the second with a fringe, ponytail and stethoscope. I drew a big heart round both. Klaus and the Doc.

"Emily, what are you thinking?" I scribbled out the unlikely lovebirds and reopened *Tess*. I attempted a few more paragraphs but, irritated with beautiful heroines, threw it down and went to the kitchen to toss Tikka some more rice and help myself to another banana.

A leisurely bucket bath and detailed ablutions took me to nine o'clock. Now what? My toenails needed cutting – my, how fast they grew! Toenails cut, I looked at my watch yet again. Ten-to-ten. At last, a reasonable time to go to bed.

Now this wasn't as easy as it sounded. My narrow single bed was smothered with a king-sized mosquito net hanging from wires strung across my bedroom, with as much excess as possible tucked tightly under the mattress. None of those little bloodsuckers would find a way into *my* bed. Unfortunately with all those spare folds, neither could I.

Lillibolero tinkled out of the radio to announce the World Service ten o'clock news and... instant darkness. Why did Sesay have to be so blooming punctual with the generator curfew?

Blindly, I fought my way through a false opening in the net curtains from hell, eventually pulling their suspension wires from the wall, leaving me drowning in a cloud of foaming mesh. I'd left my torch in the sitting-room, so I fumbled around on my bedside table and found a candle but no matches (probably just as well as I was hot and sticky enough without everything going up in flames). Praying that braving the mosquitoes for one night would not mean White Woman's Grave,

I curled up naked and sweaty on the mattress, clutching my sheet like a security blanket.

The rain had stopped, but the toads still grommeted outside my house, punctuated by the drip-drip from my overfilled gutters. In the distance I could hear the rumble of rhythmic drumming from a secret society gathering somewhere in Serabu. As a poomui, I would never be privy to any information about the secret societies, but since membership generally involved genital mutilation for both males and females, ignorance was probably bliss. The drums blended with the occasional groan of thunder that after an hour or two became almost soothing.

Light suddenly flickered through my cotton curtains. I bolted upright and went to the window, expecting to see Almamy standing on my doorstep with his kerosene lamp, come to fetch me for some dire emergency. But there was no Almamy, just some distant flashes of lightning. Finally I dozed off.

When Almamy really did start banging on my door, I was deep in dreamland, skiing after Klaus down a snowy Scottish hillside. Totally disoriented, I jumped out of bed and tripped over the voluminous mosquito net that covered the floor. Bang bang bang.

"Okay, I'm coming." I felt around for my dress.

"Dr. Em, come quick quick." Bang bang bang. It was too dark to find clothes so I wrapped myself in my sheet and stumbled to the front door.

Almamy thrust a crumpled note into my hand and held his lamp so I could read the rounded writing:

Jeneba is eight months pregnant. She get convulsions.

"Shit!" I grabbed the theatre keys and flew to Maternity, my makeshift toga flapping at my ankles.

"Kushe Dr. Em," said Laygby, the midwife. I clutched the doorway, puffing, sheet splattered with mud, gaping at the heavily pregnant teenager having violent seizures. "Dis Jeneba. She get eclampsia."

Eclampsia. One of those conditions hammered into medical students as pregnancy's greatest danger, but thankfully rarely seen in the West. Textbooks describe the soaring blood pressure and the fluid leaking into all the bodily tissues, causing widespread oedema. It had turned Jeneba's normally slim body into a grotesquely overinflated rubber doll, swamped with excess fluid. Fluid also leaks into the brain, and this, combined with the rapidly escalating blood pressure, leads to convulsions then death. In the West, mothers-to-be wonder why their doctors and midwives make such a fuss over blood pressure. Here, convulsing in front of me, was the reason.

My sheet was slipping, so I tied it more firmly over my breasts. With no Philippe to call upon, two lives now depended on me. Help! "Laygby we need intravenous diazepam," I announced in my calmest voice.

"Diazepam don finish, Dr. Em."

"What do you mean, finished?" I hissed.

"Don don. Aw fo do."

"What? No!" I nearly screamed. "Don't give me aw fo do. What about hydrallazine? Magnesium sulphate?"

"Don don."

"Damn. Find some from another ward. Break into pharmacy. Anything."

Laygby ran out with her lamp leaving me with two assistants: a fellow pregnant patient and Jeneba's mother. First I needed to secure venous access for the drugs, so Jeneba's mother clamped herself round her daughter's convulsing legs while my second assistant tried to restrain her arm for me to slip the cannula into her vein. My assistants whispered urgently to each other in Mende. Even if we had a communal language, there was nothing I could say to reassure them. Jeneba and her baby would surely die.

Things had seemed bad enough, but then Jeneba jerked uncontrollably and knocked over our remaining kerosene lamp. "Damm," I muttered, feeling for my torch and burning my hand on the overturned lamp. "Shit!" My curses needed no translation, and the room, already black, fell silent.

Moments later Laygby arrived, standing in a dim pool of light from her lamp, and we all looked at her with unified desperation. "I get diazepam."

"Well done, Laygby," I said, forcing brisk confidence into my voice. "Draw up two vials."

"No problem, Dr. Em."

Two hours later we had finally calmed Jeneba's fits and eased her blood pressure down but the only cure for eclampsia is immediate delivery of the baby. Without all the swelling, Jeneba would normally be a tiny girl and she had a very big baby. There was only one thing to do. "Laygby, we need to prepare for a Caesarean Section."

"No problem, Dr. Em."

You might not think it's a problem Laygby, but then you haven't seen me with a scalpel. "Can you get the theatre staff?" I added out loud.

"No problem. I get Almamy."

Almamy was asleep outside Surgical. Laygby sent him to round up the theatre staff from their homes in the village. No telephones in Serabush.

Tiange and Earnest, who lived in the first two houses by the hospital, arrived within ten minutes. "Where theatre keys?" Tiange yawned.

"The keys? The keys," I muttered, looking hopefully first at Laygby then the grandmother. I patted my belly and hips, as if expecting to find pockets in my bedsheet-dress. "Where are they? Where are the keys?" I pleaded. Laygby shook her head and Tiange rolled her eyes to the ceiling. Earnest scanned the floor and shone his torch under the birthing chair, then shrugged. The grandmother turned from me, clutched Jeneba's hand and started to moan rhythmically. This poomui would never save her daughter.

I dropped to the floor and crawled under the bed with my torch. They all stood and gaped.

"Well, help me look for them, dammit."

We scoured the path to my house for the keys, but our lamps and torches were no match for the puddles, mud and grass. We'd have to break into theatre, which with big metal-framed doors, would certainly cause considerable damage. MT would never forgive me.

The last person on Almamy's emergency call-out list was Sesay, and for all Almamy's faults, he always knew in whose bed to find him. Fortunately Sesay had his own set of keys for the generator room.

Laygby and Earnest were lifting Jeneba onto the theatre trolley just as the comforting rumble of the generator brought us light. And lo! There were the elusive theatre keys, pressed deeply into Jeneba's left buttock.

Once in theatre, Jeneba's swollen flesh obscured the space

between the vertebrae for Earnest to pass his spinal needle. He was distraught. "I no able feel the bones-self. Five years don pass since I miss a spinal, Dr. Em."

Good Lord, imagine giving a spinal to a patient with eclampsia? It was totally contra-indicated but our alternative was ketamine and that was even worse.

"Let me try," I offered. After a year's anaesthetics in York, spinals were one thing I was actually good at. Usually.

Jeneba's skin was like playdough, with Earnest's fingerprints and the deeper imprint of the theatre keys the only landmarks. This was going to be a stab in the dark but finally God smiled on me. The needle popped through the coverings of the spinal cord and I injected the local anaesthetic with ease. For the first time since arriving at Serabu, I felt a glimmer of confidence.

After a quick check in *Primary Surgery*, Tiange and I scrubbed with a bar of soap and bowls of water taken from the theatre drum, put on our patched green gowns and recycled rubber gloves and prayed.

"We pray that Jeneba and her baby can be saved this night, tenki ya. Amen."

"Amen," I whispered into my mask. Tiange placed the scalpel firmly into my hand and I made my incision.

Mr. Lord said a beginner should give themselves plenty of room, so I cut deep and straight and long. I worked down through the layers of waterlogged skin, muscle and fibrous coverings of the abdominal wall until I reached the womb. Blood oozed from every level, but Tiange pressed arterial clamps into my hands and I found myself calmly tying off the bleeders.

We were quickly upon the womb wall, and my hands trembled as I made a tiny incision through the paper-thin tissue to reveal a curl of damp hair at the nape of the baby's neck, immediately below my blade. Tiange took the scalpel so I could pull the womb wall open with my fingers then plunge my hands deep into Jeneba's pelvis to grip the baby's head and ease it out. I could feel the womb tearing around my wrists as I pulled the body of a floppy blue baby boy from Jeneba's abdomen. My heart sank as I felt desperately over his chest wall for a heartbeat. There was none.

The room fell silent as I handed the lifeless bundle to Laygby. All

I could hear was the snip of Tiange's scissors as she cut through the umbilical cord. Should I help Laygby at the resuscitation table, or should I stay and try to repair the gaping mess that lay before me? The baby was surely dead already, but maybe I could still save Jeneba.

"Help me, Dr. Em He no breathe," called Laygby.

"Tiange?" My eyes pleaded with the scrub nurse.

"I can pull the placenta Dr. Em. You go look the pickin."

I left Tiange to remove the afterbirth and went to join Laygby, who was now doing mouth to mouth on the tiny mite. Earnest had laid out a miniature rubber endotracheal tube and a rusty laryngoscope.

The laryngoscope may have illuminated the vocal cords of the very first baby delivered by Sister Hilary thirty years ago, but its light was not coming on today. "Come ON!" I slammed the piece of equipment against the table. The bulb flickered and I took my brief opportunity to slip a tube into Jeneba's baby's windpipe before it went out again. Laygby connected an ambu-bag to the end of the tube and I squeezed the bag gently but rapidly to pump air into our patient's little lungs. Laygby massaged his heart with her fingertips, tapping out compressions over his breastbone like a Morse code operator.

"Can you connect up the oxygen, Laygby?"

"No oxygen, Dr. Em."

"WHAT...? Of course not. Sorry. I knew that."

I kept pumping the bag until my fingers cramped. I swapped hands and kept going. Laygby did the same with her heart massage. Tiange removed the placenta, clamped the edges of the womb then covered the open wound with a warm damp cloth until I could continue. The minutes passed.

Just as I was about to give up and return to Jeneba, I felt a little resistance as I pumped the bag.

"Wait." I stopped and watched. The bag sucked in a fraction of its own accord, then a little more.

"The baby's breathing!" I squealed with delight.

"And I able feel his pulse," added Laygby.

"Let me feel." I pushed Laygby's hand away in my eagerness to confirm her report. The little heartbeat tapped my fingers from under his left nipple, slowly at first, then fifty, sixty, ninety and finally one hundred and forty beats a minute.

"Laygby, you're right!" I shrieked. "He's made it. The young survivor started to take his own regular breaths through the endotracheal tube. I pulled out the tube and he coughed, then let out a furious cry. What music!

Earnest helped me into a new pair of gloves. Spurred on by the baby's cry, I took my time and sewed up Jeneba's womb, Tiange telling me where they usually put the knots.

An hour later, I bounced out of theatre into the dawn of a new morning, my head nearly too big to get out of the door. I'd saved a life! Two! Wait till I told Morag! And Klaus! And Lindsey's granny!

It would not be a discrete little wound that could hide under a bikini but fortunately, in a society keen on tribal markings, a large and ugly scar seemed to be something to be proud of.

Break a Leg

Jeneba's baby was eighteen hours old and was screaming for his dinner. His mother lay in a coma. This wasn't promising.

"The pickin is hungry." Theresa, the first-year student nurse, took the baby and put him to his unconscious mother's breast. But no matter what angle she tried, he wasn't going to latch on.

"Any formula milk?"

"No. No milk, no bottle," Theresa answered. Normally I would have been pleased that Western marketing of bottle milk hadn't reached rural Sierra Leone, but this baby needed food.

"Well, he'll have stores for a few days." And then what? If his mother died, which was looking very likely, what would become of him? Deflated, I continued my evening rounds.

A young woman was being brought in by native ambulance – a hammock slung beneath a wooden pole with either end balanced on the heads of two men. As the 'ambulance-men' gently lowered their patient onto the bed, I recognised her. It was Musu, the orange-seller from The Junction – pregnant, recently widowed, near-starved and now with a broken leg – her tibia and fibula jutting out at a sickening angle through mud and blood. I turned to the first Good Samaritan. "What hap...? Almamy! Did you just carry Musu all the way from the Junction?"

"Yes."

"Three miles! On your head!" Quite a feat for anyone, never mind for the terminally lazy Almamy. I was so impressed that I did not ask what Almamy was doing up at the Junction when he should have been on duty an hour ago. Probably conducting a bit of his own business to the poda-poda passengers. "So what happened?"

"That passenger no pay Musu," he said. "An the poda-poda don begin go. Musu don chase am."

"Musu was chasing the poda-poda for her money?" I could visualise the heavily pregnant young woman desperately trying to get her few leones.

"Yes Dr. Em, and dat poda-poda don tip over."

"Trapping Musu underneath?" I winced. Having seen the overloaded poda-podas, it had to happen.

"Yes Dr. Em."

I made my plan: anaesthetise her with a spinal, clean out all the muck, pull the bones into anatomical alignment and support it in plaster. Not that I had ever put a cast on. But there was no time for such minor worries – the trauma had started labour and Musu's contractions were coming hard and fast, and just for added interest, the baby was the wrong way up. I needed to do whatever I was going to do quickly. Giving birth was bad enough, but a breech delivery with a dangling broken leg? Urgh!

"Kushe, Musu, I want fix that leg..." But Musu wasn't interested in my explanation. She just clicked her fingers at the peak of each contraction.

"Almamy, can you call the theatre staff."

"No problem." Almamy trotted off.

Minutes later he reappeared with Tiange and Co. We manoeuvred Musu onto the theatre trolley and headed towards the operating room. An old woman stood in front of the doors blocking our way.

"Kushe Ma, er, can I help?" She didn't utter a word. Nor did she move out of the way.

"Who's this?" I mouthed to Dauda. Short of mowing the old woman down with the trolley, I was a bit stuck.

"This is Musu's mother."

"Ah." I nodded to the unfriendly face in greeting. "What's the problem?"

"She wants the Native Healer," explained Dauda. After all, everybody knows that broken legs go to the Native Healer.

Well, I tried logical explanation, pleading and cajoling, and when that failed, shouting and stamping my foot, but Musu's mother was not going to let me put on even a temporary backslab. Spoils the magic. Tiange leaned against Surgical's doorway, peeling an orange and the patients grinned delightedly at the entertainment.

Five hours later Musu's baby arrived, bottom first as predicted. I had only ever watched a breech delivery as a medical student, and it looked scary. Okay, okay. The obstetrician had used the lithotomy position, so Theresa helped me hoist Musu's legs up onto poles, which left her foot hanging by its tendons. I grimaced in sympathy, but had to concentrate on my part of the job. Then the obstetrician had eased the baby's hips downwards… there. A limp body slid out, leaving the head stuck with the arms pinned up against the ears in surrender. God, this wasn't looking too good.

Four minutes, I had four minutes tops if I wanted to deliver a live child. Arms, he hooked down the arms, didn't he? Musu's mother holding the two halves of her daughter's broken limb steady, glared at me. Taking a deep breath, I reached inside Musu to pull down first one then the other of her baby's arms. Now it was dangling by the neck. Musu clicked her fingers a little louder as I twisted the head round… and up… and plop! Out popped out a little girl! The baby cried, I laughed with relief and Musu beamed. But still her mother did not smile.

The next morning, Musu was asleep on the bed, her baby asleep by her side and her mother asleep under the bed. Laygby had propped two sandbags on either side of Musu's leg for some support. The baby stirred so I picked her up.

"She's beautiful, what's she called?"

"Laygby."

"After you? How lovely." I smiled at the little bundle.

"Musu did not name her pickin after me." The midwife said.

"No? It's a pretty name. Perhaps if I ever have a little girl, I'll call her Laygby."

"Oh no, Dr. Em, you must not!"

"Why not?" I asked, surprised at Laygby's outburst.

"Laygby means 'I was born after my father has died.'"

"Oh." I bit my lip. "Sorry. Do we know why Musu's husband died?"

"He don dry. He no get money for come na hospital."

"Well Musu's losing weight too. We need to start her on charity feeding and get Latif to check for HIV and TB. Can you arrange all that Laygby?"

"No problem."

"Meanwhile, what about this broken leg? You've done well with those sandbags, but…"

Just then Mariama appeared in Maternity's doorway with a tiny, stooped old man wearing a gara suit much like Nat's. He was carrying a raffia basket over his arm. "Dr. Em, this is Pa Kamara, the Native Healer."

"*This* is the Native Healer?" I blurted. Where was the six-foot witch doctor covered in war paint, dressed in feathers, black cloak and a headpiece with perhaps a monkey's skull set into the front? I was vaguely insulted that my medical skills had been spurned in favour of this unprepossessing character. Mariama led the elderly gentleman to Musu's bed.

Musu's mother jumped up, prodded her daughter awake, guiltily hid the sandbags under the bed and stood to attention. Pa Kamara nodded, put down his basket and motioned for Laygby to bring him a bucket of water. I sidled towards the door, not wanting my poomui presence to interfere with the magic. Mariama caught my hand and mouthed, "You can stay."

Amidst much chanting, Pa Kamara rubbed what looked suspiciously like plassas into the broken leg then dragged his hands, sodden with the green gunge from the thigh to the foot, pulling her leg in line. As soon as he let go it flopped back to its unnatural right angle.

After a dozen pulls and humming an ever-higher note he ran his hands up the skin from her foot to her thigh, gradually straightening her leg. Musu lay still and silent, although having someone hauling on your broken leg must have been agony. Her mother offered her no comfort, standing several feet from the bed, ramrod straight and expressionless while Pa Kamara climaxed with an enormous groan and shoved the ends of the broken bones together. I was the only one to wince. Then he tied a series of little twigs round the fracture site with twine. I had to admit he made a very neat job.

Just when I thought he had finished, Pa Kamara reached into his basket and pulled out a chicken. The bird, which had been quite silent until now, had a flurry of justified panic. Pa Kamara held its body under his arm and snapped its right leg in two. He resumed his chanting while splinting the chicken's broken leg with a tiny piece of cloth and twine.

"When dat fowl walka, Musu go walka," he announced, setting the squawking chicken on the floor to hop to refuge under the bed. Poor thing. Suddenly I could visualise Tikka, tied to a rope outside my house, innocently pecking at her rice, and went off all ideas of a chicken dinner. Pa Kamara picked up his basket and left.

There was still work to do, so I moved over to Jeneba in the neighbouring bed. After two days the swelling that had so distorted her body had receded, revealing the fine features beneath, but Sleeping Beauty lay without an eyelid flickering nor a finger twitching. I cuddled her baby.

"Poor little thing. He's not going to have a mother."

"Jeneba will recover," Laygby stated.

"Says who?"

"Sister Hilary say we must never give up."

Unfortunately, we don't all have Hilary's Midas touch. I sighed.

"Does this little one have a name, Laygby?"

"He is called Problem."

"Problem? You can't call a baby Problem!"

"He is called Problem."

"Well then Problem, why are you so happy today? Have you found some milk?"

"Musu don feed him fine," said Laygby.

"What?" I turned back to the emaciated young woman with a broken leg who could scarce have stores to sustain herself and her own baby, never mind that of a stranger. And what if her husband had died of AIDS and she was also positive? But Problem needed food, and was there a choice?

Problem didn't think so. He burped and Musu smiled.

LET THEM EAT PLASSAS

Laygby went to MT, holder of the purse strings, to plead for food. "MT say money is not there."

I was in the middle of Outpatients, so I only had time to scrawl "MUST HAVE CHARITY FEEDING" in big black pen across Musu's chart. Laygby tried again and returned to say MT would allow free treatment, but Musu would have to find her own food.

"What treatment? Pa Kamara's treating her leg! And Musu's feeding Jeneba's baby as well as her own." I stormed up to Admin.

"Sister Ignatius. I insist we feed Musu."

"I would be grateful if you would knock before entering, Dr. Joy." MT glared, instantly shrivelling my confidence.

"But... but she probably has TB, she's lost her husband and has a baby to nurse. Two babies in fact." My voice was getting shrill. I could never be assertive without getting upset. "She cannot live on water. We must feed her!"

"There are too many charity cases. We have already delivered her baby for free."

"But she and her baby will die of starvation." I was pleading now. I needed to steady myself and reclaim the advantage with some logical argument that might appeal on a financial level. "If they die, we've wasted time and money." Yes, that sounded better. "Two lives saved will look better on the Annual Report than two added to the mortality figures." Inspirational.

"Very well, Dr. Joy," she sniffed, briskly signing the chart. "But if you have any more such cases you can feed them yourself." She stood up. "Now if you will excuse me."

I was dismissed.

Back in Outpatients, Ma Kpukoma told me she was unable to have a little sibling for Patricia, her exuberant ten-year old. I knew what a wonderful nanny she was to Philippe and Nicole's children and I was finding it really hard telling someone so deserving that there was nothing I could do to help.

"Kushe, Dr. Em! Kushe Ma Kpukoma!" AJ, a first year student nurse, swaggered in.

"AJ. Can't you knock!"

"I get for translate for you."

"OK. Sit down AJ."

"We go see back, Ma Kpukoma." He shouted after the dejected lady softly leaving the office. "She no able born other pickin, notto so?" continued AJ. Serabu Hospital's confidentiality policy was a bit lacking. "But she lucky-oh."

"Hardly lucky, AJ."

"But Pa Kpukoma has not left her."

"I should think not!"

"But he no get boy pickin. He get for take other wife."

"AJ!"

The cocky young student shrugged. I bit my tongue. After all polygamy was the norm and I couldn't do without a translator.

"Just try to be kind, AJ."

As the hours passed I became increasingly suspicious of the ever lengthening monologues springing from my simple sentences.

"AJ! What are you saying?" I hissed when a man with inoperable liver cancer left the room with a cheerful thank you.

"I translate fine for you!"

"I have no doubts about your linguistic ability, AJ, but why was he so happy?"

"He gladdi for meet you, Dr. Em!"

"AJ…" I glared at him.

"I don tell him the iron tablets go make him better," he said proudly.

"No they will not! He's terminal."

"But if he does not have fine blood, he will not get better."

"True, but…" I thumped the table in exasperation. "Look, you're a first-year student. Your job is to translate, not transform what I say into something you think sounds better. DO YOU UNDERSTAND?"

"No problem, Dr. Em," he beamed back. Before I could strangle him, Laygby appeared for Antenatal clinic.

"Women's business," said AJ. "We go see back."

"Phew! Okay, Laygby, who's our first patient?"

"Na me."

"You are? Congratulations!" I looked at her outpatient card.

Three-months pregnant. Hang on, one stillbirth, five Caesarean Sections....

"FIVE Caesarean sections?" Three Caesareans was pretty much the limit in my book, partly as the increasing scar tissue makes it technically very difficult, but mostly because the womb wall can weaken to the point of rupture. Uterine rupture is a catastrophe that will kill mother and baby. Laygby would never survive a normal labour, and Philippe would be gone in six months, so it would be up to me to perform her sixth Caesarean. Hopefully I'd be better at it by then.

"My first baby died after many days of labour," Laygby explained. "Sister Hilary saved my life."

"I promise to look after you, but this baby has got to be the last."

"But you are not allowed to do sterilisation, Dr. Em."

"Says who? Your man?"

"No, MT. This is Catholic hospital."

"MT isn't having her sixth Caesarean section. Nor will she be in theatre. What do you want, Laygby?"

"I wanted to be sterilised last time."

"Right. We will call it tubal ligation and hope MT doesn't notice. Will you help me with the rest of clinic?"

Nat was in his usual position, reclined on my sofa with a Star, listening to the World Service.

"Don't administrators ever do any work?"

"Shhh. Listen."

"What?"

"Maggie Thatcher has been thrown out!"

"What? No. Really?" I turned up the volume.

"...and Margaret Thatcher leaves number ten Downing Street with tears in her eyes..."

"Well, well, well. Good riddance."

"Have a heart. Don't you feel sorry for the poor dear? Her life's work in ruins."

"She's left plenty of lives in ruins."

"Forgiveness, Dr. Emily."

"Nat O'Connor, just because you are going to be a priest and ooze virtue, please don't expect it of me."

"I thought you were trying to save your soul?"

"I've got enough problems just now. So who's Prime Minister then?"

"Some chap called John Major."

"John…?"

Before I could ponder further on the identity of the mystery man who was now running my homeland, Pa George dumped a large black pot of plassas on the table with his usual verbal constipation.

"Oh please let's eat Chicken Tikka," begged Nat.

"No. We're keeping her for eggs."

Mustapha took health education and childhood vaccinations to the remote corners of Bumpe chiefdom. He was one of the first nurses to be trained by Sister Hilary but, despite his thirty years loyal service, Mustapha was particularly unpopular with MT. Perhaps it was because he was a Muslim, or even worse, because he was always fetching nonpaying patients from his Community Outreach Team.

"Sorry-oh, Dr. Em. I bring you one patient from the villages."

Pa Bangura stood, barefoot, leaning against the Landrover, his black skin ashen and the palms of his hands milky pale.

"Kushe, Pa. Can I look?" Battling with every gasp of breath, the old man just nodded. I pulled down his lower eyelid to look at his sheet-white conjunctiva and felt the racing pulse at his wrist. He was so anaemic that he'd gone into heart failure.

"We need Latif."

"Latif don check his blood count already, Dr. Em. Three grams."

"Three grams! Mustapha, are you sure?" Latif was an excellent laboratory technician, but in the UK, a blood count of five grams would normally be a ticket to the intensive care unit. Pa Bangura shouldn't really be alive.

"Three grams," Mustapha repeated.

"Who can give blood?"

Philippe had told me to avoid transfusions where possible, because of the risk of AIDS, hepatitis, malaria and bacterial contamination. With our pathetic refrigeration, a blood bank was impossible, so Pa Bangura's only hope was to find a donor.

"He only has one wife. Look at her," Mustapha nodded to a pale old lady sitting patiently in the back seat of the Landrover.

"Latif had better check her blood count too," I sighed. "Any children?"

"All the pickins don die. There is no other relative to donate."

"Oh dear. What happens now?"

"Latif will go to the village. He get a list of donors."

"Good, well let's get Pa Bangura into Medical and organise a transfusion."

"But Dr. Em, Latif get for pay the donor."

"How much?"

"Each pint, one thousand leones."

"He'll need at least three. I don't suppose Pa…" I looked at the old man's torn shorts, and bare, skeletal chest.

"No. You must get the money from the charity fund," said Mustapha. "Sorry-oh."

Nat was on Admin duty in the afternoons, so hopefully that wouldn't be too much of a problem.

"Kushe," I greeted Moses in the front office, having swapped his driver's hat for that of records officer.

"Kushe, Dr. Em. How di body?"

"I tell God tenki. Is Nat in? I need three thousand leones for blood."

"Nat don go to Mokanje. MT is on duty. Sorry-oh."

"Damn," I muttered under my breath. "What's he doing at the Mines anyway?"

The Swiss-owned bauxite mining company was just over an hour's journey away in Mokanje. Nat and I argued over the Mines' ethics, but there was no doubt we had a symbiotic relationship. Serabu looked after the Mines' families, national and expatriate, and the Mines helped us out with the odd barrel of diesel or spare sheet of corrugated iron.

"The Mines' people don radio today," explained Moses. "They get parts for the water pumps."

With the water pumps down, I knew what a priority it was to fix them before the dry season, but at that moment, I wanted Nat right here.

My best bet was to bring Pa Bangura to Admin, so MT could see his condition for herself.

"Sister Ignatius, his blood count is dangerously low, he must have a transfusion." I put my hand on Pa Bangura's shoulder as he propped himself against the table to counter-balance his heaving chest.

"Let him pay for a donor," MT said, not looking up from her accounts.

"I beg... Sister... I get... no pickin... my wife... no well..." Pa Bangura gasped.

"No." MT did not have heartstrings that could be tugged. "Dr. Joy, you had a charity patient only yesterday."

"Sister Ignatius, this is not a lost cause, but a life we can save," I begged. "Pa Bangura will do very well with a transfusion and iron treatment."

"Aw fo du. Let him eat more plassas." And she left the office with a swish of her habit.

"Mary bloody Antoinette!" Nuns are supposed to shelter heroes from Nazis, not turn sick old men away from hospitals! I kicked open the back door. "Find him some blood Moses, I'll pay for it."

I stomped out.

We may have rid ourselves of the real Maggie Thatcher, but who was going to oust Serabu's own?

A WOMAN'S LIFE

MT had opened a vein of bad-temper that I never knew I possessed. Self-improvement? Huh! Well God could just concentrate on her soul and forget mine. Philippe was due back in a matter of hours and once he arrived, I was going home. Home home. In the meantime I had my rounds to finish.

Maternity Ward did nothing to improve my mood. Jeneba remained comatose, despite my surgical meddling, and no matter what Sister Hilary might have said, I wished she'd just pass away peacefully, rather than put her family through any more suffering. Musu was still feeding Laygby and Problem, but what if she did have AIDS? Musu gave me a lovely smile, but her mother sat stoney-faced on the edge of the bed.

"Doesn't that woman ever smile, Laygby?" I snapped. "I've agreed to the Native Healer, I've brought her grand-daughter into the world after quite a tricky breech delivery and I've made an enemy out of MT getting charity feeding for *her* daughter." What was I looking for? Gratitude?

YES!

"She did not want a girl pickin for Musu."

"What?"

I could almost hear the Suffragettes weeping. Speechless, I walked out.

Patrick Kpukoma was waving a chart from the doorway of Medical. "Dr. Em. You get for sign for the blood."

"Blood?"

"For Pa Bangura-self."

"We've got blood?

"Yes, Mustapha don give one pint and Moses go give his own this evening."

"Oh well done! Well done." I couldn't believe it. They were marvellous. "You don't need me."

"Oh, Dr. Em!" Patrick Kpukoma blushed through his dark skin.

Well maybe they didn't, but I was so touched by the staff's kindness to an old man that I decided that I just might stay after all.

Philippe returned that evening with some flesh covering his ribs and Pierre's skin back to baby's bottom quality. He had also collected three letters from the VSO office. My granny's petunias hadn't survived the recent frost and our squash team seemed to be doing depressingly well without me, but what was this third envelope? I ripped it open to find two pages of school jotter covered in tiny script. Klaus!!

Opening a bottle of Star, I settled into my sofa to read a list of complaints longer than my own: no water, no electricity, no funds, no tools, no spares, a workshop full of broken vehicles, cockroaches, driver ants, prickly heat and so much plassas that he was worried he might have jaundice because his palms and soles were turning yellow. I laughed out loud. At least I was not alone.

Next morning we were on the scrounge for another pint of blood.

"Tom's anaemic." I crossed the American off my list.

"Quelle surprise. This man has always the malaria. Pah! He eats not even the fish."

"So, where to find another candidate..." My eye caught Nat, wandering towards Admin, which conveniently backed onto the lab. "Quick!" Philippe and I nipped into the lab.

"Kushe, Dr. Em. Kushe Dr. Fleep." Latif looked up from his microscope. "Wetin do?"

"Kushe, Latif. We need your services."

"No problem."

"Do you know what blood group Nat is?" I nodded through the window towards the bleary eyed red-head, still suffering from the excesses he had been forced to endure during his trip to the Mines.

"Yes, Dr. Em. I have the staff list." Latif brandished a chart. "O positive, Dr. Em. Like Pa Bangura-self."

"Great. Get him, boys."

Latif and Philippe hustled Nat into the lab and were draining blood from Nat's arm before he had time to object. He promptly fainted. Mariama appeared with a cup of tea and Philippe produced a piece of chocolate he'd brought from Freetown (and had been keeping very quiet about) which brought Nat swiftly round. Latif resumed his business of blood letting and Nat swooned again, but this time with one eye half open.

"Perhaps another piece of chocolate might rouse him, Philippe?" I suggested.

Twenty-four hours, three pints of blood and six little tablets for hookworm later, the old man was transformed. We'd treated his wife too.

"Moses don put his admission notes in the three-stone fire," whispered Mariama as we watched the Banguras sit cross-legged on the floor, sharing a bowl of Pa George's leftover plassas.

"Now all they need are iron tablets and flip-flops to stop any more hookworm burrowing in through their feet."

"A big success," smiled Mariama. "You deserve some time off, Dr. Em. Come to the celebration this evening."

"I'd love to. What sort of celebration?"

"The girls are coming out. I come for you eight o'clock?"

"That will be nice. Eight o'clock," I agreed, but Mariama was gone before I could ask what she meant by Coming Out.

"So what is it? This Coming Out?" I asked Nat over our plassas.

"The girls spend two weeks in the bush undergoing their initiation. When they come out of the bush, they are accepted into society as women available for marriage and everybody celebrates."

"Like debutantes?"

"Yes, except I don't think debutantes get circumcised."

"What?!"

"All the women get circumcised here. Jaysus, you're a doctor. You must have seen the evidence."

"Well, yes." I had seen the scars. Irregular lines of raised, lumpy scar tissue where once there was a sensitive clitoris, running down the upper vagina to the urethra.

"So why the big surprise?"

"Why would Mariama invite us to celebrate such an awful thing?" I felt a bit sick.

"It's a big event," said Nat.

"I'm not going."

"You'll insult Mariama."

"It's collusion."

"It's education. Come on Em. You've got to work with Mariama and the others for the next two years. It's a big party."

"You mean they party round these poor girls whilst they lie screaming and bleeding as some man hacks away their genitalia with razor blades!"

"No, no. They've done all that already in the bush. At the Coming Out all the girls get to wear their new clothes and are presented to society. Besides it's the women that do the circumcisions."

"Women do it to each other?"

"They do it to remove all trace of man. It's a sacred passage to womanhood."

"God."

"Will you come?" Nat leaned towards me. "Please. Mariama wants you to come, I know. Don't you see. She needs you to understand."

"I won't understand."

"Try."

"Okay," I sighed. "Okay."

Mariama arrived exactly at eight o'clock. She looked great, with her hair tied up in a colourful head-dress so that her big gold earrings could swing freely. She wore the traditional gown and lappa: a loose-fitting, knee-length poncho made in a heavily sheened deep green cotton targeted with several golden tie-dyed circles and richly embroidered in white thread across the yoke, worn over a plain green lappa (like a sarong) that fell to her gold sandals. I felt very dowdy in my short-sleeved blue denim dress.

"Oh Mariama, I need some new clothes."

"Ma Kpukoma will make gara for you, then we visit the tailor," said Mariama. "A gown and lappa would be fine for you. You get body."

Okay, okay. I am fat. I should be proud to get body. And Mariama was right, I probably would look good in a gown and lappa. At last, a fashionable outfit that would cover my bulges!

"I'd like that, Mariama."

"We de go?"

"Yes, let's go."

Nat was marching up the path wearing a new gara suit – navy blue with purple tie-dye.

"Love the new suit, Nat."

"And you ladies both look marvellous. Shall we go?" Nat offered us an arm each and we made our way to the village. It was a beautiful night, stars littered the sky around a sliver of a moon, with no clouds or streetlights to detract from their glory.

We could hear drumming and singing long before we reached the market-square. The main street was packed with people dancing, all dressed in multicoloured gara. They danced to a beat, played out by groups of drummers on goat-skin drums and children with sticks on coconuts or rusty tins. There were six or seven 'devils' working their way through the crowds – in haystack skirts and head-dresses strewn with multicoloured pom-poms. Like lap dancers, they writhed and cavorted before both men and women.

One gyrated under my nose, then rubbed his belly against mine.

"Oh!" I gasped and stepped back. He did it again. I giggled anxiously.

"He want money," Mariama told me.

"Oh he does, does he? Where am I supposed to put it? Down his grass skirt?"

"He won't mind where," said Nat, slipping my devil twenty leones. The devil twirled round in appreciation then brushed his body over mine again.

"Good Lord." Afraid of spending my two years in Serabu under a curse, I hastily handed over twenty leones. My devil took the money in his teeth, tossed his straw head-dress in appreciation, then picked another victim.

AJ appeared from behind a devil, clutching a two-gallon plastic container and three chipped cups.

"You want poyo?"

"Tenki-ya." Mariama and Nat took the cups and AJ poured cloudy liquid into each.

"What's that?" I asked, taking a sniff of the cup Mariama handed to me. "Urgh." I recoiled. It smelled like diluted vomit.

"Poyo. Palm wine." Mariama smiled and drank hers down in one. AJ filled it up again.

"Palm wine?"

"It's the fermented sap from palm trees. It's good. Drink it." Nat drank and AJ refilled.

"Hmm," I said dubiously, sniffing again. It didn't smell any better.

AJ grinned encouragement, poised with his container. There was no escape. I would have to drink. I threw the poyo over my taste buds and swallowed, concentrating hard for a few moments to make sure it stayed down.

"Well done." Nat slapped me on the back, making me gag. Nat gave AJ fifty leones to top me up and I gave the student a sick smile. AJ gave me the thumbs up and moved on through the crowd in search of more customers.

By then we had reached the market-square. The stalls had been dismantled and in their place were fifteen makeshift armchairs, covered with gara. On each of these thrones sat a girl dressed in white, holding an umbrella. Their heads were bowed and their eyes covered by cheap plastic sunglasses in fluorescent pinks and greens, obscuring expressionless young faces.

"Sunglasses!" I hissed. "Why those awful sunglasses?" I was stunned. I could imagine some gum-chewing prepubescent American wearing them, but not here. This was a celebration of an ancient tradition that I could only begin to comprehend or forgive in the context of its deep cultural roots. But to me, the sunglasses made a mockery of the whole thing.

"Your mother tells you it is the most important occasion of your life," Mariama explained. "You get new clothes. You will become a woman. You able ask for anything."

"Sunglasses?"

""The girls want sunglasses."

I was horrified. How could Mariama condone such a thing? She was so well educated. "But isn't it just the Muslims?"

"No. Also Christians. All must be initiated."

"Why don't the mothers stop it?"

"The mothers are too frightened. If a girl isn't initiated, she's not clean. Then she can't belong to her society. And then she can't marry."

"That's awful," I shuddered. I wanted to ask Mariama if she had been initiated, and if so, what it was like, but I didn't dare.

"The girls look forward to initiation."

"But do they know? Do they really know what will happen?" I insisted.

Mariama shook her head sadly.

"Good God." I wanted to cry for the girls in their longed-for sunglasses. Some were fully-fledged women, yet others could be no more than seven or eight. "But some are just children!"

"It is 'spensive to initiate a daughter. If you able pay when she is young, the men know you get money and she will marry better."

"Poor kids. Can't you refuse?"

"It is hard. No mother wants her daughter to be an outcast. I was very happy when Hindolu was a boy."

"Oh Mariama."

I thought of Musu's mother's disappointment at having a granddaughter. And Mariama, getting hit over the wrists as a girl for crying when she picked up the boiling pot. And Laygby bearing another child at great risk to her own survival. And Jeneba. God, Jeneba. I shuddered. All I had to worry about was being manless and a bit chubby. If I was a Salonean woman, I wouldn't want my baby to be a girl either.

"What for chop today?" Pa George was thumping on my bedroom door. "You are too much late."

"Okay, I'm coming." Urgh, that poyo! Tentatively pulling my dress over my thumping head, I went to open the door. Pa George thrust a dead snake under my nose.

"Look," he said. I recoiled. This was no way to treat a girl with a hangover.

"Yes, Pa George, I can see." It was over four-foot long and had shiny leaf green skin.

"I kill this today outside you door," he announced proudly.

"Thank you, Pa George. Is it poisonous?"

"Very poisonous."

"Oh. What do you call this kind of snake?" I asked, thinking I ought to know for future reference.

"This is green snake."

"Of course."

"What for chop today?"

"I'll leave it to you Pa George," I said without thinking, too busy feeding Tikka and vaguely wondering when she'd start laying eggs. Suddenly I realised I needed to be more specific. "But not the snake."

Pa George shrugged and arranged his trophy on the doorstep instead.

Philippe was striding up my path. "Bonjour, bonjour. Come quick."

Oh dear, I *was* rather late. "Is there a problem, Philippe?"

"Viens." I trotted behind my Medical Superintendent to Maternity. He held the door open for me and I froze. Sitting in the bed opposite was a beautiful young mother, tucking into a plateful of plassas whilst a baby slept at her breast.

Jeneba? Jeneba!!

I was speechless.

"Jeneba, this is Dr. Em," said Laygby.

"Kushe, Dr. Em," grinned Jeneba. "I gladdi to meet you."

I burst into tears.

A CHRISTMAS CAROL

Two months in Serabu and still only on page ninety of *Tess of the d'Urbervilles*. Tsk, tsk. At least I had managed to save a few lives.

Jeneba and Problem, the first two notches on my stethoscope, had long since been discharged, although I would have happily kept them on Maternity forever just for the ego-boost. The other good news was that Musu, Problem's wet-nurse, was HIV negative although she did have tuberculosis. But dry cough was treatable and Musu was already two stones heavier. The broken legged chicken continued to hide under her bed and had even produced a couple of eggs but there was still no smile from the grandmother from hell. I turned to page ninety-one.

"Open the door for the children,
Open the door for the ch-il-dren,
Open the door for the children
Christ is born today."

Glad of the distraction, I opened the door. Eight schoolgirls clapped their hands and banged their homemade drums, wiggling their hips in patched dresses that either brushed ankles or scarcely covered bottoms. After the opening number, they abandoned their rehearsed classroom English and lost themselves in the rhythms of their own Mende carols. The first of December obviously qualified as carol-singing season.

Patricia Kpukoma was the ringleader, and thus bearer of the group's one kerosene lamp, which swung dangerously as she danced. The song finished and they reorganised themselves into a neat line. Sixteen hopeful eyes twinkled at me from glowing faces.

Full of Christmas cheer, I gave them twenty leones each and they skipped off delighted.

"You gave them how much?" exclaimed Nat.

"Twenty leones."

"Each?"

"Of course, each. Come on, Nat, it's Christmas!"

"Hah! Just you wait. Christmas is three weeks off yet."

The dry season had well and truly begun. God had gradually turned up his thermostat and my prickly heat reared its red spotted head again. Only two weeks to the High Commissioner's Christmas party and the cooling sea breezes of Freetown's beaches. The deep-green palm trees and vegetation that lined the laterite roads were turning autumnal in colour, but it was with red dust rather than mellow fruitfulness. Without an egg to her name, it seemed that Tikka was also barren. Aw fo du. There was always plassas.

The river was reduced to a trickle and the water pumps were still broken. Thank God for Pa George who brought me two buckets a day from the well. I resolved to give him a large Christmas bonus. I was not to be the only one giving that Christmas, for my first present arrived that evening.

"Dr. Em, you want beef?" A rosy Pa Bangura stood on my doorstep with a large sack slung over his shoulder.

"Kushe! How di body Pa?"

"I tell God tenki, Dr. Em. I get fine blood now." He pulled down the lower lids of his eyes and I peered approvingly at healthy pink conjunctivae.

"Very good Pa."

"I bring you beef."

Beef? Since my arrival in Salone, I hadn't seen a single cow, but before I could ask, Pa Bangura tipped an Alsatian-sized rat onto my kitchen floor. It lay like in typical dead rat pose, feet in the air with a blind goofy-toothed stare. I stared back at it, edging my foot out from under the metre-long tail that had flopped over my sandal.

"Fine beef, Dr. Em. I catch him today," announced Pa Bangura proudly.

"Beef?" I finally found my voice.

"Na so." He was obviously very pleased with his present. "For you."

"Tenki Pa, but you should eat this yourself. Plenty iron for you and your wife." This impressive specimen was certainly nutritious, and might well have been very tasty but I wasn't eating it. Pa Bangura looked crestfallen.

"I don't know how to cook it." I changed tack. "Pa George has gone for the weekend." This should work better – we poomuis were known to be incapable of doing anything practical for ourselves.

Pa Bangura cast his eyes down. Oh hell. "Pa, this beef better for you, it get plenty protein and plenty iron." I tried a final time to convince him that his need was greater than mine.

"Tenki ya, Dr. Em. We go see back." He stuffed the rat back into the sack and slouched back down the path.

I sighed and sat down to Pa Georges' plassas. It looked surprisingly appealing.

Nat was furious. "It's a mighty insult to refuse a gift!"

"Sorry, but rat!"

"Or monkey, or snake. Besides it was a cutting-grass, more overgrown guinea pig than rat, and they're actually rather good."

"Rat, guinea pig…" I shook my head.

"You can't afford to be rude, and you certainly can't afford to be fussy. Just 'cos you've got plenty of stores…"

"Nat…" I warned.

"And I'm SO SICK of plassas! Won't you get Pa George to cook Tikka? Pleeeese. She's never going to lay."

"No!"

We sat in silence on my doorstep until Nurse Sankoh, junior entrepreneur, sauntered into view.

"Dr. Em, you want egg?"

"Eggs! Great! How much?" Nurse's timing couldn't have been better.

"Forty leones." He produced two from his pocket and I handed over the money. Nurse put it in his shoe and ran off.

"You shouldn't buy eggs from Nurse without checking them." Nat sniggered.

"What for?"

"Chickens."

"Huh?"

"You've got to check for chickens." Nat took the eggs and plonked them into a cup of water. "Yup. They're floating." He cracked them open to a tangle of feather. "Chickens."

"Urgh."

"Protein. You all need plenty protein." A new week, a new battle with the TB patients.

"You give me mericine, Dr. Em. Protein too much spensif," complained Ibrahim, six weeks into treatment, and still only nudging five stone.

"Those tablets and injections just won't work unless you chop plenty protein. Beef, fish..."

"Too spensif, Dr. Em, too spensif." Ibrahim chewed his kola nut, Africa's answer to cocaine. Kola might assuage his hunger, but he would still starve.

"Spend your money on beans and groundnuts rather than kola," I persisted. "You must eat protein. Look at how well Princess is doing." I nodded towards the pregnant Liberian refugee that we had managed to get on charity feeding a week or so earlier. But as soon as the words were out of my mouth I realised that I had chosen the wrong example.

"But Princess get charity feeding!" Ibrahim exploded into a coughing fit.

"We no get charity feeding, Dr. Em!" The others rallied to his cause.

"Give we all charity feeding, Dr. Em, then we all get fine body."

"Sorry-oh, we can't feed you all," I shouted above the outcry. "Aw fo do."

Oh why oh why had I mentioned Princess? Patrick Kpukoma glowered at me. I mouthed sorry and beat a hasty retreat.

I ran straight into Nurse, lurking outside TB ward.

"Psst. You want egg, Dr. Em?" There was little doubt that the origin of his eggs were suspect, but the appeal of an omelette was too strong to question too deeply. As long as the eggs sank. I marched Nurse up to my house to check them.

"Okay Nurse, I think these are good."

"Forty leones, Dr. Em."

"No. Those others were bad. Twenty."

"Forty leones," Nurse insisted.

"Twenty."

"Okay, Dr. Em. Thirty."

"Very well. Thirty. But no more eggs with chickens in them," I said assertively, ever so proud of my little bargaining triumph.

We were eating boiled eggs on the doorstep when Pa Ali walked past for his nightly visit to tap poyo from the palm tree behind my house.

"Dr. Em, bua."

"Bua, bise, Pa Ali." Pa Ali had the physique of a feather-weight boxer with leathery skin stretched over stringy muscles. He wore only a ragged pair of shorts

"Bise, bi gahun yena?" he beamed, revealing his three teeth in the dark. He was late tonight.

"Kayingoma. A bia be?"

"Kayingoma. Malo-hua."

"Malo-hua."

Our greeting routine was now as much a part of my daily rhythm as Pa Georges' plassas. 'Hello. Thank you, hello. Thank you, how are you? Thanks be to God, what about you? Good-bye'.

"He's too old to be up there." I watched as the wiry man hung off the prickly side of the palm tree, suspended by a loop of woven cane in the moonlight. He dug a sharp hollow metal pipe into the tree and drained the sap. The longer he left it in the large yellow plastic container, the more it would ferment.

"It's his living. From God to Man."

"What are you on about now?"

"Poyo comes straight from the tree, from God to Man. Which means 'tee-total' Muslims and guilt-crippled volunteers can drink it quite happily."

"You'd have to be desperate to drink that stuff." I cringed, remembering AJ's offering at the Coming Out.

"Listen, we *are* desperate. Our beer's don don. It really is the dry season."

"Well it's only two weeks 'til the High Commissioner's Party." I hugged myself with excitement. "I could stock up."

"Off jaunting to Freetown already? Anyway, you'd never get a crate of beer back on a poda-poda."

"Excuse me." I jabbed my finger into his chest. "All VSOs are expected to attend the Christmas Conference."

"Oh my."

"And look at you. Always off to Mokanje."

"Urgent hospital business," Nat sniffed.

"Yeah, lots of business to be done at the Mines' swimming pool."

"'Tis amazing what donations and price reductions you can get with the personal touch." Nat tapped his nose smugly.

"So why is there no water coming out of my taps, then?"

"Jaysus, you're worse than MT. You try finding parts for electric water pumps up-country," he sulked. "Of course. That's it!"

"What?"

"Your excuse to take the Landrover. *You* can find the spares in Freetown and bring back as many crates of Star as we can find money for."

"We ought to put that money into our own charity fund," I mused. "Then I wouldn't need to beg MT for food for my TB patients."

"Jaysus, you sound like Tom. Don't start feeling guilty, Emily. You'll always have more than anybody here. Most people back home could buy fifty pints of blood, feed the whole hospital and still have enough for a drink. The way I look at it, the longer you keep your sanity, the longer you'll stay and the more good you can do."

"You'll be a very popular priest, Nat."

Nat was right about the carol singers. Nat was right about everything.

They flocked to my door by twos, by tens and by twenties. Nurse, who now supplied me with a daily egg, kept reappearing, singing loudly in the front row of each group. No wonder he could afford shoes.

Adults and children sang 'Open the door for the children' and I foolishly did as instructed. VSO had not allowed for carol singers in their calculation of monthly living expenses, so I gradually reduced my donation, but obviously insufficiently to dissuade the next group. And the next. And the next. I was almost relieved to find Almamy knocking at my door late one evening.

"You get for come to Maternity." He handed me the chart.

"But this is a Children's Ward chart."

"They call the pickin Maternity."

"I see."

Maternity Sankoh, aged five, was very sick with pneumonia.

"Aisha, can you draw up the antibiotics whilst I put in an IV?"

"No problem, Dr. Em." The young nurse dashed off to find the drugs trolley, leaving me by Maternity's bedside. The little girl sat all alone on the bed. Perhaps her mother had gone to get water and would return soon. Propping herself forwards on her thin arms her chest wall heaved up and down. She desperately needed oxygen but we had none, so all I could do was hope.

"Osh, osh." I tried to take Maternity's hand, but she would not uncurl her fingers from the determined fists that made her props, so intent was she on sucking in each breath. Where was her mother? It was very unusual to find a child alone. Feeling very inadequate, I went to bed. Only six days to Freetown.

Klaus was serenading me in my dreams. I sang along, banging a drum. The tune slowly turned into 'Open the door for the children'. Bang bang bang. I beat my drum and sang 'Open the door for the children'. It was louder now, Bang bang bang.

Open the door for the children." Knock, knock, knock. My eyes snapped open.

"Open the door for the ch-il-dren."

"Oh no." I moaned and squinted at my watch. Half-past one!

"Open the door for the children." Bang bang bang. I pretended not to hear.

"Jesus Christ is born."

"It's the middle of the night. Go away," I yelled from under my pillow. The singing stopped for a second, then continued.

"Open the door for the children."

"Go away!"

"Open the door for the ch-il-dren."

"FOK-OFF!" I screamed at the top of my lungs. Footsteps shuffled off.

Our Krio teacher had informed us, reliably I hoped, that fok-off was acceptable Krio for get lost. Jesus himself shouts it in the Krio Bible to rid the temple of the wheelers and dealers. At least I had made myself understood.

MT would have been proud of me.

NURSE

"You don enjoy the show last night, Dr. Em?"

"What? Those carol singers at one in the morning!" I cringed, embarrassed that word of my bad temper had got round.

"No, no, Dr. Em, the video!"

"The video?" What was Dauda talking about? Surely there were no videos here.

"In the church hall, Dr. Em," AJ chirped. "The Liberians brought a video. Only a hundred leones to get in."

"Oh, I see."

Refugees from Liberia's brutal civil war were fleeing over the border in their thousands, and were being sheltered in Salonean homes, sharing their already meagre resources. They brought with them horrendous stories of the atrocities being committed by the rival rebel factions led by Prince Johnson and Charles Taylor. Both men claimed to have liberated the country from the brutality of the president but, so far, had proved themselves more than able to match any of his atrocities.

The Saloneans gave thanks that they were not, and had never been, involved in such a terrible war. On the other hand they had never been as prosperous as their sophisticated neighbours. Those refugees who had escaped early in the conflict had brought belongings such as televisions and generators that a Salonean wouldn't even dream of. An enterprising refugee could certainly make a nice living from showing videos in village halls.

"So what was the video?" I asked.

"The Killing of President Doe," said Dauda, enthusiastically.

Typical, I thought, a Rambo movie. Then I stopped, remembering far-off news bulletins. "Wasn't he the President of Liberia?"

"Yes. Prince Johnson don kill him," said AJ.

"Was it some kind of documentary then?" I asked, hopefully.

"Oh no, Dr. Em! The rebels don torture him then they don kill him and they don make a video!" AJ enthused.

"Oh," I said, feeling suddenly sweaty and light-headed. Good God, a snuff movie.

"Sorry-oh, Dr. Em."

"No problem," I gulped, assuming Dauda's concern was over my change in colour.

"We are sorry we did not tell you about the film," Dauda continued. "You could have come with us!"

"That's quite all right, Dauda." I found my voice. "There's enough blood for me on Surgical."

"There was plenty plenty people there, Dr. Em," raved AJ.

"Mmm hmm." My hand was still over my mouth.

"Sold out," nodded Dauda.

"Indeed." This was probably the first time any of them had seen a television, I told myself. They would have been just as excited by *The Sound of Music*.

"He was a bad man, President Doe," said Dauda.

"So I understand."

"Yes, he killed hundreds. Thousands. He deserved to die, Dr. Em."

"I'm sure. And these rebel-saints? How many have they killed?"

"Prince Johnson don cut off his ear," AJ continued, ignoring my last comment.

"And then he ate it!" added Dauda. This was too much for me. I left them to their enthusiastic conversation, went outside and threw up.

We big strong girls are not usually squeamish, but Mariama sent me home for a lie down. A hundred yards from my house, I spied a small figure bending in the undergrowth outside my back door. It was Nurse Sankoh.

What was he doing? The mid-morning sun made me squint, but I suddenly knew exactly what he was up to – pinching Tikka's eggs!

"Hoi. Nurse!" I hollered. Startled, he sprinted off. I tried to make chase but an eleven-stone white woman was no match for a wiry

Mende boy. My mind filled with all manner of un-Christmassy thoughts which were never likely to get souls saved, but I was forced to let Nurse go.

Eggs were not the bargain I had thought at thirty leones.

After a cup of water and a banana, I was sufficiently fortified for the TB ward where I found Patrick Kpukoma rollicking Musu's mother.

"Patrick, Patrick! Why are you shouting?"

"She don thief two cups of water from our drum!" His black face was purple with outrage. "For Musu!"

"Two cups of water?" I glared at our normally placid Charge Nurse. Musu's mother was not my favourite lady, but really! "Patrick, this woman's daughter has TB, a broken leg and a newborn, and you are shouting at her for fetching a drink of water?"

"She has a bucket. She get for fetch her own water from the well."

"But it's hot and she's old! Have a heart."

"The well is too far and we nurses are too bweezy."

There was no doubt that since the rains had stopped and water could no longer be collected by barrels under the guttering, the student nurses had been sorely put upon to fetch water from the village well, a good mile away.

"You're as bad as MT. Let this lady have her water, Mr. Kpukoma," I pleaded. "As a Christmas gesture?"

"No. She must fetch her own."

"But…" I stopped. Patrick wasn't going to give in. He'd obviously carried one bucket of water too many that week. "Who's first on our round then?"

Ibrahim smiled sweetly at me from the first bed, then resumed his lunch, spooning something out of a sort of cup. My jaw dropped.

Monkey brains alfresco, straight from the skull. The blood rushed from my face and the whole ward burst out laughing.

"Protein, Dr. Em," Ibrahim announced, mouth full. "You tell us we must chop plenty protein."

Four days, only four days to Freetown.

Maternity, the little girl with pneumonia, was sleeping peacefully on C Ward. The antibiotics had worked their magic and she was breathing normally. I smiled and bent to stroke her head, but then stopped with my hand poised above the sleeping child's tight curls. Bloody Nurse Sankoh was sitting on the end of the bed.

"Aisha, what's that little thief doing here? Touting stolen goods to the patients?"

"Nurse is Maternity's brother," Aisha replied quietly.

"What?" I looked more closely at the boy. He had been crying. "Of course," I whispered, ashamed of myself. Nurse and Maternity Sankoh, children of Serabu Hospital.

"He don sit with Maternity all night," Aisha continued. "Until she breathe fine."

I nodded, then managed to clear the lump in my throat to speak a few banal words. "She'll be fine now, Nurse."

"Tenki-ya, Dr. Em."

"No problem," I said, and paused. I still had not seen the mother. "Um, Nurse, is your mother here? Maternity's mother."

"I am her mother," said Nurse.

"Oh." I furrowed my brow. "What about your father?"

"I am her mother and her father," stated the ten-year-old boy.

"Nurse looks after Maternity," explained Aisha. "He don tell me he try to make plenty money so he can send her to school."

"Oh," was all I could say, before stumbling out of the ward in tears, vowing that in future I would buy as many eggs as possible from Nurse.

"He doesn't stand a chance." I shook my head.

"You have reason, Emily. We have only four bottles of insulin," he confessed. "It is too expensive. One year's insulin would use up the whole drug budget."

"Oh."

"Diabetics are like the junkies, they travel the country, searching, begging and stealing their insulin."

"But if Serabu has none, then who does?"

"A little bit in a clinic here, or a pharmacy there," Philippe shrugged.

"That's awful. Poor Gasimu. It looks like his search ends here."

"Eh, bien, we should not give up without trying." Sister Hilary's legacy lingered. "You can buy some more insulin in Freetown, peut-etre?"

"Okay," I sighed. "You're right, we can't leave Gasimu like this."

Tiange appeared in the doorway. "We do not have any saw."

"No saw? Nothing?"

"The Gigli saw," she suggested.

"Quoi?"

"The cheese wire," I told Philippe, remembering the strange device Tiange had handed me to amputate the fingers last week. "Bloody hell! You surely can't cheese wire through the femur!"

"Then we must do this option." Philippe pointed to the third paragraph. "'Amputation through the knee'."

"Hmmm."

"It says it is most easy. No bone needs to be cut. Just to cut the ligaments and disjoint the bottom from the top. Pas de probleme."

"No problem," I repeated.

In fact it was surprisingly easy. After only forty minutes we were sewing the skin flaps over the stump whilst Earnest wrapped up the leg for disposal. Most 'waste' was dropped down the pit latrines, but a leg was surely too big. Earnest could deal with it. I didn't want to know. I just stood admiring our neat finish.

That evening I returned to the freshly aired ward, with all the patients back in their beds.

"Tenki ya, Dr. Em. Plenti tenki." Gasimu clung to my arm and wept.

Nobody ever went to Freetown without a shopping list. Mine was as follows:

1: Insulin
2: HIV test kits
3: Spares for water pumps
4: Everyone's Christmas mail
5: A few thousand condoms
6: Star beer.

I mentioned the first four items to MT, hinting at the difficulties of carrying them back to Serabu on a poda-poda. It would, of course, be nearly impossible with items five and six. Amazingly she agreed. She would go to Freetown herself for the water pumps and bring me back home. Gosh, my surgical prowess must have really impressed her. Nat, eavesdropping from the back office, gave me the thumbs up, smacking his lips at the prospect of more beer.

But I still had to make my own way to Freetown.

My journey started at dawn, when thankfully it was still cool. After an hour's walk to the Junction, I had joined the poda-poda queue forming under the lone palm tree that offered the only shade. Three women, two babies, a toddler, two teenage lads, an old Pa and a goat greeted me. I smiled back and sat on my rucksack, hoping I wouldn't squash the gown and lappa that Serabu's tailor had made especially for me from Ma Kpukoma's hand-dyed gara.

I wanted to look my best for the High Commissioner's Party – you never knew who might be there.

"Kushe, Dr. Em. You want orange?" I looked up into the hard eyes of Musu's mother. She was looking after her daughter's orange-selling patch.

"Tenki ya."

She peeled off the outer skin, sliced off the top and handed it over. Never being one to roll a toothpaste tube from the bottom, I grabbed it by the middle, threw my head back, and squeezed the juice straight into my mouth. Delicious. I tossed the skin to the Pa's goat, who munched it down. I handed over the money for another.

At noon a poda-poda finally appeared, by which time frustration and eight oranges had given me indigestion. Musu's mother had done a roaring trade from the queue of thirsty passengers and the goat was also looking pretty pleased with itself. The driver prised in my travelling companions, their luggage and the goat, but refused to let me on board.

"Place not there," he said, shaking his head at the fare I held under his nose.

"What?" My stomach acid production doubled. "But you've just let all these people on!"

"Poomui woman no go manage," he added simply.

"Of course I'll manage. Let me on," I demanded. What was this strange form of racism that suggested that poomuis were too soft to tolerate the journey when they had waited over four hours like everybody else and there was unlikely to be another poda-poda coming along that day and they had friends to meet, seas to swim in and a High Commissioner's Party to attend. Huh?

Remarkably, my saviour turned out to be Musu's mother who ordered two lads to climb onto the roof, leaving a tiny space for me on a bench down the middle. Once squeezed in, I was sardine canned from all four sides by bodies, from underneath by the goat and three chickens, and from above by the metal roof bowing under the weight of the boys on top.

"Tenki ya," I said, rather uncertainly to Musu's mother. She nodded back.

Thirteen hours later, my body contracted into the foetal position, I wished I had heeded the driver's warnings at Scrabu Junction. Poomui or not, I never wanted to get into a poda-poda again. Thank God for MT, my angel of mercy, for promising me my own personal seat in the Landrover for the return journey.

But I had arrived! The big city! I needed to find my VSO comrades, so armed with my torch to avoid the potholes and storm drains of the dark streets of central Freetown, I picked my way to the VSO rest house.

I was so looking forward to seeing everyone again. Even Mike. Perhaps he'd show me his stump, so I could compare it with Gasimu's. I quickened my step. Wait till I told them all that I was a surgeon now. I had saved lives! I had amputated a leg!

THE HIGH
COMMISSIONER'S PARTY

Not unreasonably for two am, everybody was fast asleep. It was probably just as well, for I was truly exhausted. I crawled through the mosquito net of the last bunk in the rest house and within seconds had joined my friends in the land of slumber.

Morning came and I opened my eyes to an escapee from Hammer Horror hovering above my mosquito net. The shaven head was cracked and peeling, with blood oozing from the sores around the corners of the lips.

"It's the Doc! They let her out!" cried the head.

"God!" I sat up abruptly and pulled the netting aside. There stood Klaus, as cachectic as my TB patients, clothes hanging from his body and his clan covered with the most dreadful eczema.

"What happened to you? You look awful!"

"Great bedside manner, Doc. You, however, are the absolute picture of health," he said, trying to smile through the sores.

"You mean I haven't lost an ounce?"

"Yep. Still the same big strong girl."

"Hmmph!" I was going to complain further but he really did look a mess. "What are you doing about that eczema?" I asked, almost kindly. "You should go home."

"Na. Morag's given me a prescription for some lotions and potions." Klaus put his arm round an unfamiliar girl beside him. With her cropped hair and sensible glasses I assumed she was one of VSO's old guard.

"Kushe." I held out my hand. "Emily Joy."

"Em!" she spluttered. "It's me!"

"Huh!" I reached for my glasses under the bunk. "Goodness, Morag! You're nearly as bad as Klaus!"

"Lost my contacts, cut my hair and can't stand plassas. You look great, though!"

"Well yes, I probably do, compared to you two. You three," I corrected, spotting a waif sitting in the corner, peeling an orange.

"Kushe, Susan! And there's Lindsey, Hi!"

I squeezed Lindsey and Morag tightly, and Klaus a little less tightly in case he should snap, and they introduced me to some of the more-established VSOs who were down for the conference. There were nurses, teachers and even a tailor known as Squeezebox Tim (for reasons that became obvious at the party).

Tim taught tailoring at a vocational college, far out East in Kailahun, whilst his house mate Jo taught secretarial skills. They'd been in Salone for two years and it was obviously home. Jo had a Salonean boyfriend and Tim had a crush on Chandra, a black American Peace Corps.

So relationships were possible. I had been having doubts, surrounded as I was by professional celibates. Good for Jo though. That was one in the eye for the High Commissioner and his dire warnings. Meanwhile, she had a three-inch boil under her arm that needed sorting.

"Where there's pus, let it out." Morag and I quoted in unison.

"After you, Emily."

"Help!" Jo looked anxiously from Morag to me.

"You'll feel a lot better," I assured her whilst Klaus set a pan of water on the kerosene stove and started boiling up one of his razor blades.

It is always satisfying squeezing pus out of nice juicy boils and Jo's was no exception. She grudgingly admitted to feeling better whilst Morag and I sat down to compare Panguma and Serabu.

"I'm so jealous!" laughed Morag. "Amputating a leg, I can hardly believe it!" I preened a little but attempted modesty by saying nothing. Morag had a real surgeon that she could send her major cases to, only ninety minutes away at Segbwema Hospital.

"Listen. Segbwema's going to give me some surgical training at Easter," she continued. "Why don't you come?"

"Great!" I enthused, immediately planning ways to get time off. Philippe would cover me, no problem, he was leaving in May and owed me a week anyway, but I would need to put a business case to MT – something along the lines of improved surgical skills attracting more custom. "Now, how to get there…?" I mused.

"I'll take you," offered Klaus.

"What? Really?" I said, delighted, then paused. "How?"

"I've done myself up one of CARE's old Honda trail bikes. I'm not spending two years fixing up all their vehicles without doing one for myself now am I?"

"Klaus Von Hondabenda!" exclaimed Lindsey. "Your own transport, you lucky sod."

"A hundred and fifty miles on the back of a motorbike? On these roads?" I wasn't so sure, but hey, anything would be better than a poda-poda, and I'd be with Klaus. I smiled. "It's a date!"

"Easter, then Doc?" We shook hands.

"If you haven't been med-evacced by then," I eyed his skin.

"Nah. I won't be joining Mike."

"What do you mean?"

"Don't you know?" Lindsey exclaimed gleefully. "Mike and his wife have gone home in a huff."

"Home home?"

"Last week," Klaus added. "His project collapsed after he sacked half his staff in the first month. The rest walked out."

"Oh dear," I said. "Any relation to MT?"

"MT?"

"Maggie Thatcher, my boss."

"Maggie Thatcher?" asked Lindsey, and off we went for a happy few hours comparing stories.

Morag's prescription for Klaus' eczema wasn't available in any of Freetown's pharmacies, so he had to make do with potassium permanganate soaks in Nick's bath which turned both him, and the bath, first purple then splodgy brown.

"You really should go home," I suggested mildly. "Get out of this dreadful climate."

"Naw. Too many beautiful women here," he smiled. Gosh! Did that include me?

"It's tempting though, decent food, decent beer, a game of squash…"

"You play squash!"

"Yeah."

"We'll have to play." Why was I so excited by this sudden revelation of common ground?

"Naw. Wouldn't want you to embarrass yourself." He smiled a knowing smile.

Gosh, he must be good. He was such a modest chap.

"A coaching session then."

"You find the court and I'll play."

"You're on!" I agreed enthusiastically, although I couldn't imagine who would build a squash court here. "But a sweaty game of squash is the last thing your skin needs. I'm being negligent, not telling the Field Director to send you home."

"Don't you dare!"

"He'd never let him go," Jo piped in. "He's far too useful."

Klaus had apparently already wired up the VSO office to its new generator, fixed the water supply in the rest house and mended the VSO Landrover.

"Is there anywhere with air conditioning?" asked Morag. "That would help."

"You could hang around the Lebanese supermarket, Klaus," said Jo.

"Or my operating theatre."

"Or get yourself an invite to the High Commissioner's compound," Lindsey suggested. "They must have spare rooms."

"He'll be lucky," Squeeze-box Tim snorted. "Scruffy VSOs are only allowed in for the Christmas Party."

"They'll think I'm trying to infect the High Commissioner with the plague and bounce me at the doorstep. Aw fo do."

"We'll lynch 'em if they do," said Tim. "There's more of us."

"Cheers, mate," Klaus laughed. "Perhaps I'll just go for some sun, sand and salt-water treatment. Anyone coming?"

"Yes," chorused twenty voices. The Health, Education and Politics on the Conference agenda could wait.

The High Commissioner's party was a scene taken straight from the last days of the Raj. I only spotted five black faces: Jo's boyfriend, Sule; Tim's date, Chandra; and three waiters. By rights we should have stuck by our VSO principles and boycotted it completely, but principles are there to be broken at the prospect of unlimited free food and booze.

A tall black waiter dressed in a white suit with gold trim handed me my fourth pink gin. I giggled and accidentally sloshed some onto the speckled marble floor. The waiter raised an eyebrow. I flashed him a smile and hastily slipped out onto the white columned veranda to join the others on the lawn.

Everybody was dressed in competitively garish gara outfits. Everybody, that is, except Susan, who still wore the same high necked lacy blouse and brown corduroy skirt that she had had on in the check-in queue at Gatwick, only now they hung limply from her body. Poor Susan. All that worry about Tampax was wasted as stress and weight loss had put a firm halt to her menstrual cycle.

The rest of the girls wore dresses made from an assortment of stunningly coloured gara material, or the gown and lappa with headdress. Chandra's was the best of course, since she had her own pet tailor to make it for her. Tim had made himself an immaculate gara suit in rich blue and green tie-dyed circles, but even he was upstaged by our field officer – Nick was an Adonis in a white robe of shiny embellished material, trimmed in gold. Klaus, in comparison, was a pale Belsen refugee in what looked like embroidered brown pyjamas, but at least his skin looked better. He was laughing at Chandra, a natural comedienne, telling us how she spent her first weeks shouting back at the Saloneans "Sister, I'm blacker than you!" when they insisted on calling her a poomui too.

"Chandra's only twelve miles from you, Em," said Klaus.

"Hey girl, you're my nearest neighbour – come visit Sumbuya."

"That'd be great. I could cycle – Tom's got a bike."

"Woah, it's still twelve miles!"

"No problem! I'd walk it for an excuse to escape Serabu."

"Well then, second weekend in January?" Chandra suggested.

"Great!"

Everybody was happy, swapping experiences and invitations to visit. Even our Field Director looked relaxed and remarkably handsome with a pretty brunette on his arm.

"Who's she?" I asked Nick.

"Juliet. His wife. She teaches at the blind school in Freetown."

"Gosh, life's hard enough here, without being blind."

"Juliet's blind too."

"Gosh! Now that is brave, coming to Salone."

"She's got a good husband. He spends his free time at the school, or ferrying children to Connaught Hospital with TB or broken bones. Pays their medical fees too."

"He does?"

"Yes. He's always worrying about some child or other."

"Leaving him no time to worry about us volunteers?" I suggested ungraciously.

"Ah, but you are big and strong, Emily. Nobody need look after you," laughed Nick.

"Yeah."

"Dance?" Nick held out his hand. I perked up.

Nick whirled me around the impossibly green lawn of the High Commissioner's humble home. The grass was framed with palm trees and beautiful flowering shrubs and stretched down towards the horizon. Behind us Tim's accordion blended with the chatter of guests and the gentle hum of the generator.

The waiter called us to dinner and, oh boy, did we feast. My VSO comrades joined me in hoovering up turkey, real potatoes, brussel sprouts and Christmas pud. We even raved about the cabbage. Ecstasies over cabbage? The High Commissioner and his wife looked on, smiling with a mixture of indulgent patronage and disgust as their buffet table was reduced to crumbs and their drinks cabinet dwindled.

We wondered just what High Commissioners did all day, but with our heads woozy with alcohol and our bellies full, we were glad to see that ours was fulfilling at least one useful function.

There were several other expatriates at the party, presumably to provide moral support for the High Commissioner. They clinked their ice cubes in long glasses and made polite conversation with the plucky young people from up-country.

Susan avoided the expatriate contingent completely, refusing to be associated with their Capitalist exploitation and Colonialist attitudes, but as far as I was concerned they were just another audience to whom I could boast about amputating legs. I gave them the full olfactory-visual experience in between mouthfuls of mince pie.

"... diabetes is bad enough at the best of times, but I'm damned glad I'm not diabetic in this country," I proclaimed. One of the middle-aged ladies in the group then announced that she had been diabetic since childhood.

"Oh." I choked on my mince pie. Tact was never my strong point.

"Never mind dear. From your story, I too am glad to have been born in Britain," she said, more kindly than I deserved.

"Where do you get your insulin?" I asked tentatively. Having dug my hole, I might as well jump in to get the information I needed. My last three lunchtimes had been spent unsuccessfully touring the pharmacies in Freetown for insulin. Even the pharmacist at Connaught Hospital, the main government hospital, had laughed in my face at my request.

"I brought my own supplies," she explained. "I don't let diabetes interfere with my social life, although I can't eat quite as many mince pies as you dear."

Touché, I thought, wiping the dusting of icing sugar from my upper lip. "How long have you been here?"

"Only two months, visiting my son. I'll be sorry to go home tomorrow."

"Tomorrow?" I asked, my brain slipping slowly into gear through the fog of gin. "Forgive me for sounding rude – well, even ruder than I've already been – but would you, er, have any spare insulin?"

"Yes," she smiled. "Six bottles. My GP told me to bring triple supplies."

"Sensible GP."

"Would you like it for your patient? If you can come before ten, it's yours."

"Oh, yes please!"

The High Commissioner spoke to each one of us individually – for a least a minute.

"So what do you do?" he asked.

"I'm a doctor at Serabu Hospital."

"Indeed. That must be very interesting."

"Yes, I…" But he had turned to Squeeze-box Tim. Hmmph. I had had longer conversations with Pa George. Perhaps the High Commissioner had been talking to the diabetic lady's group. They had probably warned him that if he wanted to avoid twenty-minute monologues on rotting legs and cheese wires, then on no account should he give the big girl in the blue and purple tie-dyed tent any opening whatsoever. Klaus was the only one to engage him for any length of time.

"So, Mr. High Society," I teased. "What was all that about?"

"I was suggesting he should consider solar panelling."

"He seemed very interested." I had to agree. "But what do you know about solar panelling?"

"I did a module at University."

"*You* went to university?" I hadn't meant to sound quite so surprised. "Where?"

"Cambridge. Oh, there's Lindsey, she promised me a dance."

Well, well, well. Handy, intelligent, modest…

"You'll have to come to Serabu to discuss solar panelling. Diesel's so expensive…" I started conversation as soon as they left the dance floor. Perhaps the boy just needed an excuse to visit.

"They call him Mr. Electricity at his project," said Lindsey, slipping her arm through his.

"Very good!" I laughed over-heartily, one eye on Lindsey's fingers resting on Klaus's forearm.

"Yeah, Serabu sounds like fun, I've got my bike, and it's only eighty miles from Moyamba," he mused. My heart leapt into my throat. "I know, Lindsey can come too, up from Freetown."

"Great!" said Lindsey. My heart slumped back to its rightful anatomical position. Why couldn't Lindsey come another time?

"Great," I agreed.

"Good, it's another date then." Klaus smiled and turned to Lindsey. "Another dance?"

"Absolutely," said Lindsey. I smiled idiotically as he led her back onto the dance floor, then glugged down the remains of my gin and went to find the drinks waiter.

Next morning I woke with salt caked into every pore and the nausea of a woman two months into a twin pregnancy. It was small consolation that morning sickness was not something I was ever likely to suffer, if my current record was anything to go by. With a determination borne of rejection, I had out danced and out drunk everybody at the party. I had challenged Klaus to Strip the Willow and dragged him to the floor. I took a certain satisfaction in flinging him from partner to partner as we spun down the set, which, I am sure, is against all rules of attracting men.

Now, feeling wretched, I crept out of my bunk and tiptoed to the bathroom. At least there would be no competition for a bucket bath from the snoring bodies behind the mosquito nets, so I spun the taps wide open. Not a drop. So much for the big city.

I stuffed my sweaty gown and lappa into the bottom of my rucksack and put my slightly less smelly dress on for the journey back to Serabush. MT had given me a noon deadline, which left four hours to pick up the insulin then find my way downtown to the National AIDS office for HIV test kits and condoms. There was no time to say goodbye to anyone, which was just as well since maintaining jollity would have been be hard that morning.

Leaving my sleeping comrades at the rest house, I started the two mile walk back up to the High Commissioner's compound. My mind was too busy with the implications of last night to notice my aching feet, battered and blistered from hours of barefoot dancing.

Why shouldn't Klaus fancy Lindsey? She was, let's face it, the most attractive girl in the group. And nice. And funny. And clever. And probably a squash international too. But why should I care anyway? They were probably just flirting, as we had all done from day one. We were just a big group of fond siblings, that was all.

"Silly me," I said to myself, as I gave the security guard on the Compound gate the hand-written letter requesting that I be allowed to pass. He waved me towards one of the back buildings.

"Good morning," I chirped, my jovial façade firmly reapplied.

"Well, it's the dancing doctor. Good morning. I must say I didn't expect you so early." She looked me up and down and, without actually sniffing, added "Come in for a shower."

"Great," I replied, too excited by the prospect of my first shower in three months to take offence.

"The bathroom's this way."

I followed her eagerly through the air-conditioned apartment, to the strains of Beethoven. The bathroom was a sanctuary for smelly VSOs, with its clean white suite trimmed with gold, shower cubicle, flowers in a vase on the windowsill, soft powder-blue bath mat and six matching towels on the rail. Soon I was revelling in the massaging force of water, the hot needles, helped by copious amounts of moisturising shower gel, flushing the sweat out of my pores. Humming along to Beethoven's sixth, I worked my hair up into a satisfying lather, rinsed it off, doused my scalp in almond conditioner then rubbed myself down in one of the oh-so-soft towels.

"That was heaven," I said, surfacing a clean pink, wrapped in a fluffy white bathrobe like a baby in a fabric conditioner advert.

"Glad you enjoyed it, dear. Lemonade?"

"Please." I accepted the long frosted glass, and flopped onto the cream cotton sofa. I slurped my cold, cold drink and listened to the ceiling fan swishing gently round. My hostess brought me her six bottles of insulin, two freshly baked bread rolls with real butter from the Lebanese supermarket and a large piece of fresh pineapple. Life in Sierra Leone was not hard for everyone but this lady was certainly sharing her good fortune.

An hour later, I was delivered back to the VSO office by her son's driver. I popped in for a final check for Christmas mail. There was nothing from home in my pigeonhole, but there were four little notes:

Had to get an early poda-poda if I'm to make it to Panguma today. See you in Segbwema. Love Morag.

Where were you? We've gone to the Crown Cafe for breakfast. Love Lindsey.

How's the head, Doc? See you at the Crown. Love Klaus.

How'd you get up so early? Hope to see you at the Crown. Guess what? Lindsey tactfully rejected Von Hondabenda last night, but everybody is still friends. A little birdie tells me you might be relieved. My lips are sealed. Tim.

I shredded the notes and threw them in the bin. Tim was right, I should be relieved, but instead I felt somehow insulted. And how did Tim know anyway? Was it something to do with being a fellow sufferer of unrequited love, or had I been that obvious? How embarrassing! The therapeutic effect of my morning shower evaporated. At least I wouldn't have time to face them at the Crown for party post-mortems. I scribbled super-cheery little Christmas messages to leave in their slots, then made my way heavily out of the office, down the stairs, past the cluster of refugees outside the Red Cross Office and along the street to Connaught Hospital for my midday rendezvous with MT.

NO SOCKS, NO SEX

"WOMEN, NO ONE FOOT SUCKS, NO SEX!"

I stood outside the National AIDS Office, deep in the bowels of the Connaught Hospital, trying to decipher the hand-painted banner. *Foot* was Krio for leg, and *one foot* was the penis. No penis sucks, no sex. Goodness, what was it suggesting? Oral sex to avoid AIDS?

Our own HIV posters, assiduously vetoed by MT, depicted couples holding hands with no hint of a kiss, never mind fellatio. Smiling at the thought of AJ and the rest of the students trying to design our sweet posters without mention of sex or condoms, I jumped when a little man flung open the door.

"Kushe, kushe. Welcome to The National AIDS Office!"

"Oh, kushe. I'm Dr. Joy from Serabu." I looked round the cubbyhole, filled from floor to ceiling with boxes of condoms. Before I knew it, I was the caretaker of three thousand Trojans and a box of HIV test kits.

"Thank you." I flicked off the dust, searching for the expiry date. "But, er, aren't these test kits out of date?" I was sorry to sound so ungrateful to one so generous.

"Aw fo do," he answered, his grin never wavering. "No more 'til Easter-time."

There was no time to argue, it was already noon I was quite sure MT would leave me behind if I was late. Unable to face another poda-poda journey, I dashed to Connaught's main entrance, balancing boxes of condoms like a waiter clearing up after a Greek wedding. Puffing, I spotted Moses rattling round the corner in the Landrover.

"Kushe, Dr. Em." Moses jumped down to open the back doors.

"Kushe, Moses. How di body?"

"I tell God tenki. I get your beer." He pointed to six crates strapped to the roof.

"Six! I only gave you money for three. Yours?" I asked doubtfully.

"Too 'spensive for me." Moses grinned.

"For MT? No! Really?" MT reclined across my imagination with a bottle of Star in one hand and a bible in the other.

"Quick, Dr. Em." Moses grabbed my arm. "MT de come."

I threw the thirty bumper boxes of condoms into the back seat and hastily covered them with my newly purchased yellow and green gara.

"Dr. Joy, you are here. I could not find the required items for the pumps." MT was not one for small talk. "I hope you were more successful."

"I have everyone's mail and some insulin, but the HIV kits are out of date."

"No use, Dr. Joy, no use at all," she tutted. "Latif has tested 3% of our potential blood donors as positive. How can we combat the scourge of this terrible disease with inadequate testing?"

"There are other ways," I suggested, settling myself innocently against my secret stash of condoms. "At least they're less out of date than our current batch."

"And when is the next delivery?"

"Easter."

"Well I'm quite sure we will not be wasting fourteen hours of diesel coming down again." MT lifted herself into the front seat and arranged the layers of her dark-grey, ankle-length, polyester habit. Little wonder she was bad tempered. I was sweating in my knee-length cotton dress.

"Back to Serabu, driver," she instructed, straightening her veil for action. Poor Moses had been driving round Freetown at her beck and call all day without a break. Without so much as a sigh, he put the Landrover into gear.

Failing to get the spares for the water pumps had put MT in an even worse mood than usual. I took some comfort from the thought that even she had to suffer bucket baths and dispose of her bodily wastes without water. My head thumped and my stomach churned, so I leaned out of the window for some air while the beer bottles clinked accusingly in their crates. Hour by hour we crept closer to Serabush in miserable silence.

One year, nine months to go. Bloody hell. Look on the bright side Emily, that's one year nine months to convince Klaus of your charms. Or one year nine months for him to convince Lindsey of his charms. Not that she was the only competition – female volunteers far outweighed the men, both in the VSO and American Peace-Corps' ranks.

Aw fo do. Remember, you amputated a leg! You are a surgeon, you can be proud of yourself.

The proud surgeon stood in a washing-up bowl and tried to wash seven-and-a-half hours of dust off with a bucket of water without spilling any so there would be enough to pour into the toilet for the daily flush. Welcome home. My oil drum was empty and we were now rationed to a single bucket a day. My shower at the High Commissioner's only that morning seemed as long ago as my last soak in a hot bubble bath in Scotland.

Next day I went straight to Gasimu's bed, eager to see how my first amputee was progressing.

"Kushe, Gasimu. How di body?"

"I tell God tenki, Dr. Em. How di Freetown?" he smiled weakly.

"Fine," I shook his hand.

Dauda appeared with the dressings trolley. "I get for do Gasimu's dressing."

"Good." I watched Dauda peel back the layers of gauze. But it was not good. Gasimu's stump was swollen and leaking pus.

"You'd better remove those stitches," I whispered.

Dauda did as I bid and I stood with my hand over my mouth. The whole wound fell open, revealing a writhing mass of maggots. I froze, transported into a horror movie with all my boastful words being shouted back at me from the screen.

"AJ, do ya, bring me water," said Dauda calmly.

"No water," AJ replied.

"Then fetch some from the well," Dauda ordered.

"But the well is ten-minutes walk!" AJ, king of the student nurses, did not want to demean himself with women's work.

"Quick quick," Dauda snapped. AJ glared at him, but marched out of the ward to find a bucket. "Don't worry, Dr. Em. I go clean the place," Dauda added kindly. "You go to Maternity."

"Thank you," I whispered and lurched for the door, unable to look into Gasimu's tortured face.

An hour later, Dauda and Mariama had cleaned and dressed Gasimu's leg with fresh white gauze. Perhaps I should have left the maggots in to debride the wound? Too late now. Gasimu, pale and sweaty, still managed a smile for me.

"Insulin don don," Mariama whispered.

"I brought more from Freetown."

"Tenki ya, Dr. Em." Gasimu grasped my hand, obviously understanding every word that we were saying, but I looked away. I couldn't accept his gratitude.

We had been so pleased with our tidy, impressive-looking wound. But that neat little line of stitches had been our, and more importantly Gasimu's, undoing.

"*Never, EVER, sew up an infected wound.*" Mr. Lord' words hammered against my skull. "*Where there's pus, let it out.*" His fist pounded the table.

"The bone-self don begin rot," Dauda told me once we had left the room.

"We'll have to amputate higher," I said, struggling to maintain a pretence of competence.

"You are trying, Dr. Em," said Dauda.

To try was a great compliment in Sierra Leone, whatever the outcome, but perhaps sometimes it's better to give up gracefully. Oh why had I ever come back from Freetown? There had been plenty of flights that would have taken me home in time for Christmas.

Home. I leaned against the doorway of Surgical. No one need know I had been a failure in Africa. I would just write "three months in Sierra Leone" on my CV, adding a touch of the exotic to give me the edge in the job market, then return to being a GP – a job I was good at. At least my Salonean experience should curb my moans about the state of the NHS. The main problem would be telling Nat and Philippe that I was leaving. Oh poor Philippe. In all decency I should at least give a month's notice, so they had chance to find a doctor who had the ability and the stamina that I lacked, but could I even survive another month?

"Come and see the baby Jesus, Dr. Em."

"What?" I jumped. It was Theresa.

"Come and see the baby Jesus." The student nurse took my hand.

"I..." But I was already being led across the compound to a newly built raffia shack. Moses and Tom were twining palm leaves and flowers to form an archway around it.

"Look at him, Dr. Em," said Theresa.

I peered into the shack to see baby Jesus and Company housed within. I smiled at the exquisitely carved figures framed by a halo of flowers.

"How sweet." I wiped away a tear.

"Hey girl, what's wrong?" Tom gave me a hug.

"Nothing." Tom looked hard at me. "Oh Tom, its everything. Gasimu's going to die. His leg's crawling with maggots and it's all my fault."

"The diabetic man?" Tom asked.

"I sewed up an infected wound."

"You've given him your best."

"My best isn't good enough."

"You're only a novice, Em, and you've already saved lives. Look at Jeneba, and Pa Bangura."

"You're being very kind, Tom." I looked into the gentle eyes of the American. "But it was such a basic mistake."

"Hey, I'll bet you've never saved so many lives in your life, and now you want to save them all." Tom looked at me square on.

"I want to go home."

"Don't you dare!"

"Oh Tom, what am I doing?"

"You're trying to help."

"It makes it so much worse that Gasimu has no one. Why is he the only patient without a relative?"

"Diabetics are expensive and he's had two major operations," sighed Tom. "He'll have a huge bill."

"Well he's going to die anyway. Even MT can't charge a corpse."

"She can charge the relatives and withhold the body until they pay."

"You're jo… No, you're not. Poor Gasimu has to suffer alone so his family won't get landed with the bill? And I'm not helping, I'm just too ashamed to face him."

"I'll talk to him," Tom offered. "My Krio's real good now. And I'll get my students to spend more time with him too."

"Thanks, Tom. He badly needs a friend."

Friends are indeed wonderful things. Tom's pep talk was enough to get me through Outpatients and when I surfaced at four, the whole compound seemed to be in bloom. How had I never noticed before? Flowers tumbled round every corner and threw their perfume into the air. A little wind fluffed their petals and I wondered if perhaps it was just a little cooler. Bolstered by the hospital's unexpected beauty, I went home for lunch. I lifted the blackened lid off Pa George's pot and there, where there should have been orange palm oil congealing on green sludge, there sat a fluffy yellow omelette. Hallelujah! Thanks be to Tikka!

After such a gourmet dinner, I felt strong enough to look back in on Gasimu. There he was, sitting up in bed, laughing at a book of cartoons that Tom had lent him. And I had thought he only read the bible. Not wanting to spoil the magic Tom's human touch had worked on my patient, I closed the side room door quietly and went over to TB ward.

Standing in the doorway was Musu, with baby Laygby strapped to her back.

"Musu!" I gaped at the young woman. "You're walking!"

"Kushe kushe, Dr. Em." She beamed and gave me a twirl. Her mother stood behind her, grinning from ear to ear.

The evidence before me was hard to believe – Pa Kamara, you're an orthopaedic genius. "So. How's the chicken?" I had to ask.

"Very good. We don chop am."

Sleep came easily as I fell exhausted into bed. Unfortunately it left just as easily when Almamy banged on my door two hours later. There was a very sick girl on Surgical.

Christiana's blood pressure was unrecordable, her skin was

clammy and her belly was full of blood. AJ was already putting up a saline drip.

"Well done, AJ." It pained me to have to praise one so cocky, but I was secretly most impressed. He was, after all, only a first year student nurse. "What's your diagnosis?"

"She get ectopic, Dr. Em."

"Yes, I'm sure you're right. Tell me about ectopic pregnancy."

"The pregnancy try for grow in the Fallopian tube instead of the womb-self. Then space is not there and it bursts, so everything bleed too much inside."

"I couldn't explain it better myself."

"I take her to theatre, Dr. Em. You get for do surgery quick quick."

Unfortunately he was right about that too.

"Her blood count is less than four grams, Dr. Em," Latif shouted through the window. "Them relatives no get the right group."

"Can you look in the village?"

"I de try," Latif shrugged, and went off into the night to knock on doors of villagers who might be willing to donate.

This was hopeless. My confidence slumped back to the lows of that morning. What was I doing in the middle of Africa at two in the morning faced with more impossible surgery for a patient who would probably bleed to death on the table long before I had time to look up the instructions in the book? Even Sister Hilary couldn't turn salt water into blood.

Well perhaps I could learn something from Gasimu. I should work within my limitations and accept that I couldn't save everyone.

"I'm going to let Christiana die in peace, AJ."

"Too late, Dr. Em," AJ piped in. "Earnest don already give the anaesthetic."

"Damn!" I looked at the ashen girl, breathing shallow irregular breaths and was about to order Earnest to withhold further anaesthetic when Tiange held out my gloves.

"You get for do the work, Dr. Em," she ordered. "No time to scrub."

"But..."

"Quick, quick." She shoved a scalpel in my hand.

I was sure that even Hilary had never disobeyed Tiange, so I made my incision. As soon as the knife cut through the distended abdominal wall, an oil well of blood burst out. Tiange jumped deftly aside but I was too slow. Christiana's warm blood spurted against my chest and ran between my thighs, down my shins and into my theatre wellies.

"Oh…" I howled, but Tiange was not sympathetic.

"Dr. Em, you waste the blood!"

"What do you mean, waste it?" Tiange ignored me, grabbed a jug from her tray and started scooping up blood. Then she was pouring it through a sieve into a bottle.

"What are you *doing*?" I gasped. "You can't just…"

But Tiange had already handed the bottle to Earnest who was running Christiana's recycled blood into the drip. They couldn't be serious! However, who was I to argue with Tiange? I took my own jug and started bailing in the blood until we had collected another two pints to transfuse. Once we'd cleared the blood, I found the tube containing the misplaced pregnancy and tie it off to stop further bleeding. Heaving a sigh of relief, I sneaked a look to the head of the table. Christiana was still breathing.

The operating theatre looked like a battleground with blood splattered over the patient, the drapes, the floor and me. But with the help of one more pint from Latif's nocturnal search, Christiana's blood pressure finally stabilised. Earnest wheeled her back to Surgical whilst AJ and Tiange washed down the floors.

With Christiana settled on the ward, Tiange, AJ and Earnest returned to their beds, spotless despite their toils, whilst I traipsed stickily back to my house.

It was now four thirty. Dismayed, I stared at the trickle of water at the bottom of my bucket. Lady Macbeth couldn't have cleaned herself with that, and she only had a spot of blood to worry about. I was covered from the waist down. Where could I find water? AJ had already pilfered from most of the wards to wash down Theatre's floors and I was too tired to walk the mile to the village well in the dark.

"Aw fo du." I rubbed off the worst of Christiana's blood with my towel, dampened with water from the toilet cistern. Bloody hell!

Okay, I knew I had been toying with contracting a serious illness to buy me a free ticket home, but AIDS wasn't what I had in mind.

"Kushe kushe, Dr. Em. Morning-oh." I lifted the sheet from my head and peered at my watch. Seven o'clock. What was AJ sounding so cheerful about? Hadn't he been up in the middle of the night with the rest of us?

"Morning, AJ. What is it?" I called from my bed.

"Dr. Em, Tiange say you don make too much mess last night."

"Hmmph!"

"So I bring you water."

"WATER? Great!" I dashed to the front door. AJ stood, daisy-fresh on the doorstep, a bucket of water on his head.

"Thanks, AJ, that's great. Plenti tenki."

"But, Dr. Em, I get no socks."

"Sorry?"

"I get no socks."

"You get no *socks*?" I repeated like an idiot. Well I supposed socks and shoes were quite a status symbol. Perhaps I could give him a pair of mine in return for the water? After all, I'd never had occasion to wear them here. "What size are you, AJ?"

He looked at me blankly.

"Would mine fit you?" I persisted.

AJ's brow furrowed. Obviously I wasn't breaking through the language barrier, so I stepped up to him and measured my foot against his. This was too much for AJ.

"Dr. Em! *Trojans!*"

"Ahhh... Socks!" I blushed. "Condoms!"

'NO ONE FOOT SUCKS, NO SEX.' The AIDS office sign finally made sense. Admittedly the wrong vowel for *socks*, but since so few could read, spelling mistakes were scarcely important.

Still, AJ got his socks and I got my water. I rushed off to have a bucket bath in celebration.

MARIAMA'S WEDDING

Mariama and Ben were married on Christmas Eve. Their baby, Hindolu, was to be christened on Christmas Day. This laudable open-mindedness bumped Father Joe several notches up in my estimation. The fifty-something priest reserved a rather stilted bonhomie for we volunteers, but he always had a kind smile and would invite us round for the occasional beer. His sermons were delivered in a rather mechanical monotone, made comical by Patrick Kpukuma's animated line by line translation into Mende. But Joe was well loved by his community and his church was always full on Sundays.

MT, as an honorary man, always sat on the left; Nat and Tom sat on the right with the women and children – Nat because it was more fun with the children, and Tom because it was politically correct behaviour befitting a tee-total Christian vegetarian who would rather die of malaria than swat a mosquito. I was invariably late, so sat wherever there was a pew. Today there were none.

The pews were overflowing with smiles and multicoloured well-wishers – including the Muslim staff members and villagers. The men were clad in gara suits, the women in gowns and lappas and new hairdos. Most had tight braids twisted with beads or ribbons sweeping across the scalp to the sides or back or, like Theresa, whirling round in elaborate swirls, but a few sported nests of little black snakes twisting Medusa-style around their heads. My ponytail and kirby grips, which kept my overlong fringe from sticking to my forehead, were a bit of an embarrassment. At least Pa George had taken the charcoal iron to my gown and lappa after the High Commissioner's party.

Mariama outshone everyone; even the net veil dotted with little flowers couldn't disguise her radiance beneath. Ben, by her side, wouldn't have looked out of place in the City in his slate-grey three-piece suit were it not for his huge smile. The service ended with Nat's beautiful singing filling the church.

Smiles finally gave way to laughter as the bridal couple walked down the aisle together, ducking under each flower entwined palm-frond until they reached the doorway and stepped into the sunshine. The congregation spilled out behind the happy pair, throwing flower petals, dancing, singing and banging drums. Even MT was smiling.

The party continued at Mariama's house. The Bride and Groom changed into traditional white gara, yokes and sleeves embroidered in gold thread. Hindolu bounced on his grandma's lap, drooling happily over his own golden embroidery as the three of them sat like angels at God's table, surveying the rest of the throng as we danced.

What I lacked in style on the dance floor, I compensated for with vigour. Laygby tried to teach me the secrets of the Mende bottom and hip gyrations but, even if I had had any natural rhythm, I was too busy struggling to keep control of my clothing. Legs were traditionally covered in Sierra Leone, and thighs were a definite no no. My thighs were a definite no no anywhere, so I really had to keep the lappa tied round my waist. How had I managed to Strip the Willow with Klaus? Oh yes, I had just cast my lappa aside. Aw fo du. I didn't really care what the High Commissioner thought, but I couldn't snub Mariama with such socially unacceptable behaviour.

"Kushe, Dr. Em." A beautiful young woman interrupted.

"Kushe," I replied, trying to place her.

"You look really fine in that gara, Dr. Em."

"Thank you." I looked down at my once smart outfit, now soggy with sweat.

"You want poyo?"

"Tenki ya." It wasn't water but at least it was fluid. Smiling graciously I held out my glass while I racked my memory banks.

"Poyo, Mr. Nat?"

"Tenki ya, Christiana."

"Chris...? Surely not Christiana!" I couldn't believe it. "What are you doing out of bed?" I admonished.

"I notto dance, Dr. Em," she grinned. "We go see back." The girl whose blood had covered my body only three days ago vanished into the crowd.

"But... but, your stitches!"

"Well now, doesn't she look just grand, Dr. Emily?" Nat gave me a friendly shove. "Perhaps you'll be staying with us a little longer after all?"

"What the hell does she think she's doing at a party?" I snorted, trying to cover up the little flush of pleasure creeping over my cheeks. "But she does look good, doesn't she?"

"Mighty," agreed Nat.

"So what's she doing here?"

"Latif invited her."

"Oh he did, did he?" I laughed. "I can see why, but he better not let MT find out he's been chatting up his patients."

By dusk the party was winding up, so I made my way home. Theresa met me on the path.

"Kushe, Dr. Em. It was a fine fine wedding notto so?"

"Lovely, Theresa. Have you got a patient?"

"We get one woman who don labour for many days now. I think say, you get for do Caesarean."

"Okay, I'll just fetch the theatre keys."

"But you must come quick. Onita get belly ten times but she no get pickin. They say she is a witch. If this pickin die, they no let her go back to her village."

"Ten Pregnancies. No baby. Oh Theresa, that's awful!"

I jogged home as fast as my lappa allowed. Fifty metres from my door there was a crack of lightening and a rumble of thunder and within seconds, I was drenched. An hour earlier I would have revelled dancing in the cooling rain but now I had work to do. Where had that downpour come from? This was supposed to be the dry season. At least it might help our water problem. Once inside, I scooped up the keys, retrieved my umbrella and stepped back through the curtain of water at my front door to slide and slither down the path that now rivered its way back to Maternity.

Theresa was rolling out two large oil drums to collect the water flowing from the guttering of the ward.

"Any sign of Tiange or Earnest yet?" I shouted above the clattering of rain on the tin roof. I hadn't heard the theatre bell, so probably neither had the staff. "Have you heard the bell, Theresa?"

"No, Dr. Em." She listened for a moment. "That rain – too noisy."

"Damn," I muttered.

Onita was breathing heavily with sweat clinging to her brow. Theresa turned her limp body onto its side as I struggled to pick up the baby's heartbeat – it was very faint. There was a knock at the window. A drenched Moses stood outside with his face pressed to the mosquito mesh. He refused to come inside, so I had to join him in the dark and rain. Even an educated Mende-man would not enter the labour room.

"Dr. Em, I rang the bell many many times, but no person able hear it," Moses panted. "I done go to Tiange and Earnest's houses, but all two are not there."

"Are they at Mariama's?" I asked, trying to squeeze myself further under Maternity's narrow eaves for shelter. Onita's baby was going to die and Onita would be an outcast, all because it was raining.

"No. I done check. Only Sesay and Almamy are there, drinking poyo."

"At least Sesay can turn on the generator, but what about the others?" This baby should have been delivered two hours ago and if we left it much longer, Onita herself would not survive much longer in labour before she died of exhaustion or a ruptured womb.

"Will I get Dr. Fleep?" Moses suggested.

"Philippe's already gone to Mokanje for Christmas. Bloody hell," I cursed. "Yesterday there was no water, today there's too much."

"I go look for am again."

"Thank you Moses. Theresa, who's on Surgical?"

"Hawa."

"And Medical and C Ward?"

"AJ and Mohammed."

"First-years only, no trained staff?"

"It is Saturday. Aw fo do."

"Okay. We'll manage with students."

Ten minutes later, I had five eager first years, and Theresa, in her second year. I gave the spinal and put Theresa in charge of Onita's vital signs. Only AJ had actually done his two-month theatre placement which, unfortunately, made him the only choice to be my assistant. AJ was delighted with his sudden promotion. My, how he would boast to the other students now! He slapped the scalpel confidently in my hand, his eyes alive with excitement above his mask.

AJ's euphoria only served to accelerate my palpitations. I had never operated without Tiange, and we were surely too late for Onita's longed-for baby. Taking a deep breath, I focused on trying to save the mother.

Five minutes later, I lifted a floppy dusky-blue baby boy from Onita's womb.

"I can only just feel a heartbeat. Has anybody resuscitated a baby before?" A creeping silence gave me my answer. Could I risk leaving Onita with AJ whilst I tried to bring the baby round myself? I knew just how important this baby was. An alarming gush of blood spilling from Onita's womb made my decision for me.

"Theresa what's her blood pressure?"

"Too low to make a reading, Dr. Em."

"Turn the drip full on, Theresa. Hawa, take the baby quick. You must try to revive him," I called, turning my attention to the bleeding points.

"Dr. Em I have never…" sobbed Hawa.

"TRY!" I shouted at the poor girl.

Just then the theatre doors swung open and an angel in theatre greens entered.

"Mariama! What on earth…?"

"My mother told me Moses came looking for staff."

"But this is your wedd…"

"Where do you want me, Dr. Em?" Mariama snapped on rubber gloves.

"Help Hawa with the baby. Quick."

Hawa gladly relinquished responsibility to Mariama, who was calmly asking for the ET tube as I tied off blood vessels to stem the flow of blood from Onita's womb. The theatre was so quiet that I could hear the gentle puffs of the ambu-bag as Mariama filled the baby's little lungs with air. Only AJ seemed to be breathing, his masked face close to mine as he held clamps steadily or passed over suture material for me to sew up the layers. I focused on Onita's abdominal cavity, too scared to ask how either of my patients were doing until I was finished.

"Thank you, AJ. Well done." I watched my fledgling assistant put a dressing on the wound. "How is Onita, Theresa?" I asked, not daring to look up.

"Onita's blood pressure is one-twenty over eighty."

"Really? Is she conscious?"

"Yes, Dr. Em. She is watching Mariama."

It couldn't be helped. We didn't have room to hide the resuscitation attempts from Onita. "And the baby?" I whispered.

"We have a heartbeat of one hundred and forty," Mariama announced.

"What? Do we?" I perked up. "That's great! Is he breathing?"

"Yes. He's straining on the tube. I get for pull it." Mariama's last statement was punctuated by a loud cry, followed by cheers from the students.

"Mariama, you're terrific!" I exclaimed, watching the new bride carry a screaming baby over to his mother. "Now for goodness' sake you'd better get back to that husband of yours. You can't spend your wedding night in an operating theatre."

"It was worth it," she beamed, nodding towards Onita, who was cuddling her first living child while tears of joy splashed onto his wrinkled little face.

At midnight, bolstered by my success, I joined the rest of Serabu round a huge bonfire that blazed at the back of the church. Thankfully the rain had stopped in time for the Christmas festivities to go ahead. Everyone lit a candle from the flames then, singing, we formed a candlelit procession which snaked into the church and down the aisle, still arched with flower-entwined palm fronds.

Squeezing back into the pews poda-poda tight, we watched the Mother Mary with baby Jesus bring up the rear of the procession. I looked again at the young woman. It was Jeneba walking tall and proud with two month old Problem in her arms! She lowered him into a basket crib before the altar where, surrounded by candles and flowers, he fell asleep. Lucky baby Jesus. By two-thirty, I was nearly crying with fatigue, so slipped off to bed. In my defence, O Lord, it was the second time I had been to church that day.

WHERE MI KRISMAS?

M y Christmas alarm call came at six-thirty.
"Dr. Em, where's my Christmas?"

I peered through my bedroom window to see Nurse Sankoh, junior entrepreneur, with a gaggle of children on my doorstep.

"Where mi Krismas?" They chorused.

"Dr. Em, where mi Krismas?"

"Dr. Em?"

"Dr. Em…"

Now, much as I admire the adage 'Ask and it shall be given,' this direct approach rather clashed with my British upbringing of hanging around, being good and looking quietly hopeful.

I was going to have to get up anyway, if I was going to do a ward round before church. They were only kids and they didn't have the vocabulary to be subtle. I gave them each a balloon from a bumper bag of fifty I'd bought from a Lebanese supermarket in Freetown specially for Christmas day.

Twenty sad pieces of multicoloured rubber drooped from uncertain fingers.

"Okay, watch." I blew up a balloon and tied off the end. My audience watched with rapt faces. Nurse quickly got the hang of it and punched his balloon in the air to squeals of delight from the others. I helped some of the smaller children to blow up their own balloons and they skipped back down my path to show off their 'Christmas' to their friends.

Smiling, I wandered down my path, lined with expectant children (and adults). I was out of balloons before I even reached the wards.

"Dr. Em, where mi Krismas?" chanted the patients as I arrived on Surgical Ward. They had to make do with a "Happy Christmas" and a fixed smile. I swallowed my irritation when even the nurses demanded their own 'Krismas'.

The only person not to ask me for anything was Gasimu. He just quietly wished me Happy Christmas. It was his leg that shouted out for further attention. What a mess. I'd have to take him back to theatre and clean it out thoroughly under anaesthetic.

"Dauda, Can you ask the theatre staff to come in after church?"

"No problem, Dr. Em."

Ten o'clock saw the church full for a further two-and-a-half hours. Father Joe and the congregation carried on as enthusiastically as they had left off just a few hours previously. I slipped out as soon as Hindolu was baptized.

Gasimu's leg was even worse than I'd thought. Philippe wouldn't be back for hours from his Christmas dinner in Mokanje, so it was up to me.

After half an hour of cutting back the muscles, it took another twenty hard minutes with the Gigli saw to cheese wire through four centimetres of thighbone. I handed the cross-sectioned stump to Tiange and wiped away the fine layer of bone dust to see what was left.

There was still a long thin pocket of pus running up Gasimu's inner thigh to his groin. Shit. Even an orthopaedic specialist would balk at taking his leg off at the hip (and it wasn't mentioned at all in *Primary Surgery*), so I could only wash it out with sterile saline and pray.

This time I didn't suture Gasimu's stump – instead Earnest swaddled the raw end in gauze and bandages. I knew I hadn't done enough, but I wasn't capable of more.

Bright sunshine greeted me as I stepped out of theatre, constricting my pupils so severely that my vision blurred. But not enough to obliterate the crowd of children heaving towards me.

"Dr. Em, where mi Krismas?"

I squeezed my eyes tightly shut, hoping to somehow magic the little army away. It didn't work. They started chanting, "Where mi Krismas, where mi Kristmas." I wanted to scream. I wanted to go home. I wanted... help!

Aisha provided a rescue of sorts, shouting behind the mob, waving a medical chart above their heads.

"Dr. Em, you have a patient on C Ward. She get convulsions."

"I've got to go," I muttered, pushing my way through the crowd.

As I was trying to thread an IV into the fitting child's tiny vein, I heard my name: "Dr. Em, where mi Krismas?"

I looked into Almamy's pleading eyes and something finally snapped. Just as I was sucking in breath to scream abuse at him, MT appeared. "Peace and Goodwill to you all on this happy day," she proclaimed. "I bring your Christmas." MT held up a basket stuffed with little parcels. Aisha and I gaped as the skinny, grey and white Santa made her rounds, giving a parcel to each nurse, each child and each mother and wishing them the blessings of the day.

"I don't believe it," I muttered, watching the children's faces light up as they unwrapped their little rubber balls whilst the mothers were equally delighted with their cake of soap and tin of sardines.

This sudden surge of goodwill from MT was almost too much to bear. I scribbled instructions on the child's chart, thrust it back to Aisha and stormed off the ward, my soul far, far from salvation.

It was late and Pa George had taken the day off, but maybe Nat would have some food left from the lunch he had promised me. I marched down to his house and banged on the door. No answer.

"Gone to the staff Christmas picnic? You selfish bastard!" I threw myself against Nat's locked door. "It's Christmas Day, what's my blooming Muslim cook doing with the day off?" I shouted into the nearly deserted hospital compound. "What for chop today? I... want... my... lunch." I punctuated my frustration with kicks at Nat's door, then slumped down on the doorstep, dropped my head in my hands and started to cry.

I wept because I had only slept for six hours across the past three nights, because my ignorance had left a man rotting to death, because I was hungry and hot and all my family would be at home, stuffed with food and alcohol. I wept because there was nowhere to hide from nurses looking for me to sort out impossible problems, or from children wanting their Christmas present and because my once generous personality had sunk to a level lower than Scrooge himself.

Then to top it all, bloody Klaus fancied someone else and Nat was not even in for me to talk to. I lifted my head and sniffed.

Come on Emily, big strong girls don't cry. I dragged myself to my feet and headed home.

Pa Ali passed me just as I reached my path.

"Bua, Dr. Em."

"Bua bise, Pa Ali," I muttered into the ground without breaking stride, waiting for the inevitable demand for a Christmas present. It never came.

"Bi gahuyena?" he asked, as usual.

Surprised, I stopped, then answered "Kayingoma," looking at him expectantly.

"Kayingoma. Malo-hua." He waved and headed off to his palm tree. Here was somebody who expected nothing from me.

I ran inside, fished out a handful of twenties from my carrier bag and thrust the notes in Pa Ali's palm.

"Happy Christmas."

"Happy Krismas, Dr. Em." He looked perplexed. "I bring poyo for you?"

"No, Pa Ali. No poyo. Happy Christmas."

"Plenti tenki, Dr. Em," he beamed. "Malo-hua."

"Malo-hua."

My brief surge of Christmas cheer fizzled out five minutes later.

"Dr. Em, Gasimu's brother de ya," Dauda called through my mosquito mesh. "He want tok with you."

"Gasimu has a brother?" I said, surprised. "Good! Finally, a relative. Okay, I'm coming, but let me finish my lunch."

"Only bananas, Dr. Em?" Dauda pointed to the pile of black skins lying on the table.

"I'm just a poor little poomui," I replied. "I've nothing else, so don't dare ask for your Christmas."

There was no private place to talk to relatives so I stood outside Surgical with Gasimu's brother, running my hands through my hair and telling him that Gasimu would surely die in the next few weeks.

"Aw fo do," he said quietly. He had just walked thirty miles from Mokanje. My struggle to find some words of comfort was interrupted by Latif, tanked up with poyo from the staff picnic, throwing his arms round me and wishing me Happy Christmas in between declarations of my brilliance.

"Thank you, Latif. Can I have a few minutes with this gentleman now?"

"No problem, Dr. Em. She a fine fine Doctor sir, fine, fine…"

"Latif, please!"

"No, no. A fine doctor. Dr. Em, where mi Kri…"

"Latif!"

Thankfully Latif weaved off, and Gasimu's brother shook my hand warmly.

"Tenki ya, Dr. Em, you don try." I forced a smile in reply as he left for his thirty-mile return journey.

"He's walked such a long way, Dauda, why won't he stay awhile with his brother?"

"He is too much scared that MT make him pay."

"Of course… oh…"

"Dr. Em you really have tried for Gasimu. Do not cry."

"You're so kind," I sniffed.

"Look, I don bring your Krismas!" Dauda smiled, proffering a sardine sandwich made with his morning's gift from Santa MT.

"Oh Dauda!"

I was about to pay a Christmas visit to 1B ward when Philippe's truck crossed the compound and headed towards my house.

Twenty minutes early! With a yelp of glee, I run towards them. My enthusiasm was soon tempered by a gang of children approaching from the wings, their sights fixed on fresh prey to torment for Christmas presents. I broke into a sprint.

"Quick, quick. Inside!" I rattled my key in the lock. Philippe and Nicole exchanged glances. I pushed Philippe into my living room and pulled Nicole through the door as she clutched Simone, slamming the door behind them, just as a wall of children's faces appeared at the window.

"Qu'est que c'est…?" started Philippe. A plaintive wail came from behind my door.

"Maman!" It was Pierre. I had shut him outside with the Christmas present seekers. Sheepishly I opened the door, but just enough to guide Pierre in.

"Oh, I'm so sorry Pierre."

"I think you have had a bad day, yes?" observed Philippe, cuddling his sobbing two-year-old.

"They just want their Christmas," I sighed.

"Ah yes. And you want yours. There's a Christmas dinner marveilleuse waiting for you at the Mines. No, don't tell me about the problems, I'll soon find out. Bon appetite." Philippe bundled his family back into their truck like a bodyguard removing celebrities from the paparazzi. He slammed the door and bounced off to their house with the bounty-seeking children skipping behind.

An hour later we were off to the Mines: Nat, Tom and I singing carols in the back seat of the Landrover. Father Joe clapped along and even MT was humming as I belted out the words, spoiling the harmony between Tom's rich baritone and Nat's beautiful tenor, still piccolo clear, despite a heavy afternoon on the poyo at the staff picnic. No matter what he might have imbibed, he could not have felt as elated as I did at that moment. I was free!

Six miles down the road we passed a lone figure trudging slowly towards the sunset. Oh no, it was Gasimu's brother. "Moses, can we give him a lift?" I asked. Well, what else could I do? "He lives in Mokanje."

Moses pulled the Landrover up on the side of the road and Tom pulled him in by the arm. "Do ya. Come inside, sir."

"Who is this man?" demanded MT. "Serabu hospital is not a taxi service."

But Gasimu's brother had already sat himself next to me and was shaking everybody's hand.

"It's Christmas, Ignatius. We can give the man a lift, dear." Father Joe patted MT's arm.

"Drive on Moses," MT instructed, a kitten in the hands of the kindly priest.

"On… the… FIRST day of Christmas, my true love gave to me," Nat started, as soon as we were moving. I cringed. He couldn't know that only hours ago, I'd been telling this man that his brother was dying.

Selfishly starting to wish we had just driven straight past him, I gazed out of the window and dreamed of my family breaking open their Christmas champagne by my granny's roaring fire. They would be laughing and joking, surrounded by presents, new clothes, CDs, clever gadgets and computer games and boxes and boxes of chocolates.

"Seven swans-a-swimming. Come on Emily!" Tom nudged me out of my self-pity. I looked round to see Gasimu's brother singing along with the others, a huge smile on his face.

"Six geese-a-laying. FIVE GO-OLD RINGS!" I shouted. What the hell, it was Christmas.

HAPPY NEW YEAR

New Year dawned with a teenage girl weeping on my doorstep. "My father don die, Dr. Em." The young stranger lifted her tear stained face.

"Oh. Sorry," I said hesitantly. Once a patient died and the bill was paid, the relatives took the body away. We doctors were no longer wanted or needed.

"Who is your father?"

"Gasimu Kallon."

"Oh." He had a daughter?

"I'm sorry," I repeated inadequately to the girl. Why hadn't I spent a bit more time talking with him, instead of always finding excuses to leave? "How long have you been here?"

"Yesterday, Dr. Em." At least Gasimu had not died alone. I was glad of that.

"They did not tell me my father was ill," she started to explain. "I don come quick but my village is near Kailahun."

"Kailahun! How did you get here?" Kailahun was where Jo and Tim were posted, a hundred and fifty miles to the East.

"I walked."

"You walked!" The girl had scarcely reached puberty. "Alone?"

"I get no mother and no brother."

So the responsibility for transporting her father's corpse back to their village now rested on this child's shoulders. And the bill – all those dressings, all those antibiotics and insulin, not to mention the surgery – God, it would be enormous. Remorse suddenly overwhelmed me. I had failed Gasimu in every way and my biggest failure was to treat him as a medical problem rather than as a person. My horror at his condition and the language barrier were no excuse. I wished I had held his hand. Just once.

I felt quite sick at the thought of this girl, or anyone, having to pay for my failings. I had to help her now. I glanced at my watch. It was still early, and a hospital holiday. We had to get her father out of the compound before MT was back on duty and confiscated the body. We had twenty-four hours.

"Okay, come with me. Your uncle works at Mokanje, notto-so?" She nodded as I slipped my feet into flip-flops and tied my unbrushed hair into a pony-tail.

By nightfall Gasimu's body was gone, with a lot of help from Nat's Mines' connections. We would face MT in the morning.

We lied.

"Sister Ignatius, sadly the diabetic patient on Surgical died yesterday. He'd been very ill and suffered greatly," I waffled, wringing my hands and shuffling my feet. "We tried to save him by amputating his leg, but it became infected and we had to amputate it higher, but that didn't work either and his diabetes got out of control and the infection took over his whole system and I managed to scrounge insulin in Freetown so at least we didn't have to pay for that bit of it. Anyway…"

"His body vanished in the night, Ignatius, before the bill was paid," Nat interrupted.

"Aw fo do," said MT, her head bent over her calculator. We stood and gaped.

"Aw fo do," I mouthed to Nat. "Is that all?" He shrugged.

"Now I'm sure you young people have work to do," MT added. "I must finish the annual report."

"Yes, yes, of course," said Nat, pulling me out of Admin office.

"I don't believe it," I exclaimed, as soon as we were out of earshot. "What's got into her? Aw fo do? I was expecting a lynching!"

"Well you know why don't you, Dr. Emily?"

"No, I don't. Enlighten me."

"It's the annual report. Attendances are up nearly fifty percent this quarter."

"Really?" I exclaimed.

"Yes. You must be the first atheist to make it into MT's good books."

"Agnostic," I corrected. "It's the curiosity factor. As soon as the patients discover I'm no Dr. Pat, attendances will slump back to normal."

"Maybe they did come to test you out," mused Nat. "But you try for them and you laugh a lot. Two things that go down very well here."

"Nonsense," I retorted, unused to a direct compliment from Nat but I was pleased. Perhaps I actually could help save Serabu Hospital.

1991 assumed a nice little rhythm. The Harmattan blew in some cooler weather, banishing my prickly heat which lifted my mood considerably. At work, my surgical skills would never be the greatest, but they were good enough and attendances crept up steadily, taking my confidence with them. Pa George served his plassas and gradually my waistbands loosened. As for my love life? Well, you couldn't have everything but my social life was very pleasant: girly chats with Nicole, beers with Nat and Philippe, cribbage with Tom and Joe, or Scrabble with Mariama, Earnest and AJ. Fellow volunteers popped in from time to time, and I even cycled to Sumbuya to spend a weekend with Chandra, my Peace Corps pal. When alone, I wrote long letters home with the World Service as my constant companion. The news from the big bad world outside scarcely touched me, even when I heard that we were at war with Iraq. But The Gulf seemed very far away, whilst I was safe in peaceful Sierra Leone, a country that had never known war.

"Why haven't you told us about Mr-Dr-Em?"

"Mr-Dr... What are you talking about, Tom?"

"Your man."

"I don't have a man," I snapped.

"Well, who was your visitor today?"

"Huh?"

"You know, the little guy who fixes things."

"What?!!! Klaus? He came to visit?!"

"That was him. Hey you see. She's blushing. He must be Mr-Dr-Em."

"Rubbish." I tried to gather myself. Why did the staff assume Klaus was my other half? Had he insinuated it somehow? That was very hopeful indeed. "He's just another VSO," I added hastily.

"Come, come, Dr. Emily. You can't be telling us there isn't something going on," teased Nat.

"So where is he?"

"Oh, he left long ago."

"You mean he's gone!"

"Sorry. Hey, Nat's right. You really like the guy!"

"Hmmmph!" I was doing my best not to burst into tears. "Didn't he... why didn't he come and find me?"

"You were busy in theatre."

"Couldn't he wait?"

"He waited for nearly three hours, Em. He came on his motorbike and wanted to get back before dark."

"Oh."

"Hey, his trip wasn't wasted," Tom continued. "Nat collared him and guess what?"

"What?" I asked in a flat voice.

"He fixed our water pumps!"

At least he had left me a note. I read it once I was safely free from my audience of Philippe and Tom who were enthralled by the thought of me having a fancy man.

Dear Doc,

How di body? Sorry to miss you. Aw fo do. I heard you were up to your knees in blood, so couldn't bear to disturb you. Next time. I've got this bike running like a pussy cat, so if I can scrounge some petrol, I'm on for that trip to Segbwema. Meet you in the Peace Corps rest house in Bo on Easter Saturday? Radio CARE to confirm. You owe me a big kiss for fixing your water pumps. We go see back!

Love,

Klaus xxxxx

I cheered up a little. He'd signed his letter with love and five kisses and said I owed him a big kiss! I cheered up a little more. And he still wanted to take me up to see Morag at Easter. And he'd even fixed our water.

What a star! I had a shower and flushed my loo for the first time in six months.

SAFFA AND SCOOBY

Saffa was seven and he had rabies. Three weeks earlier he'd been bitten by a dog and all we could do was to clean the wound and put him on antibiotics – his father couldn't afford the rabies vaccine and neither could we. MT only allowed those bitten by dogs proven to be infected (and who would catch, cage and feed a potentially rabid dog for ten days when there was not enough food to feed their own families?) or those wealthy enough to pay, to get the vaccine. Horrible though this was, even I could see that egalitarian principles were useless if the hospital bankrupted itself on one or two cases.

I had never seen rabies outside of the textbooks and I never want to see it again. Saffa could no longer swallow as even his own saliva started excruciating spasms in his throat. His young body twisted in pain, saliva frothing from his mouth.

"Saffa's father wants to take him home," Mariama told me, as I stood, helplessly watching the child suffer, despite huge doses of sedative.

"Not like this," I exclaimed. "They live fifty miles away!"

"His father wants him to die with his family," Mariama persisted.

"No!" I snapped. "No," I repeated more gently. I fully understood that his father should want Saffa to die at home, especially after we had failed him so badly, but how would he get him there? "Look, Saffa can't possibly go on a poda-poda." The memory of my own journey in the glorified cattle truck was still fresh in my mind. "We can't cram a child drooling rabid saliva into a truck full of people! And the journey will be a nightmare for the boy."

Mariama spoke at length to the father in Mende, then turned to me.

"He wants to take Saffa home alive. Poda-poda drivers charge double for dead bodies."

Aghast, I struggled to give a civil reply. "This child is suffering."

I spoke to Mariama without looking at the father. "The journey will be a nightmare – I doubt he'd even survive it. Let Saffa die here where at least we can sedate him."

Mariama nodded and spoke again to the father.

"The father has agreed."

"Well done, Mariama. How did you persuade him?"

"If Saffa died during the journey, it would cost five times as much."

A fist of anger encircled my heart. How could this man be so mercenary when his own son was dying in agony?

After a few deep, calming breaths, I gathered myself for Outpatients. My first patient was Pa Ndanema, an old man who'd lost a leg many years ago and now his stump was breaking down. It was probably a side effect of TB. I sent him to X-ray.

"Another patient is there in X-ray," said AJ.

"Really? Who?" I hadn't sent anybody and Philippe was in bed with malaria.

"A patient sent by Dr. Momoh."

"Oh yes." We did have an agreement that Dr. Momoh, the Mines' official doctor, could use our X-Ray facilities, even though we had little faith in Dr. Momoh's visual or medical faculties. We charged extra of course, and always sneaked a look at the pictures before they went back to exclude major problems. "So who is it?"

"I don't know. He get swelling on his jaw," AJ told me. "He named Scooby."

"Scooby? Not a Mende name, surely?" But with children called Nurse and Problem, I refrained from further comment.

"He black Dr. Em, but he notto Mende man." AJ shook his head solemnly.

"AJ what are you trying to tell me?"

"Mr. Scooby Doo is not well." AJ was laughing now.

"Scooby Doo! A DOG?!"

"Dr. Joy what is going on? There's a dog in X-Ray!" MT stormed into my office. "This is a gross misuse of precious facilities. I demand an explanation."

"Ask Dr. Momoh, Sister Ignatius." I threw my hands up defensively, "They've just told me."

"Dr. Joy, are you laughing?"

"No, Sister," I replied with great effort.

"This is no laughing matter. Are you not aware of the funding crisis that may force my hospital to close in a matter of months?"

"Of course, Sister. Shall we go and investigate?" I offered.

"I have work to do. Dr. Momoh will be hearing from me personally."

MT left abruptly and suppressing a smile, I went down to the little X-ray room. An expatriate couple sat outside, stroking an old black Labrador with a large swelling on its cheek.

"Dr. Em, look at this X-ray." Latif pushed a picture of the dog's jaw under my nose.

"Well there's a swelling, but you don't need an X-ray to see that." I handed back the film.

"Doctor, the vet's on holiday and Scooby's swelling is just getting bigger," the tearful middle-aged lady told me. Gosh, was there a vet in Sierra Leone?

"How old is Scooby?" I looked into the cloudy brown eyes gazing mournfully into mine.

"Nearly fourteen."

"Fourteen!" I exclaimed. "Wouldn't it be kindest to put him to sleep?" A double dose of out of date anaesthetic would probably do the trick. Perhaps triple to make sure.

"Oh please doctor, is there nothing you can do until the vet comes back?"

My knowledge of dogs was based entirely on James Herriot books, but surely Scooby wouldn't even survive until the vet's return. Poor old boy. I tentatively touched Scooby's swelling and he licked my hand.

"The swelling is soft, and there's pus dribbling into his mouth," I mused. "It might just be an abscess."

"Could you lance it?"

"Well I suppose so, but I've no idea how to safely anaesthetise a dog. You'll just have to hold him down." Dogs might be the only thing not covered in *Primary Surgery*, but I was sure 'where there's pus, let it out' still applied.

155

Except it wasn't an abscess. Not a drop of pus drained out of my incision. Scooby never released me from his placid brown stare, flopping a paw onto my thigh as I knelt beside him and probed inside the swelling with a gloved finger. All I could feel was a soft mush of rotting tissue.

"I'm sure it's cancerous. Okay, Scooby, I've finished." I stroked the dog's head. "I should put him to sleep. I'm sorry."

"We'll wait for the vet," the woman gulped. Her husband mouthed thank-you, then scooped up Scooby and carried him to their truck.

"So Emily, what about Mr-Dr-Em? Confess all to Father Nat."

"Just dish me out my chop." I shoved my plate over to the would-be-priest.

"A mighty choice."

"Hmmph!"

"Not as handsome as me, of course, but anyone who can fix our water is a friend of mine."

"No wonder he couldn't wait to leave – before you roped him into a hundred more jobs."

"Jaysus, is that all the thanks I get for providing running water!"

"Excuse me, who fixed the pumps?"

"The mark of a good Administrator is knowing the right person for the job," Nat sniffed. "I was after thinking he'd be a bit bigger though."

"Why?" I snapped. Was this a slur on my size, or Klaus'? Either way Nat realised our friendship was hitting rocky territory and rapidly changed the subject.

"So how much do you we charge the Mines for veterinary services?" he asked.

"Double at least."

"Poor dog." Nat shook his head. "Anyway, I'm afraid we still haven't heard from the new doc who's replacing Philippe."

"Perhaps he's waiting for the July review. There's not much point coming if Serabu's going to close. I'm trying not to panic about being left alone."

"Talking about, er, being left alone... I've, um, got something to tell you..."

I didn't like the way he was fiddling with his earlobe. Nat was never hesitant. "Tell me."

"I'm leaving." He coughed. "Father Gregory has asked me to work at the seminary in Makeni from Easter."

"What?! But that's next month!"

"I know. I'm sorry."

"What can I say?"

"You can come and visit, it's less than a day's journey north."

"Yeah great. MT will never let me out – especially if there's no replacement for Philippe!"

"I'll visit Serabu."

"Hmmph. Looks like I'd better enjoy my trip to Segbwema, then – my last escape."

"Have a beer."

"Hmmph."

Three days later a smartly dressed young Salonean man interrupted our plassas.

"Kushe, Dr. Joy. Dr. Jalloh from Freetown."

"Pleased to meet you Dr. Jalloh." I shook the outstretched hand. Who on earth was he?

"I am most grateful for your assistance with my patient."

"No problem." I smiled politely. "Um. Who are we talking about?"

"Scooby."

"Scooby." I glanced over to Nat who was raising his eyebrows as he put his flip-flopped feet on my table. "So you're the vet?"

"Indeed I am the only vet in Sierra Leone." Dr. Jalloh bowed. "U.S. trained."

"Congratulations. I obviously don't have your training, but Scooby seemed very sick to me." Had this man really made a seven-hour journey to discuss a fourteen-year-old dying dog?

"Yes, very sick," agreed Dr. Jalloh. "I wanted to know if Serabu, the best hospital in the country, can do angiograms?"

"Angiograms?!!" I spluttered.

"What's an angiogram?" Nat asked sweetly from the corner.

"An angiogram is a specialist X-Ray examination where radioopaque dye is injected into the blood vessels to delineate the arteries," explained Dr. Jalloh.

"I see," Nat nodded in mock understanding. "Can I ask how this test would help Scooby?"

"Scooby's mass is undoubtedly a cancerous growth. An angiogram would outline the extent of the lesion more effectively than a plain X-Ray."

"I see." Nat rubbed his chin and nodded. He was enjoying this.

"We scarcely have enough resources to perform even the most basic X-Rays on our *own* patients," I said with forced politeness. Why were we even discussing hugely expensive treatments for a dog when we didn't have the money to give rabies vaccines to children? "This is a dog we're talking about. And a very old dog at that."

"I wish only to formulate an accurate treatment schedule," said Dr. Jalloh. "Scooby's owners are very upset."

And Scooby's white middle-class owners were rich enough to pay his juicy veterinary bills too, no doubt.

"Yes, of course." I folded my arms. "It must be hard to see a loved pet suffer so." Admittedly Scooby was a nice dog.

"Yes. So you no able help me?"

"No. Aw fo do."

"Aw fo do. I better get back to work." Dr. Jalloh shook my hand. "It's been nice to meet you, Dr. Joy."

"Good-bye."

"Nice to meet you too, Dr. Jalloh." Nat waved from the sofa.

"Angiograms!" I snorted as soon as the door closed.

"Such is the advantage of a Western education!" Nat collapsed in a fit of helpless giggles.

The irony was no longer amusing by morning. Twenty feet from C-Ward, my feet froze on the baked ground as Saffa's father left the ward. He was cuddling a white shrouded bundle close to his chest, making no attempt to wipe away the tears that rolled silently down his face.

Saffa's father loved his son – that much was painfully obvious. Who was I to stand in judgement? We had sacrificed Saffa for the survival of our hospital, just as this father had had to make impossible financial decisions to ensure the survival of the rest of his family. We had failed Saffa but would try to save the next child who came to us. Saffa's father had lost his son, but he still had to struggle on to provide for his other children. God, what a life. I brushed away my own tears and did my rounds. Only four weeks to Segbwema. Oh Emily, don't start that again.

CREATURE CRAWLING IN
ABDOMEN

"Som ting de walka na me belly."

Dr. Dan raised a quizzical eyebrow at Patrick's rounded handwriting.

"Have you had Krio lessons?" I asked.

"Hey, I only arrived yesterday. I know 'kushe', though," Dan volunteered.

I still couldn't believe that we had a new doctor. His letters had gone astray so the first we knew of his arrival had been a radio message the previous morning, leaving Moses to attempt a record breaking journey to Lungi Airport.

"Kushe will get you further than you think." I smiled at my handsome new colleague. Married, unfortunately – his wife was coming in a couple of weeks.

"Well that's a relief." He tapped the patient's card. "So, what's the system?"

"The nurses triage the Outpatients and, send those that need tests straight to the lab. They'll treat anything simple, then send the rest to us after recording their histories."

"It's sure no use if they put it all in Krio."

"Don't worry, they usually use English but 'Something walking in my belly' is the no.1 symptom here – sometimes translated into 'creature crawling in abdomen'," I explained.

"D'ya mean worms! Isn't that just a great expression?"

"Creature crawling in abdomen covers everything from a little tummy ache to full-blown peritonitis. And worms, of course."

"I guess worms are so common here that most people don't even notice. Unless they cause secondary complications like anaemia with hookworm infestation," he mused.

That was the trouble with Dan. He hadn't been with us for twenty-four hours, and already he knew it all.

The latest recruit to Serabu's medical staff was in his mid-thirties, an athletic all-American male. He wore little round glasses, just like mine but, where mine with their hint of verdigris shouted NHS, his gave him that serious but trendy look – like Harrison Ford in a Heroic Doctor role, putting me, more of a Dawn French sort of character, on the defensive.

"Kushe, Bockerie. How di body?"

"Kushe, Dr. Em. I no better," announced my first patient on Medical.

"But I drained four pints of pus off your chest!" Surely he felt just a little bit better?

"I still de cough, I still no able blow fine, I still get fever…"

"Okay Bockerie, let me listen in."

AJ stood unhelpfully at the end of the bed as I struggled with Bockerie's chest drain.

"AJ, are you going to help?"

"No problem, Dr. Em." AJ saluted and swaggered forward.

I sighed. So much for the humble student nurse with undying admiration for the doctor.

"Probably TB," said Dan, examining Bockerie's X-Ray. Sure enough, Latif arrived with sputum results to confirm Dan's diagnosis.

"Aw fo do, Bockerie," chirped AJ. "You get for go na TB ward!"

Bockerie was not impressed. Nobody wanted to go to TB ward.

"Sorry-oh," I muttered. I could have hit AJ for his insensitivity. Bockerie did hit him.

"Careful AJ, he's frail." AJ was shoving Bockerie back onto the bed.

"He done hit me, Dr. Em!"

"You asked for it, AJ." But my words were lost in a Mende shouting match that had suddenly developed between student nurse and patient. Bockerie now had AJ's crisp white uniform by the lapels.

"Shall we continue?" I asked Dan, who stood gaping.

"Shouldn't we break it up?" he suggested.

"No. Sister Ignatius can sort it out."

"Who's Sister Ignatius then? Does she pump iron?"

"Er, not exactly. She's our seven stone administrator."

"I'm quivering in my shoes," laughed Dan.

"Believe me. Quiver."

Dr. Dan chewed gum and diagnosed all my patients quickly and decisively, confidently suggesting treatment appropriate to a Third World situation. I cursed Philippe for making me show him round – I just wasn't impressive enough.

"But you will soon be his boss, yes? Dr. Emily, the Medical Superintendent of Serabu 'ospital," Philippe had teased, before trotting off to Outpatients, Dan and I continued our rounds.

The first three cases on Surgical had nasty wound infections. I knew they were all excusable given the poor condition they had been in on arrival and yes, they would all heal eventually, but it just didn't look good. Dan stayed tactfully quiet – until Ansumana.

"Ansumana fell out of a palm tree sustaining multiple intestinal perforations. Somehow he survived three days walk to the hospital," I told Dan. "When he reached us, he was septicaemic with a grossly distended belly."

"Really? Well ain't that amazing he's alive?" Dan enthused.

"Yes, isn't it," I preened. "It was tricky surgery, especially in a moribund patient."

Keen to show off my handiwork, I pulled off the dressing with a flourish. "Oh no!"

"Gee, what's that orange stuff and white flaky bits?"

The gauze dressing was soaked orange with palm oil and grains of half-digested rice oozed between the stitches. Having your patient's dinner coming directly out of the wound was not a good way to advertise your surgical skills. I was speechless.

"Hey girl, even with proper equipment, anaesthetic and a real surgeon in the States, he might never have made it." The newcomer slapped me encouragingly on the back and continued to chew his gum, no doubt wondering what sort of place he had come to.

Why couldn't I find a miracle recovery to show him? Jeneba for instance, or Christiana? Like the rest of us, Dan hadn't had any surgical experience before coming to Africa, and with three cases scheduled that morning, I was going to have to teach him. Or rather Tiange was.

"This is Tiange, Dan. She'll teach you everything you need to know about surgery."

"Real pleased to meet you, Tiange." Dan stepped forward and firmly shook her hand. Tiange actually smiled. How did Dan manage that?

"You don't mess with Tiange, our queen of theatre," I whispered to Dan as we scrubbed up.

"I'll remember that."

"Last week Tiange asked a patient five times if he was chewing gum. He denied it every time, despite her dire warnings of what could happen if he inhaled it whilst unconscious under anaesthetic. When he woke up, she had plastered the gum across his forehead."

"I'm real glad I spat mine out," Dan laughed. "Where's the antiseptic?"

"We just have that bar of soap. Usually we don't have as many post-operative wound infections…"

"Hmm." Dan was not convinced. "Tell me about our patient today."

"A lady with a large abdominal swelling. She's quite elderly, although no one really knows how old they are here. Saloneans measure time by today, tomorrow and yesterday, or wet or dry season."

"So what do you think? An ovarian cyst?"

"Probably. Just last week, I removed cysts the size of basketballs from two separate patients."

"Gee! That's amazing."

Pleased that at last I had the chance to impress Dan, I made a confident incision in the abdominal wall. Separating the sides of the wound with my hands, we looked inside. The nature of the mass became quite, quite obvious.

"She get belly!" Tiange exclaimed.

"She must be nearly six months pregnant!" echoed Dan.

Gulping back tears of humiliation whilst Dan and the nurses gulped back tears of laughter, I closed the wound without disturbing the foetus any further. Tiange reassured the patient, who was still awake under a spinal, that her pregnancy would proceed quite normally. The patient, apparently unconcerned, asked why we didn't just remove it as she already had eight children.

Once we were finished, Dan picked up her Outpatient card and succumbed to helpless guffaws. Embarrassed, I snatched the card from him to see what had caused such mirth.

The presenting complaint read: *Creature crawling in abdomen*.

RAISING THE ROOF

Serabu Hospital was one man down for the annual Hospital vs. Serabu Village football match.

"Wouldn't it be mighty if there was a doctor on the hospital team?" Nat suggested innocently.

"Well, Philippe's off to theatre with Dan champing at the bit to get stuck into his first Caesarean."

"That leaves our favourite lady doctor. Even better!"

"What about their favourite Administrator?" I prodded my terminally unsporty Irish friend.

"Ah, Emily, they'll be needing me to organise the supporters."

And so it was that the big strong girl became Serabu Hospital's left back. I jogged onto the field amidst much chuckling from the spectators. A poomui playing football was funny enough, but a woman?

Determined to do female caucasians justice, I ran doggedly round the lumpy threadbare pitch in futile pursuit. Every time I came within striking distance of the ball, our supporters who consisted of students, nurses, relatives and TB patients, roared with delight. The hysteria was palpable on the four occasions I actually made contact with the ball. Even Tiange was cheering.

Tom, malaria free, turned out to be quite a sportsman and achieved honorary black man status for his prowess, even if he did cheat by wearing trainers rather than playing barefoot. With AJ and Tom on side, our boys managed to sneak a 3-3 draw.

With two minutes to go, Patrick Kpukoma, as ref, awarded the hospital a penalty kick. This was debated so ferociously by the village lads that the match could only continue when Patrick agreed to let them choose who out of our team would take the shot.

Since I could now barely stand, I assumed I would be the obvious choice to mess up a penalty kick. I was eternally relieved, and rather flattered, when they unanimously yelled out "Mr. Nat!"

Nat, never one to think of taking offence, high-stepped on to the pitch, his pasty arms held aloft to the cheers of encouragement from the supporters. He bowed, picked up the scuffed and patched ball, blessed it with the sign of the cross, kissed it and placed it gently on the ground. He took three deep breaths, crossed himself, then blasted it between the two bamboo stick goal posts.

Well, Scotland winning the world cup at Wembley couldn't have generated more jubilation. Nat was hoisted high on the victorious team's shoulders and paraded round the field. He gave me the royal wave before vanishing for his lap of honour, round the entire village. I managed a weak thumbs-up in reply before staggering home to drink my water filter dry.

"Bua bise, Pa Ali. Bi gahun yena?"
  "Kayingoma. A bia be?"
  "Kayingoma."
  "Malo-hua."
  "Malo-hua Pa Ali."
The wiry old man jogged to the base of the palm tree – he was busy after the football. Placing his empty yellow two-gallon rubber container on the ground, he slung his woven raffia halter round the trunk and shinned up. In the half-light, he vanished into the umbrella of leaves, so I returned to thinking about Nat. We were going to have a last supper together in Bo on the Friday, before he travelled North to his new posting and Klaus took me East to meet Morag at Segbwema.

How would I survive without Nat? At least I had my consolation prizes – the surprise arrival of Dr. Dan, the whole of next week to turn Klaus into Mr-Dr-Em, a chance to see Morag (and the opportunity to learn a bit more surgery of course).

"What for chop today?" My daily alarm call thundered through my bedroom door as the sun rose. Every wooden muscle in my body nailed me to my bed.

"Morning, Pa George," I groaned. "Plassas please."

"Cassava ten leones, bonga thirty leones…"

"Okay," I sighed. "I'm coming." I rolled my aching body off the bed, gave Pa George his money and limped down to the hospital.

"Kushe, Dr. Football!" Sesay called out.

"Look, Dr. Football de come!" AJ and Latif dribbled imaginary footballs round me. I stuck out my tongue and side-stepped into Maternity, where I thought interest in football would be minimal.

"Yo! Here's our soccer star!" Dan slapped me on the back.

"Dan," I coughed. "You're early."

"Come to check on my first Caesarean."

"And how is our new surgeon's patient?" I asked.

"She's real great." Indeed mother, baby and doctor were all radiant.

"And this little fellow is called Dr-Dan." He picked up his namesake.

"You're obviously a natural," I laughed, but stopped short when I caught the eye of a stony-faced man standing, arms folded, by the bed opposite.

"Can I help, sir?"

"This is Isata's man," explained Laygby.

Isata was one of my series of wound infections following a delayed Caesarean. She had crawled into the ward a week ago, nearly dead with exhaustion, so I hadn't expected her husband to be dressed in a tailored shirt and trousers, set off with shiny leather shoes and a gold watch.

"I done tell him Isata no able go home today, so he is angry."

"Kushe." I offered my hand but it was left hanging.

"He say it he no able wait for that wound to heal," Laygby told me. "Isata get for work on the farm."

"I see." I folded my arms. "Let's see the wound then, Laygby. You removed the stitches yesterday, notto so?"

"Yes. Plenty pus came out, but I done clean it fine today." She pulled back the gauze to show a long gaping wound, exposing muscle underneath.

"It doesn't look too good," whispered Dan.

"It's clean," I retorted. "Laygby, can you reassure Isata that her wound will heal. It just needs time. And tell that man that leaving his wife to labour for three days, then making her walk to the hospital, will have exacerbated the infection."

"He speaks English."

"Good. Then he understands what I have just said?"

"Yes, but he say the infection is your fault, so he no go pay the bill."

"Isata is lucky to be alive at all after her ordeal," I snapped. "This wound will heal. It may take two more weeks, but it will heal."

"He say that this ward no get ceiling-self," Laygby continued.

Dan and I looked up simultaneously. Sure enough, there was no ceiling. "And them bats drop their kaka in the wound."

"Her wound is covered with fresh dressings every day. I promise it will heal," I stammered, pulling Dan out of the ward behind me.

"Hey, girl," he grumbled.

"You think I was rude to that man?"

"Mmm. He had a point, Emily. I sure did see some bats up there."

"Well, I thought I was remarkably civil. That man refused to pay for transport, so Isata had to walk ten miles to get here." I could feel my voice rising with anger. "She and her baby were moribund. So now he's concerned for her welfare? This is his first appearance, you know – a week later."

"Hmm. He sure had a nice watch," Dan agreed.

"Bloody man!" I snorted. "This is one chap who deserves the full wrath of MT, bats or no bats."

That evening I returned to Maternity to find a seven-month pregnant Laygby bending behind Isata's bed, beating a bat to death with her flip flop. Fortunately there was no sign of Isata's husband. Looking up, the rafters were alive with flapping shadows. How had I never noticed before? I had to admit a ceiling was probably a good idea, and went to confront MT the next morning. Maintenance was her area.

"Good morning, Sister Ig... er... hello?"

"Good morning." A sweet smiling lady in a blue dress covered in tiny yellow flowers, looked up from MT's desk. Her hair was very black and cut fashionably short to frame a girlish face. I would have put her in her late thirties had it not been for the simple cross hanging on a gold chain that brought the eye to the age-spots clustered on the sun-damaged skin at her throat.

"Er, well, I was really looking for Sister Ignatius. Sorry. Er, I'm Emily." We shook hands.

"Hello Dr. Emily, I'm Bernadette," she introduced herself in a lovely Irish lilt. "I'm sorry we have not had chance to meet but let me offer a belated welcome to Serabu."

"Oh. Er, thank you." Bernadette? Ah yes, Nat said there was a Bernie coming back from sabbatical.

"I hear you're doing great work altogether, Dr. Emily."

"Pleased to meet you too," I stuttered, unused to compliments. "Er, where's Sister Ignatius?"

"She's got malaria, I'm afraid. I'm back in Admin."

"Oh. Is Ignatius all right? Should I take a look at her?" I felt obliged to ask, although I couldn't imagine what sort of doctor-patient relationship I would have with MT.

"Thank you. Joe has driven her to convalesce at our convent in Bo. Hilary will look after her."

"Of course." Obviously I wasn't good enough.

"Now how can I help you, Dr. Emily?"

"What?" I'd forgotten why I'd come. "Oh yes. Did you know there's no ceiling on Maternity Ward?"

"No... ceiling?" Bernadette raised an eyebrow. "Since when?"

"Well I don't really know. It's just that it's not very hygienic, with the rafters full of bats dropping their droppings into patient's wounds."

"Dr. Emily, are you telling me that in the six months you have been here there has been no ceiling in one of our wards?"

"Well, um, yes. I, er, don't usually look up."

"Didn't Ignatius ever notice?"

"Possibly," I shrugged. Most probably, I thought, but new ceilings cost money.

"Very well, I'll see what Sesay can do. Moses can take you and Nat to Bo in the Landrover tomorrow, if you don't mind collecting the materials for him to bring back?"

"Of course," I said demurely. (Fantastic, a lift!) "Won't you be a bit pushed in Admin without Nat and Ignatius?"

"We'll manage," said Bernadette. "It's time we gave Moses more responsibility. Meanwhile you have a happy birthday and enjoy your break in Segbwema."

"You know about my birthday?"

"I always note down birthdays from the volunteer details."

Now this was how nuns were supposed to be. Didn't MT have the same God?

The Rebels Are Coming

"The rebels are coming!"

"Huh? What rebels?"

"The rebels have invaded from Liberia, and are heading towards Bo," announced a stern-faced, pony-tailed American. Nat and I looked at each other in disbelief. We were sitting at Ma Coker's bar, the favourite volunteer hang out in Bo, having just treated ourselves to a special birthday dinner of egg and chips.

"I'm evacuating everybody to Freetown. The Peace Corps trucks leave at dawn," our harbinger of doom continued.

"You're joking," said Nat.

"But I'm meeting Klaus tomorrow, we're going to Segbwema," I protested.

"Not now you're not," said the grim-faced man. "There are six thousand rebels invading the east and south. Kailahun and Segbwema are the worst affected. There are convoys of villagers coming west as we speak. Get back to the rest house and pack your bags."

"Who was that?" I gasped, breaking the silence that followed the departure of the American.

"Our Field Officer," mumbled a Peace Corps.

"Was he for real?"

"I sure don't know, but I'm getting another Star."

"I'm with him," said Nat. "Two Stars please."

"Shouldn't we do as he says?" I asked, never one for disobeying authority.

"Don't be an eejit, you're already packed. Have a Star! Happy birthday!"

The next morning Nat and I joined an unruly gaggle outside the

Peace Corps rest house, feeling a lot less blasé now as the Peace Corps Field Officer repeated his ominous sermon. The rebels had come in from Liberia across the border south of Sumbuya, and from the eastern border through Kailahun and Segbwema. Oh God, Morag was supposed to be in Segbwema, Chandra in Sumbuya and Jo and Tim were in Kailahun. It had seemed like some sort of surreal adventure last night, but now I felt sick with anxiety.

And so we were whisked down to Freetown with a crowd of Peace Corps, Nat entertaining them with his usual banter, whilst I looked anxiously out of the back window, wondering where Klaus was. Perhaps he was speeding towards the frontline on his motorbike, desperate to rescue me from the clutches of the rebels. Or more likely the CARE grapevine had kept him well informed, and he was sitting in Moyamba, drinking Star.

An hour down the road we passed Chandra, trying to hitch a lift in the opposite direction.

"Where do you think you're going, Chandra?" the Peace Corps Field Officer yelled through the passenger window.

"Yo, what's your problem?" Chandra put her hands on her hips and eyed the full Landrover. "I'm headed back to Sumbuya, hard worker that I am. Where are *you* all going?"

"Kushe, Chandra! There's trouble," Nat called from the back. Nat knew just everyone.

"Hey, Nat. It's not like you to travel economy."

"Very funny," retorted Nat, but his face softened quickly. "I'm sorry Chandra but rebels have invaded."

"No way!"

"We're evacuating everybody east and south of Bo, and that includes you, girl."

"But I just left Freetown! Nobody mentioned squat."

"The radio's not manned before nine," said the Field Officer wearily. "Don't argue. Jump in."

"Where? On the roof? It's worse than a poda-poda in there. God, there's even a couple of Brits in the back."

"Irish, please!" Nat bristled.

"I could hardly leave them behind, though heavens knows, it's not my job to be evacuating VSOs," the Field Officer complained. "Just get in and be thankful."

"I'll ruin Tim's made-to-measure dress."

"Get in!"

"Okay, okay."

Five hours later, the Peace Corps Field Officer dropped Nat and I off on Siaka Stevens' Street. Nat turned North to Santano house, the priests' Freetown hostel, and I headed South to the VSO office.

"See you at the Venue tomorrow?"

"If we don't get shipped home," snorted Nat, then gave me a hug. "We go see back. God bless."

"Okay. Bye. I'll just report to VSO," I said. "I must say Freetown seems very much business as usual."

The VSO office was also business as usual, or rather business as usual for a Saturday – closed. Even the Red Cross office downstairs was closed, with no sign of the usual crowd of displaced Liberians hanging around outside.

Strange. Things couldn't be that bad. Well, I'd go and see if Klaus was at the VSO rest house with all the other evacuees. My step quickened in anticipation. I skipped up the stairs, expecting to walk into an excited reunion with my fellow VSOs – comrades rallying together in the face of adversity, hugs all round, Klaus holding me tight and thanking God that I was safe.

The place was empty. There was not even a bag or a book or an erected mosquito net to suggest that anyone was staying. I stood on the balcony, looking at life carrying on below. There was a tailor on the corner, pedalling furiously on his sewing machine, whilst a woman hung his finished gara suits around him. Opposite was a stall that sold teabags, miniature tins of condensed milk, bananas, cigarettes and matches. Children played in the pot holed street and, even in the big city, the women carried water and firewood on their heads. There was no sense of any impending danger. Had it all been an April Fool?

What was I supposed to do now? No one had a telephone of course, but I supposed I could make my way to Nick's house. Our Field Officer was bound to know what was going on and would probably feed me a couple of beers too. And he was gorgeous. Now if only I could remember the way – it was over six months since we'd crashed at his place. It was a couple of miles uphill, I knew, just below the High Commissioner's Compound. Right, Emily, big strong girls don't just sit around. Better make a move before it gets dark.

I headed out of town with my pack on my back, marching through two miles of corrugated rust, twisted with decaying wood and torn clothes drying in woodsmoke. A child squatted, passing liquid motions into a storm drain. Further along the same drain lay a dead dog, the gases of putrefaction distending its abdomen. I hurried past to reach the tarmacked road that wound up expatriate hill.

Slogging up the hill, the shanties gave way to larger white or pink-washed residences, with tiled roofs, verandas, walls and iron gates. This was where the Lebanese and other expatriates lived, and with Freetown bay stretching out to meet the sunset below me, it was obvious why they had made their choice.

After an hour's brisk walk, I stopped to catch my breath under a reassuringly familiar billboard advertising cigarettes. It stood, I remembered, half way between the British High Commission Compound on the top of the hill and Nick's house. Too relieved to spot the landmark to be disapproving of its content, I headed two hundred metres back down from the sign to the inconspicuous lane that led to Nick's door.

There was no sign of the VSO Landrover, and Nick's house stood dark and quiet in the fading light. I banged on the door anyway. A young Krio lad appeared from round the back.

"Kushe. Where Nick?"

"He don go," the boy replied. To bravely go to evacuate his flock in the East and South, I assumed.

"Gone where?"

"Mr. Nick don go Otamba Kilimbi for de weekend."

"Otamba Kilimbi! The National Park?" That was just great. Here I was evacuated to Freetown, the country riddled with rebels, and my fearless leader was off looking for hippos and chimpanzees.

"For look dem hippos."

"Yes, yes. Thank you." I flopped down on Nick's doorstep. At least it was a bit cooler up the hill.

"You want orange?" the lad offered.

"Oh, that would be lovely." He came back with four. I squeezed one after the other, into my mouth, not caring about the juice that dribbled onto my cotton dress, making big spots in the layer of dust that had collected during my journey from Bo.

Now what? I knew our Field Director didn't live on the Des-Res expatriate hill because his wife couldn't appreciate the view, choosing instead to live by the sea so Juliet could hear the ocean. However, he kept his actual address on a need to know basis (and believed we volunteers didn't need to know), so all I could do was head back down to the rest house.

Night was falling and the expatriate houses started rumbling as their generators fired up. At least it meant there was light from their windows to illuminate my step. Once I hit the uneven streets of downtown Freetown though, there was only the occasional kerosene lamp hung by the street-stalls to guide me between the treacherous potholes and away from the storm drains. Although streetlights lined the pavements, they had not been lit for years. After a few wrong turnings into very similar-looking streets, I finally found the rest house. Surely somebody would have arrived by now.

The night watchman stirred as I banged on the door, and sleepily let me in. All was dark and silent.

"Where is everybody?" I asked the watchman.

"They don go Otamba Kilimbi."

"Of course." Over half the VSOs were teachers and the schools and colleges were on their Easter break.

I dumped my bag and went to buy candles, matches and a little tin of condensed milk from the stall. Then, sitting alone by candlelight, spooning condensed milk and listening to the World Service, I chortled at a book of Far Side cartoons. Gary Larson's mean spirited bugs, beasties and exploding mosquitoes had all surely been drawn specifically for volunteers in Salone. There was no mention of trouble in Sierra Leone on Focus on Africa, so I went to bed, curled up alone in the best bunk in the rest house.

It was Sunday and the lady at the stall actually had fresh bread rolls and processed cheese triangles! There were some benefits to be had in the big city. I sat on the rest house balcony eating my cheese sandwich, drinking black tea made on the kerosene stove and wondering if Serabu knew where I was. Were they evacuating the hospital? Were there even any rebels? I tuned in to the morning edition of Focus on Africa but again, there was nothing on Salone. The VSO office wouldn't open until Monday morning, so really the only option was to go to the Venue.

A Freetown taxi wasn't like your usual taxi – it went where it was going, and would squeeze you in if you wanted to go there too, even if you had to share a seat with the driver. This time I only had two companions in the back seat of the old Ford Cortina, so I stretched back to enjoy the luxury of topping thirty miles an hour with *Lucky Dube* blaring. But as soon as the driver hit thirty-five, he turned the engine off.

"Engine trouble?" I asked.

"Petrol spensif."

"Huh?" The car cruised down to ten miles an hour, before the driver spluttered the ignition and accelerated back up to thirty five... then coasted back to ten. We did this five or six times before we finally arrived.

It was midday and the Venue was full, but not with VSOs – I couldn't see a single familiar face. To console myself, I guiltily bought myself a Star beer with the Maternity Ceiling fund. Hell, refugee status should confer some rights. I had another.

On my third bottle, I spotted Chandra, who waved me over to a table of excited Peace Corps. Chandra herself was unusually subdued, worrying about her Salonean friends back in Sumbuya, and Tim in Kailahun.

Apparently all remaining Peace Corps from the East and South had been evacuated to Freetown that morning. Serabu was in the south, but since the closest Peace Corps had been Chandra, twelve miles away, nobody had any news about my friends or the hospital. Perhaps they were all en route to Freetown, or soldiering on, regardless of the threat? I prayed that everybody was safe.

"Oh Emily, I'm so glad someone else is here!" a breathless voice panted over my shoulder.

"Susan!" She was still wearing that lacy blouse. "I was beginning to think I was the only VSO left."

"Isn't it awful?" gasped Susan. "They bundled me into a Peace-Corps vehicle before I could even get my stuff."

"Have you heard about any of the others? Klaus?" I asked hopefully. "Morag? Jo and Tim?"

"They tell me Kailahun has been burnt down. I do hope… I hope Jo and Tim…" she broke down.

"Let me get you a beer, Susan." What else was there to say?

"You know I don't drink."

"This sounds like a good time to start," I tried to joke, but Susan was not in the mood for joking. Neither was I, really. We fell into awkward silence, surrounded by the remainder of the Venue's clientele who were swapping evacuation stories at the top of their voices. Susan stood, twisting the handles of her plastic bag, which contained all she had been able to grab as she left – ten green oranges, *Pride and Prejudice* and her passport. "Look, have my seat," I said. "I'll get you an orange juice."

I went to the bar, absorbing the heady mixture of adrenaline, smoke and alcohol. Finally our drinks were served and I barged my way back through to our table.

"Look who's arrived." Susan motioned toward our Field Director ambling in, deep in conversation with his wife. They stopped in the basket weave entrance, Juliet tensing before the sea of bodies blocking their way to the bar. "I don't believe it! He's got no idea what's going on!"

"You're right, Susan, they've just come for their Sunday swim." I watched in fascination as the Peace Corps Field Officer pulled him aside – presumably to whisper news of rebels in his ear. "Whoops!" Now, by the look of smug satisfaction on the Peace Corps' face, he was doubtless detailing the Peace Corps' efficient evacuation of their troops. Our Field Director's face sagged and he started looking wildly round for any of his own volunteers. He spotted us and fought his way over.

"Kushe," I said. Susan stared into her orange juice.

"Is this it? Only two of you?" our Field Director demanded.

"Looks like it," I replied. "Most of the others have gone with Nick to Otamba Kilimbi for the holidays."

"Bloody hell. We'll have to get them back."

"How? I doubt there's a mission radio at the park."

"Damn."

"Let them have their holiday – it's probably safer there."

"How would you know if the North's safe, Emily?" he snapped. "Ten minutes ago I thought the whole country was safe. Hell, hell, hell. How can I evacuate anybody with one Landrover down? The Peace Corps Field Officer claims there are six thousand rebels bearing down on Bo. He tells me they've invaded Kailahun and Segbwema. God!" He sat down with a thud. "Jo, Tim... Morag."

"Sorry," I said. "We've been trying to find out if any of the Peace Corps have heard any news of anyone, but..."

"I don't believe this! Right, you two, back in the rest house by six. I'm going to speak to the British High Commissioner."

"Well, if he wants information, he'd be better staying at the Venue." Susan broke her silence as soon as the Field Director had gone. "The British High Commissioner will be the last person to know anything."

Susan might be frightened, but she was sharp. I laughed uneasily. Her observation was not very comforting, if indeed we were caught in the midst of civil war.

THE REFUGEE

Susan sat in the corner of the VSO office, pulling at her pearl earring, reading *Pride and Prejudice*. It was Monday morning and we were none the wiser. A few VSOs had turned up over the course of Sunday evening, but there was no sign of Klaus, Jo, Tim or Morag. Moyamba was well clear of the borders, so the absence of Klaus was merely a disappointment, but the others were posted right in the trouble spots. All we could do for our friends was worry, as we lolled around the VSO office, without jobs to do, or any idea if we were all to be sent home in the next few days. Suddenly the office door flew open, and an Irish intruder infiltrated the ranks of VSO.

"Nat!" I leapt out of my chair. "What are you doing here?"

"It looked like you were after having a party."

"Yeah, hanging around like idiots, waiting to be sent home."

"Are things really that bad?" Nat said dubiously. "Santano House has contacted everyone except Kailahun and Segbwema. They're transmitting in Gaelic, in case the rebels intercept messages. Isn't that great now?" I smiled weakly at the Boy's Own excitement on his face. "Panguma's closest to the action and they're all fine," Nat gushed on. "Your friend Morag is refusing to leave! A mighty woman!"

"Workaholic," I muttered, irritated at how impressed Nat was at Morag's heroic stance. "What about Serabu?"

"I spoke to Bernie herself this morning."

"Are they all still there? Are they okay?"

"I could hardly hear a word now, there was so much hissing and crackling, but it sounded like business as usual."

"Good," I said dully, now feeling just plain guilty. "So what about you? Are you off up to your Seminary?"

"I've cadged a lift North tomorrow with Father Gregory. Now, would I be seeing real instant coffee?"

"Help yourself," I said. "One spoonful of milk powder for me."

"Buy your own coffee." The Field Director rescued the last few grains for his own tenth cup. "Yes Susan, I promise to get you on the first flight home. Emily, make yourself useful and radio Klaus from CARE's Freetown office. I want the Moyamba volunteers back, ASAP."

"Well, that's put a smile on your face," teased Nat, following me down the stairs.

"What do you mean?" I asked, struggling to keep the excitement out of my voice. It looked like I'd be seeing Klaus by evening!

"Mr-Dr-Em. Look at you! We're positively running to CARE."

"Can't you keep up?" I retorted.

"Of course. I will not delay love's true course."

"I hate you, Nat."

Preston, the CARE director, greeted us. Unlike the VSO HQ, CARE's office was an air-conditioned oasis in the heavy heat and grime of downtown Freetown. Its well-building operation was a huge project, run professionally across the whole country. They relied on their vehicles – all based at Moyamba – to get their equipment out to the remote villages. And they relied on Klaus to keep them on the road.

"So you're the famous Dr. Emily." Preston shook my hand. The famous Dr. Emily? Really? Gosh, what had Klaus said? This was most encouraging. I beamed back at Preston.

"Well, Doc. I suppose you're here about this rebel business?"

"I'm afraid so. Our Field Director wants Klaus and the other Moyamba VSOs back in Freetown today."

"I thought as much. Our Peace Corps have already taken an unscheduled rebel holiday and now you want Klaus, my greatest asset?" Preston sighed, but obligingly reached for his radio.

"Aw fo do." I smiled my most charming smile.

"Freetown to Moyamba. Do you receive me? Over."

"Loud and clear, Preston. Over." The familiar Cockney voice made my heart jump.

"Kushe Klaus. Rebels have invaded the south and east. Over."

"So we hear. The Peace Corps have all vanished. Any danger? Over."

"We don't know. Your Field Director wants all volunteers evacuated to Freetown by this afternoon. Take one of the CARE vehicles. Do you read me? Over."

"Loud and clear. I will have a vehicle ready by noon. Over."

Preston paused before continuing, "Very good, but if the rebels advance they may try to commandeer vehicles. Over."

"Quite likely. What's your point, Preston? Over."

"Will you stay behind to immobilise our vehicles if necessary? Over."

"Okay. The others will be on the truck at noon. Over."

"Thanks, Klaus. Out."

"No problem. Out."

Well thanks a lot Preston. Everybody else has to evacuate quick quick, big emergency, but Klaus has to stay and face hordes of rebels. So much for my romantic plans. On the other hand, I could not help being impressed. I had visions of Klaus trashing the vehicles with a sledgehammer then fleeing on his motorbike amidst a barrage of bullets. My hero!

The only sensible option was to return to the Venue, even if it meant swimming in my T-shirt and knickers. I hadn't come prepared for the beach.

So we sat there all afternoon, drinking our beers and gossiping, whilst rebels were destroying entire villages. And all I could think about was that Klaus wasn't coming.

Volunteers trickled back from up-country and by Tuesday night the rest house was getting decidedly cosy, but there was no Morag, Tim or Jo. However, at midnight a dishevelled figure appeared.

"Tim!" we chorused, looking up from our candlelit poker.

"You're here!"

"Er. Kushe, everybody."

"Where's Jo?"

"Are there thousands of rebels?"

"Are you all right?"

"What have you done with Jo?"

"Were you in Kailahun?"

"What happened? What about Jo?"

"What do the rebels look like?"

"Have the rebels got Jo?"

"Is she okay?"

"How did you get out?"

"Where's Jo?"

"Steady," laughed Tim, despite his obvious exhaustion. "Jo's gone to Otamba Kilimbi with the others, presumably having a wonderful time."

"Thank God for that!" There was a collective sigh of relief.

"But has anyone heard about Chandra? Sumbuya…" Tim's voice tailed off anxiously.

"She's fine. Down at the Peace Corps, waiting for a flight home," I said.

"I tell god tenki."

"Is Kailahun as bad as they say?" asked Lindsey.

"I don't know. I think it's pretty bad. Me and my students were drinking poyo when we heard gunfire. We all ran into the street. There were buildings in the town on fire and people streaming towards us. Then two Red Cross trucks appeared. They piled everybody in and drove us to Bo. That's it," he shrugged.

"That's it!"

"How many rebels?"

"Were they advancing?"

"Was anyone hurt?"

"I don't know," Tim sighed. "There were ten, maybe twelve, buildings on fire and several rounds of gunfire. I never actually saw a rebel. Everybody on our truck was fine though. Some people stayed of course, to find family, but Jo was out of town and I already had my squeeze-box, so I just hopped on with the others. It made a poda-poda feel positively deserted. Now is that a bread roll I see over there?"

"Of course," Lindsey jumped up. "Cheese triangle?"

"Cheers! A cheese sandwich and a glass of water, then I think I'll nip over to the Peace Corps rest house…"

"Tim, it's after midnight…" started Lindsey.

But he had already bounded back down the stairs to look for Chandra.

By Wednesday we were getting restless – our volunteer stipends were insufficient to have a prolonged good time in the big city. Even Maternity's Ceiling Fund had been depleted. The Field Director was busy arranging flights home for those that wanted out. In fact he was positively encouraging it – everyone who flew home was one less for him to worry about.

"Emily, what about you?" he asked. "BA have put on an extra flight. There's a seat on Friday."

"What?" For some reason I was stunned by the question. Home? Chocolate in two days! Here was my longed-for escape route handed on a plate.

"But I don't want to go home!"

"But Serabu is right in the official danger zone," exclaimed the Field Director. "And how would you get back there?"

"CARE's bound to have a vehicle going to Moyamba, then Serabu can pick me up from Klaus'." Inspirational!

"I don't know…"

"Everybody else stayed at Serabu," I complained. After months of dreaming up excuses to leave, here I was begging to stay. "Not even Philippe and he's got a young family." I was warming to my theme, my head filled with visions of Klaus and I holding hands by candlelight. "And Morag hasn't left and she's much closer to trouble."

"Believe me, if I could drag your friend Morag down here by the scruff of her neck, I would!"

"But Serabu's so quiet! I'm more likely to die of boredom than rebel bullets."

"Bloody doctors!" The Field Director rose from his desk and went to look at his map on the wall. There remained a few red pins in the north, a cluster in Freetown, plus one in Moyamba and a lone pin out east in Panguma. The rest of the map was sprayed with miniature bullet-holes, where pins had once stood, including, to my dismay, only a pinprick left to show for Serabu.

"Serabu has a radio. And three vehicles," I persisted. "And four other volunteers. Even Americans!"

"Not Peace Corps surely!"

"No, admittedly not Peace Corps, but we definitely have an American."

The Peace Corps had got their fingers burned in Liberia, finally evacuating their volunteers amidst artillery bombardment of the capital. This time they were steering well clear of the flames and had already sent three-quarters of the Salonean volunteers back to the States.

"No, Emily. We can't be sure it's safe, we just can't be sure," the Field Director mumbled.

"Oh please..."

Our argument was interrupted by the door bursting open.

"Kushe, kushe, everyone. How di...?" Nick froze in the doorway.

"What's everybody doing here? It's the middle of the week!" He flung his arms out in amazement. "Even you, Emily! Do you not have lives to save in Serabu?"

"Right now, I'm saving my own skin. There's a slight problem."

"This is Salone," Nick gave his continental shrug. "There is always a problem."

"Rebels," said our Field Director wearily.

"Rebels?"

"Yes," he snapped. "While you were holidaying, Liberian rebels have crossed the borders into the south and east."

"Rebels? No! This is too hard to believe."

"Believe it," said the Field Director. "Sierra Leone has been invaded."

"But we heard nothing," Nick shook his head. "And I always listen to Focus on Africa."

"It was all too quick for the World Service. Fortunately the Red Cross got Tim out of Kailahun just in time."

"Kailahun!" Nick's colour leached out.

"All VSOs are in Freetown as a precautionary measure. Apart from Morag and Klaus, who are just being difficult. Are you alright?"

The ever-cool Nick had slumped into a chair and dropped his head in his hands.

"Jo and Diane!" he moaned.

"Who's Diane?" asked the Field Director.

"Jo's friend. She's here on holiday. I left them to hitch back to Kailahun four hours ago."

THE REFUGEE RETURNS

Thursday. Still no further reports of rebel activity. The six thousand rebels could just as easily have been sixty, or perhaps even six. There was no Kate Adie, or BBC film crew to update us. No one in Britain had even heard of Sierra Leone, never mind cared if there were a few rebels causing trouble. The World Service had started to report the rumours but, since their reporter never left Freetown, he was unlikely to have gleaned any more information than us.

Tim was our only eyewitness, but even he had only heard gunfire and seen some smoke before he was caught up in the scramble to escape Kailahun. Perhaps there had been only one rebel with a gun, but then perhaps that's all it took to decimate a defenceless village. The grapevine talked of homes plundered and people killed in the villages round Kailahun. The rebels may or may not have gone, but the villagers were too frightened to return to find out.

We tried to convince ourselves that Charles Taylor, having depleted his forces in seizing power from his rival Prince Johnson, had just sent his rebels over from Liberia on a food foray. Even a rebel needs sustenance and, since there was nobody left to kill and nothing left to burn in Liberia, they had come to plunder the homes and farms in placid, disorganised little Sierra Leone. We had no way of knowing, but the Liberian refugees that had flooded in over the past two years had told the Saloneans so many tales of the atrocities in their destroyed homeland that there was an understandable terror that such a thing should happen in Sierra Leone. We could all be forgiven for over-reacting.

On Friday morning, a familiar figure marched in to the VSO office.

"MT! Good Lord, what is she doing here?" I gasped, slumping

deep into my chair.

"I am Sister Ignatius and I wish to know who is in charge?" she demanded.

"I am," said Nick. "The Field Director has gone to the British High Commission."

"And are you responsible for abandoning these girls to hitch back into the arms of the rebels?" she thundered. Jo and Diane appeared sheepishly at her shoulder. Jo gave us a little wave behind MT's back.

"Er. We had some difficulties with communication…" started an unfortunate Nick.

"Communication difficulties! We found them wandering the deserted streets of Bo alone at midnight. Come with me." MT dragged Nick into his own office by the elbow. The door clicked shut behind them.

"Whoops," said Jo. Tim grabbed her hand and squeezed it tight.

"I was worried about you."

"We're fine," insisted Jo. "And you?"

"I tell God tenki," said Tim. "I tell God tenki."

"And Sule?" Jo added in a whisper. "Did he get out?"

"I don't know." Tim hugged her. "But Sule can take care of himself, I'm sure. That bloke of yours is a real Rambo."

"Yeah," Jo sniffed into Tim's bony shoulder.

"Sister Ignatius has been such a sweetie," Diane enthused.

"A sweetie!" I spluttered on my coffee. "MT?!"

"All the nuns were," agreed Jo, tears wiped and brave face firmly applied. "Sister Ignatius is your boss, isn't she Emily?"

"I'm afraid so."

"I wish I had such a nice boss," said Diane.

"Huh?"

"She said she had business in Freetown, so she'd give us a lift," Jo continued.

"Oh? Why?" MT didn't make unscheduled trips to Freetown. Diesel was too expensive.

"She said she had to collect the Easter drug order and take you back to Serabu."

"I see." So I was her ulterior motive – get that skiving doctor's nose back to the grindstone.

"The nuns fed us chicken and Star beer and everything!" Chicken and Star Beer – the ultimate accolade.

"Almost as good as Majorca," agreed Diane.

"Majorca?" Tim raised his eyebrow.

"Diane usually goes to Majorca."

"Much more exciting here," said Tim.

"She's moaned nonstop about the primitive conditions, and that's even before she's seen our house. Oh." Jo's banter died suddenly. "Oh, Tim. Our house? Our friends? Sule?"

"Oh, Jo, I'm sorry." Tim hugged her again.

MT reappeared from the office, ten minutes later. I couldn't hide forever, so I stood up to face her.

"Ah, Dr. Joy. You are well?"

"Yes, thank you, Sister Ignatius." I thought I had better go through the motions of etiquette. "Are you feeling better?"

"I am well. I believe we have a hospital to run."

"Yes, Sister."

"Very good. We leave tomorrow morning. I have cleared it with your Field Officer."

"Oh. Okay." Hmmph! Was my opinion not important here? Admittedly I had spent the morning pleading to go back, but that was my decision, my bravado and under my terms. This way, MT made me feel like I'd been caught truanting. Why hadn't Nick vetoed her? Serabush was supposed to be in the danger zone for heaven's sake. But he stood no chance in battle with MT, especially not with the embarrassing episode of Jo and Diane in her weaponry.

"Seven o'clock at Santano house, Dr. Joy."

"Tomorrow then," I muttered. What about my trip to Moyamba to see Klaus? I didn't want to go with *her*.

"Do not be late. Good afternoon."

I closed my eyes. Oh why hadn't I just accepted the Field Director's plane ticket when I had the chance? Who wanted to be a bloody pin stuck in a map of some obscure war-torn country anyway?

"This Sister changes the tune very quickly," Nick grumbled loudly once MT was safely out of earshot. "I am the bad boy for the mistake of allowing Jo and Diane to go to Bo, but she does not worry about taking a young woman to Serabu, which is much closer to the rebels, just because she needs a doctor."

"Aw fo do," I chirped. The trendy Nick calling me a young woman cheered me up enormously.

"Well I suppose Serabu at least has a radio…" Nick mused. "Okay. Be careful. Do not travel outside Serabu and if we radio you to come back, you come immediately. Do not accept any arguments from your Sister Ignatius. Understood?"

"Okay," I agreed, happy to slip into this new heroic young woman role. "The least you can do for sending me back into the lion's den is to buy me a beer." It was worth a try. I couldn't afford any more beer otherwise.

"I send you to the lion's den? You've been nagging the Field Director all morning to go back!" Nick snorted.

"That was this morning," I said, sweetly. "Aren't I allowed to change my mind?"

"No!" Nick folded his arms. "Serabu needs a doctor and I need you out of my office. You're a big strong girl, you can look after yourself."

"Hmmph!" So much for the heroic young woman. "Now you definitely owe me a beer."

"And us," Jo chipped in, camouflaging her anxieties with jollity. "I need to be very drunk until I hear that Sule's okay."

"Okay, okay," Nick sighed. "I will take you all to the Venue."

Windows down to clear my head of the after effects of Nick's generosity, I stretched out in the front seat of the truck. Sister Ignatius sat beside me at the wheel. So here I was going back to Serabush with MT, hung over, just like the last time, and without any progress with Klaus, just like the last time. Only this time the country was no longer a peaceful haven, but a victim of hostile rebel activity and, even worse from my egocentric perspective, there would be no Nat to cheer me up and soon there would be no Philippe or Nicole either. I began to regret my impulsive rejection of the Field Director's no-strings, no-shame, free flight home.

Several volunteers had already gone, including Susan, who left clutching her plastic bag containing her Jane Austen and a change of underwear. The High Commissioner would not give clearance for any British subjects to go anywhere near Kailahun, so Tim was leaving too. With a glint in his eye, he had booked his flight for over a week's time, giving him that little bit longer to woo Chandra.

Jo, however, managed to persuade the Field Director that he needed a secretary at the VSO Office. She could not go looking for Sule (she certainly would not get any help from the British High Commissioner), so she would just have to wait for him to find her. The Field Director's initial objections were soon silenced as she made herself indispensable by sorting out all the annoying administrative complications that the rebels had landed on his plate. Meanwhile Klaus and Morag bashed on at work.

I squirmed in my sweaty plastic seat. The journey was taking twice as long as usual. Over twenty soldier's checkpoints had appeared between Freetown and Serabu. I had offered to share the driving but MT did not want to relinquish control. Her tactics, if not her motives, were sound, as dressed in full veil and habit and wearing her most determined expression, MT was enough to send the young soldiers scurrying to lift their wooden barriers with a tug of their forelocks. Since my services were obviously not needed, I settled down for a snooze.

Suddenly we screeched to a halt. A soldier stood, pointing his gun through the windscreen.

"Take me to Mokanjo, Sista."

"Oh shit," I gasped.

"Please," MT corrected the soldier. I clutched the dashboard. Good Lord, how could she argue the finer points of etiquette looking down the end of the barrel?

"Please, Sista. Take me to Mokanje."

"Very well. Dr. Joy will get in the back."

"I get in the back, Sista, no problem."

"In the front, soldier, so I can see you." MT ordered.

"No problem, Sista, I get no ammunition."

"Well let us thank the Good Lord for that. Seatbelt."

Soldier boy fumbled with the buckle, then started to chat away as though MT was a long lost aunt.

"I done kill two rebels, Sista."

"Indeed?"

"Yes, Sista, I get for show you."

"That will not be necessary."

"They are very close. I go show you." MT did not reply, although I did hear the slightest of sighs.

Five miles down the road he called out. "Here, Sista! Look Sista. Stop. Stop!"

MT slowed down a little. "Look. Look at my rebels." He pointed to two human skulls adorning the side of the road.

"Oh God," I whispered. Until that moment, this whole rebel business had seemed like a Famous Five adventure. Suddenly I realised it was all really happening.

The skulls were displayed on three-foot wooden poles like a pair of ghoulish lollipops, with bits of flesh still hanging from the cheekbones. MT hit the accelerator with a hint of unsisterly irritation. I gaped in horror at the skeletal mirage departing through the back window.

"Did you see them, Sista?" he enthused. "You see, I go protect you from the rebels."

Back at Serabush, Bernadette greeted us at the convent door.

"Welcome back, welcome back. We are so glad to see you both." Bernadette gave me a hug and smiled warmly at Ignatius. "I hope you are fully recovered from your malaria, Ignatius."

"I am ready to return to work, Bernadette," she answered. "There is much to be done in this troubled time."

"It's good to be back, Sister Bernadette," I said, as was expected of me.

"I will take a bath if you will excuse me, Bernadette," said MT.

"Very well, Ignatius. We will speak this evening." Bernadette touched her colleague's shoulder. "Now Emily, you must tell me all about it. Come in for tea."

"That would be lovely. How is everyone? Was there any trouble with the rebels? How are Philippe, Nicole and the children? When are they going home? How are Mariama and Hindolu? Is Laygby's pregnancy progressing safely? How's Dan doing? What about Tom? Has he had malaria again?"

"Everyone's just fine, Emily," laughed Bernadette. She motioned me to one of the wicker chairs in the convent sitting-room. "After all you've only been gone ten days. Tom has managed to stay well and Dr. Philippe and his family will be leaving next week. When Ignatius radioed to tell us the good news that you were returning, I asked her to book their flights." She patted my knee. "The break has done you good. I must say you look very well indeed, you've put on a bit of weight."

"Hmmph." Putting on weight was one of those inevitable consequences of a diet that blissfully did not include plassas, but Bernadette just meant to be nice. "So how is Dan settling in then?"

"We are all very impressed with Dr. Dan. He is doing extremely well."

He would be.

"Kushe, Dr. Em, how di holiday? You don get body," Sesay called out as I walked up to my house with my weekend backpack.

"Dr. Em welcome back. You get body." Mariama hugged me with her free arm, holding Hindolu on her hip with her other. Hindolu gurgled and pulled my ever-growing ponytail.

"Kushe, Dr. Em, you get body."

"Emily! Bonjour, bonjour. Ca va bien? You have been getting good food in Freetown, yes?"

"Kushe, Dr. Em I see you don enjoy you holiday. You get body."

"Well hi Emily, you're looking well fed and contented, you lucky thing. I'm jealous. Ain't the food here just awful?" Dan must have lost at least ten kilos in as many days.

"Kushe, Dr. Em, we gladdi for see you. You get body."

"What for chop today?"

Good old Pa George. At least he didn't tell me I was looking fat.

POST EVACUATION BLUES

"Bua, Dr. Em."

"Mmm, bua bise, Pa Ali. Bi gahun yena?"

"Kayingoma, a bia be?"

"Kayingoma."

"Malo-hua, Dr. Em."

"Malo-hua, Pa Ali."

Well, it was life and death as usual at Serabu hospital, which had obviously functioned very well without me. The only change was a new hospital signpost in proud red and blue pointing the way to Serabu.

The good news of the week was that Ansumana's dinner had stopped leaking from his abdominal wound and exited, duly processed, from the appropriate hole. He was hardly an example of slick surgical procedure – two months in hospital, three stones lighter with an angry crusted red scar bisecting his abdomen – but he would live. Isata's wound, however, healed even better than I had dared hope. Her husband paid the bill in full and arranged transport home for his wife and son. He even arranged for some men from his village to erect a basket weave ceiling on Maternity!

My glow of satisfaction from Ansumana, Isata and our swish new ceiling, was soon replaced by post-evacuation blues. Rebel fever kept admissions and outpatients down and with Philippe having a last surge of workaholism before he departed and Dan whirling enthusiastically round the wards, I was feeling pretty redundant. The new boy was doing so well, already performing solo Caesareans, that there seemed little need for me to hold his hand while he settled in. Why had I bothered returning?

The staff all raved about Dan – even Tiange! He obviously had a touch of Sister Hilary about him. It was not just Ansumana and Isata – all the patients seemed to be smiling their way to recovery.

So after only four days back in Serabush, I was bored, bored, bored. It was a Friday night and I sat alone on my velour sofa, *Tess of the d'Urbervilles* still only half finished on my lap. Tomorrow was Saturday and Dan was on call for the weekend, with Philippe available to assist in the unlikely event of somebody arriving that Dan couldn't deal with. So what was I going to do?

I watched a mosquito fly round the stub of a candle that was dribbling its last down the sides of a beer bottle. "Come back, Nat. All is forgiven." I scratched my latest crop of bites until my shins bled. It was only going to get worse once Philippe and Nicole left next week. Even Tom was due to leave.

And since the Field Director had grounded any volunteers left in country, there was no chance of Klaus, Nat, or anyone else for that matter, dropping in for a visit. It was all too depressing. I blew the flame maliciously into the mosquito's wings.

"Ha! That'll teach you to mess with me," I gloated as the insect fell to its death in the pool of wax on the table. Oh dear, murdering God's creatures wasn't a good way to curry favour.

I had a banana and an orange and went to bed.

Normally I drank very little coffee: too hot, too dehydrating and the local stuff had to be filtered through your teeth. However, the reappearance of Sister Bernadette from her sabbatical had revived the tradition of the Saturday coffee morning at the convent for the sisters and volunteers. It was the one time that we met the sisters socially. So at ten, prompt (I had been counting the minutes, I was so bored), I turned up at the convent. Dan jogged over. "Hey, girl!"

"Dan, aren't you on call? Too efficient by half, you Americans," I teased.

"Outpatients is real quiet today. I guess the patients are all still worried about rebels."

"Welcome." Bernadette appeared at the door in another pretty flowered dress. "Nice that you could join us, Dan. God bless this beautiful day."

"Good morning, Sister Bernadette," we chanted. She ushered us into the front room, kept cool by the protective layer of guest rooms above. Tom was already seated, sipping a glass of water, whilst MT poured out coffee for Philippe, who was flopped in a wicker chair.

"Did I hear you talking again about rebels, Dr. Dan?" MT always addressed Dan as an equal. Must have been those all-American looks. "Did you hear some news from the outpatients today?"

"No ma'am. I was just saying that the hospital is very quiet as though the people were still afraid to travel."

"Oh dear," said Bernadette.

"What is going to 'appen wiz your wife, Dan?"

"Gee, I just don't know."

"Perhaps you can make a telephone call from Freetown?" Philippe suggested.

"Can I? It would be just great if I could speak to Cyndi. I don't want her to worry."

"At least it's unlikely that our minor skirmish will hit the news in America."

"I guess you're right," agreed Dan. "But the airline might say something when she tries to confirm her flight for next month."

"Coffee, Dr. Dan?" asked MT. Dan politely proffered his cup. "I'll be surprised if your Embassy will let her come now. I suppose that means you'll have to leave us?"

"I hope not, Sister Ignatius, but now you mention the Embassy, I never did register. Y'all whisked me straight here when I landed."

"Too keen to get you to work," I teased.

"Dan! We must get you registered," Bernadette exclaimed. "No wonder you weren't pulled back to Freetown with the rest of the Americans."

"Nor Tom," added Philippe.

"No one contacted you either, Philippe," said Tom. "And with Nicole and the children…"

"There is no Belgian Embassy," Philippe shrugged. "We are the only ones."

"I guess I've stayed longer than my year," mused Tom. "Perhaps they think I've gone already."

"Dan, you must go to Freetown to telephone your wife and visit the Embassy," said Bernadette. "Perhaps while you are there, you can check that they still know about Tom?"

"Of course."

"Can you wait until the Landrover takes Philippe and Nicole to Lungi airport next Sunday?" asked MT, ever mindful of economy.

"Fine. By then it should be clear that things are safe and Cyndi can start packing. That's if Emily can manage alone for a few days."

"Of course!" I bristled. "Nice and quiet, as you said, so I'm quite sure I'll cope without any male doctors around."

"She has just had her holiday in Freetown, yes," teased Philippe.

I gritted my teeth in his direction and he raised his coffee cup back at me. We spent the rest of our coffee morning discussing a party for Philippe and Nicole – at my house (the biggest) with six crates of Star to be donated by Bernadette and MT!!!

With the details of the party duly sorted, Philippe went back to his family, Dan returned to Outpatients and Tom took his final year students for a revision class.

Unfortunately I had no pressing engagements, and there was still three quarters of a weekend to get through, so I searched the convent library for something I was more likely to read than Thomas Hardy.

The dusty shelves were devoid of Judith Krantz or Jilly Cooper – not being on your usual nun's reading list. However, a battered box caught my eye on the top shelf – a jigsaw puzzle!

The extraordinary sense of glee I felt at the prospect of putting a thousand cardboard pieces together to make a bowl of fruit proved that things were getting bad. With the box under my arm, I dashed home in excitement.

"What for chop today?"

"Pa George, it's Saturday."

"You don take too much holiday," he grunted, as explanation. At least he had deferred his appearance to late morning. "Wetin dis?" He peered over my shoulder.

"A jigsaw puzzle. Look, you put the pieces together to make a picture. This piece, for instance, goes there." I popped a piece of banana in place.

"Hmmph." Pa George picked up a piece of red apple and rammed it into a hole in the middle of the oranges. "Why?"

"Well…"

"Do they pay you?"

"What? Who?" I laughed. "No, they don't pay me."

"Hmmph. What for chop today?"

Pa George was lighting the three-stone fire when Mariama appeared at the door. "Dr. Em?"

"Do you do jigsaws, Mariama?" I called to my friend, still focussed on the puzzle.

"It's Pa Ali," she said quietly. I looked up.

"What's happened?"

"He's fallen out of the palm tree."

"Is he all right?"

"They've carried him to Surgical," Mariama answered.

I ran down to the small gathering round Pa Ali's bed on Surgical. He lay motionless

"Bua, Pa Ali." I took his limp hand.

"Mmm. Bua bise, Dr. Em," he replied, opening his eyes briefly.

"Bise. Bi gahun yena?" I asked, knowing he had broken his neck.

"Kayingoma. A bia be?"

"Kayingoma." Thanks be to God. I bit my lip.

"Malo-hua." He closed his eyes and died.

PHILIPPE'S PARTY

The house was ready. Hawa and Theresa had painted a big Good Luck banner to string above the table. On it sat Pa George's massive pot of plassas, MT's crates of beer, two gallon rubbers of poyo and Dan's tape-recorder.

American volunteers weren't expected to survive on only twenty-five kilos, so where I had a short-wave radio that could fit in a shirt pocket, Dan had a three-foot ghetto-blaster plus two sets of spare batteries that would allow us to party long after our ten o'clock generator curfew.

Tom, Dan, Mariama and I sat expectantly on the doorstep, drinking Star by moonlight.

"To Pa Ali." I raised my bottle.

"God bless," Tom replied.

"Poor old Pa Ali," said Dan.

"He was too old for climbing palm trees."

"It was his living," said Mariama.

"He'd have made a real fortune tonight," sighed Dan.

"But he will be happy that AJ will make that money," Mariama added. "I done see him up his father's tree this evening."

"AJ?" I asked, incredulous.

"Ali Junior, Pa Ali's son," confirmed Tom.

"Really. AJ? He seems so, well…" Cocky little devil, would-be sophisticate, student leader, smartarse, suave dresser, pushy, clever, ambitious… "Assertive," I finally said, remembering the unassuming old gentleman who had given some serenity to my daily routine.

"AJ told me how his Dad worked so hard to provide his son with the chances he never had," Tom explained. Tom's knowledge of his students made me ashamed of my ignorance of the lives of the staff.

We bantered at work or we exchanged greetings at the market or outside church, we played Scrabble or occasionally met for a cup of poyo in the village, or a cup of tea at Mariama's, but still I lived in a different world.

"Gosh. How will AJ fit tapping poyo in with his exams?" I asked.

"AJ can't lose his father's patch – he has to fund his training somehow." For someone who seemed to spend life with his nose in a bible, Tom had a firm grip on the realities of life.

"So hey, we'll have poyo after all tonight." Dan tried to lift the mood. "I'm real keen to try it."

"What a treat!" I teased.

"It is very fine," said Mariama.

"Nat knocked it back like lemonade."

"But from my brief knowledge of Nat, any alcohol would do," Dan retorted. "Hey Tom, surely I can rely on you, my fellow American, to give me the low-down on poyo."

"You know I don't drink."

"It's from God to Man, Tom. Can't I tempt you?"

"Thanks, Emily, but so is plain water."

Several Stars later, we were still only four.

"Where is everyone?"

"Punctual doesn't translate into Mende, Dan," said Tom, looking at his watch.

"Still, it *is* late," I remarked, the anxious hostess.

Just then Moses came running up the path.

"The rebels done reach Buma!"

"What?!!"

"Buma!" Mariama paled.

"I thought those damned rebels had gone," said Dan.

"Buma, that's just twenty miles away. How do you know?" I asked.

"The soldiers done just kommot Buma," Moses puffed.

"Returned from Buma?" Tom frowned. "Um, didn't you just say that's where the rebels were?"

"Them soldiers never reached the place. They don go make checkpoint at Buma, but they don meet the villagers running away."

"So, didn't they stay to defend us?"

"The soldiers say they get puncture. Now they don go to Mokanje…"

"But isn't Mokanje even further away?" asked Dan.

"Thirty miles at least," I agreed. "Couldn't Sesay fix their puncture? I'm sure Serabu Hospital would be more than happy to assist."

"I saw no puncture." Moses shrugged.

"Ah, our brave boys!" I exclaimed.

"You no able blame them. They get guns but not ammunition and the government don always forget to pay them" explained the ever-understanding Mariama.

"Everybody is too much frightened in Serabu," Moses continued. "Many are fleeing to the bush."

"Bonsoir, bonsoir tout le monde." Philippe was striding cheerfully up the path, Pierre perched on his shoulders. "Sorry I am late but Ma Kpukoma did not appear to look after the childrens. This is very unusual for her. Perhaps we bring them and they can sleep in your bedroom?"

"There seems to be a problem," I said, sorry to kill his good mood.

"Ah yes, there is always a problem."

"Moses tells us that the rebels are in Buma," said Tom.

"I think our party is off." I bit my tongue. As if anybody was worried about the party.

"Mon Dieu, Buma?" He lowered Pierre to the ground and sat down next to us, pulling his son onto his lap, "Is this true, Moses?"

Moses retold his story, then excused himself. "I must go to my family."

"Of course, Moses. Will you leave too?" I asked.

"Serabu is our home," Moses stated. "Aw fo do."

"And the rest of the staff?" Tom pressed on.

"The thiefmen will come even if the rebels-self do not. They will thief everything. I think-say most of the staff will stay." Moses shrugged. "Perhaps I will come to your party later."

"Will you go to your man, Mariama?" Tom asked. "He's with the Red Cross, isn't he?"

"Ben wrote that he get for go to Kailahun." Mariama tried to hide the fear in her voice. "I must stay here so he able find me. Now I will go and check on Hindolu and my family."

"Let us pray it is another false alarm," Tom squeezed her hand.

"We go see back," Mariama smiled optimistically.

They left us, four pale faces sitting on the doorstep in stunned silence, with dance music thumping on regardless from Dan's ghetto-blaster.

"Bloody rebels. First they mess up my birthday and now Philippe's farewell. We were going to give you such a good party, Philippe."

"Aw fo do." Philippe adjusted Pierre on his lap, and got to the point we were all avoiding. "Perhaps Emily and Tom should come to Freetown with us tomorrow?"

"We'll just panic everybody if we leave," said Tom without hesitation. "I'll stay, if you could just let our Embassy know I still exist, Dan."

"Sure thing, Tom."

Bloody Tom, always putting others first. Now I would have to stay too. "There's been no message from VSO, so it must be safe," I said in my bravest voice.

"God willing, the rebels will come no further, but perhaps we should pack essentials?" Tom suggested.

"Well I'm packed for my Freetown trip already," said Dan. "I'll guard the beer."

"Eh bien." Philippe stood up. "Tom will go to pack and I will go and tell Nicole, then we start our party in one hour. Yes?"

"No problem."

"So, Dr. Em, it's just you and me. Gin rummy?" Dan polished his glasses.

"You're on. Just give me a minute to throw my passport and some undies in a bag."

"Mon Dieu, I have a very bad head today. It was a party merveilleuse."

Philippe loaded the last of his belongings into the Landrover.

"Yep, those guys sure know how to party," agreed Dan, climbing into the back seat.

"Including most of the night staff," laughed Tom. "Not sure who looked after the patients."

"They came too. Pa Ndanema and Bockerie were knocking back poyo in my kitchen."

"What? My new patients!" Dan exclaimed. I had handed TB ward over to Dan at the earliest opportunity. "As soon as I get back from Freetown, I'll show them who's boss."

"Eh bien, bonne chance Dan. Those TB patients get bored too much and look for trouble. This is why I handed them over to Emily."

"Oh, so now the truth comes out…" My words were lost as Philippe, Nicole and the children were smothered in hugs, kisses and back slaps by the assembled crowd of well-wishers. Ma Kpukoma was in floods of tears, clinging onto Simone and Pierre.

"They're really letting it all hang out," Dan whispered to me through the open window. "Probably high on fear."

"I suspect farewells are always like this, especially for those as loved as Philippe and his family."

"Yeah, you're right. Take care now. I'll see you in a few days." Dan kissed me on the cheek.

"Give AJ my compliments on his poyo, Tom." Dan and Tom shook hands.

"Don't worry. I'll tell him he is a worthy successor to his Dad."

"Enjoy the big city, Dan," I added, just with a hint of jealousy.

"Sure will. I've got my swimming trunks packed."

I smiled and fought through to get my turn to say goodbye.

"How will I manage without you?"

"Pas de problème." Philippe ruffled my hair before lifting Pierre into the seat next to Dan.

"I'll miss you," I sniffed.

"We all will," added Mariama. Her feelings were chorused by the throng.

There were more hugs and tears before the Landrover finally pulled away, followed by a crowd of children, skipping and waving.

"Au revoir tout le monde. Malo-hua Serabush!" Philippe called as they turned out of the gates and past Serabu's shiny new sign. "And au revoir to the new Medical Superintendent." A bony thumbs-up stuck out of the front window and they were gone.

Medical Superintendent. That was me. Oh shit.

GUARDING THE HOSPITAL

Just as the dust settled from the departing Landrover, another truck lurched into the compound. It screeched to a halt, scattering the residual well-wishers outside the convent. Father Andrew from Sumbuya burst out of the passenger seat and stumbled into the arms of Sister Bernadette.

"The rebels have come to Sumbuya," Andrew gasped. "Everybody has fled. The Lebanese family at the store have been killed."

"Oh no! May God be with them." Bernadette crossed herself. "Are you all right, Andrew?"

"Yes, yes. I had to leave everything. I just…" He sucked in a lungful of air "… came to warn you."

"Are Serabu's staff and patients in danger?" MT got straight to the point. "Should we make evacuation plans?"

"No. No, I think that would be over reacting. There were only five maybe six rebels. We think they just came for a… a day trip," Andrew snorted. "Serabu is twelve miles away."

Twelve miles didn't sound very much to me. Hell I'd cycled to Sumbuya just five weeks ago. And Chandra and I had bought milk powder and stock cubes from that Lebanese store. We'd even shared a beer with the owner.

"What do you think Emily?" asked Bernadette. "As our only doctor and Medical Superintendent, will you stay?"

"Me? Er, yes. Of course." It was hard to refuse when she put it like that.

"Very good. We will have an emergency staff meeting," announced MT. "In one hour."

"Will that give you time for rounds, Emily?" asked Bernadette.

"No problem," a little voice answered. Meanwhile my mind raced over visions of skulls on sticks perched all round the hospital.

"Mariama, call the senior staff from the village."

"Of course, Sister Ignatius."

"Moses, fetch Father Joe."

"No problem, Sister Ignatius."

"Good." MT turned and went back into the convent.

"Come inside for a cup of tea and a wash, Father Andrew," Bernadette guided the traumatised African priest into her sanctuary.

Ten of us sat in the convent. There had been no mention of any further trouble on the World Service, but then we would probably be the ones to report it. MT had managed to radio Mokanje, but they knew no more than us. There was only one Sunday transmission on the Catholic mission radio network, and it had long since finished. We wouldn't receive more news until morning.

"How does everybody feel about staying?" asked Bernadette.

"We should stay," said Joe. "Serabu hospital will be needed more than ever."

"Hear hear," added Tom. I forced a smile. I didn't really fancy the thought of rebels running around waving their guns, but didn't want to be the only wimp.

"Most of the staff have no place to go. We will stay," Mariama was announcing. "But we understand if the volunteers and sisters get for go to safety. You no able take eighty staff with you in a Landrover."

Her matter-of-fact words suddenly made me realise all my idealistic VSO principles of equals working together without any 'us and them' was rubbish. When the crunch came, we could jump on a plane home, but this was their home. Mariama might have my education but she just did not have my choices. And my choice right now would be to get the hell out.

"God willing, there will be no need for any of us to leave." MT's voice broke through my thoughts.

"There's no need to panic," agreed Joe. "Our brother Andrew suspects that the few cowardly rebels that attacked Sumbuya have already gone."

"Good," added Moses. "If the poomuis stay, then we get for feel safe."

"So we agree things are not that bad," MT said briskly. "Business as usual."

"Business as usual," Tom, Bernadette and Joe echoed.

"And our Medical Superintendent?" MT prompted me.

"What?" There were those skulls again. Oh God, how bad did 'that bad' need to be? "Yes, yes. Of course."

We came out of the convent into the midday heat. A rare little breeze gave momentary relief, ruffling the beautiful blossom-laden trees in the courtyard, releasing their perfume and carrying a few petals to the ground. I stopped and listened for shouts and screams or distant gunfire, but heard only a solitary bird song. Silly me, there couldn't possibly be any rebels here.

My ward rounds finished, I went home and opened the door to the forgotten debris of the previous night. Empty Star bottles lay on a floor that was sticky with spilt poyo. The same gentle breeze that had blessed the convent blew through my mosquito mesh, carrying a waft of stale beer and bodily fluids.

What was I doing here, with a crashing hangover, clearing up a house rank with unspeakable odours, in a strange country with rebels only twelve miles down the road? I was not made of the stuff of heroes. Why hadn't I just jumped onto the Landrover with Philippe and Dan? I could easily have justified myself to the sisters and staff, perhaps by blaming VSO. At least it would have got me out of the tidying up.

"Aw fo do," I sighed, picked up a few empties and plopped them into their crate. Three smiling faces appeared in the doorway as I wiped the sweat from my specs.

"Kushe, kushe, Dr Em. We come to help," called Aisha, Dauda and Theresa.

"Tenki ya," I smiled back. Within thirty minutes the place was sparkling cleaner than it had ever been since my arrival. Cleaning was neither my, nor Pa George's, forté.

By Monday morning I seemed to be missing several patients.

"Have they gone to fetch water?" I asked Mariama.

"No. They have run from the rebels."

"Oh."

One of my few new arrivals was Rose, who would have been a sturdy picture of health had it not been for the cancer that had taken over her whole breast. It was too late for a mastectomy, not that I had ever done one, and of course there was no radiotherapy or chemotherapy. The tumour was in overdrive, pushing up mounds of pink tissue round a creviced and smelly central crater. Theresa had cleaned it up nicely so at least the odour had gone. This was as good as it was ever going to get.

"There is no more I can do, I'm very sorry," I explained to Rose and her mother as gently as possible. "You can do her dressings at home."

"But we get money, we able pay," her mother objected. "We able pay for surgery-self."

"I'm sorry," I repeated. "It has spread too far."

"We get for pay extra for you to do surgery. Please Dr. Em. Help my daughter."

"It's not the money," I sighed. "I can't operate. It's better that you take your daughter home and care for her in the family."

"Do ya, Dr. Em. Please," she begged. I couldn't argue that we didn't have enough beds, as the rebels had left the ward as empty as I'd ever seen it. Taking the easy option, I agreed to let Rose stay for daily dressings.

The rest of my rounds were rather subdued. I even wished that the TB patients would torment me with their usual teases and complaints, but even Pa Ndanema placidly accepted his medication while Patrick dressed the TB abscess that had made such a mess of the stump of his leg. Only Bockerie seemed oblivious to the rebel threat, setting up his draughts board outside the ward.

"You want play, Dr. Em?"

"I'm working, Bockerie!"

"Nobody will come today, they are too scared," he shrugged and moved the first black man a square. "You are the white man."

"Thanks Bockerie, but I must get to Outpatients."

"Look at the bench Dr. Em. Those rebels don make your job too easy."

I glanced over to the empty bench and sighed. "Okay." I moved my man one square and sat down.

Five minutes later Bockerie was grinning beside a tower of white discs and a black plague on the board. Fortunately, Pa Ndanema gallantly rescued me by throwing down his crutches in challenge to Bockerie. I left them to it and went home.

Pa George was surprised to see me back so early. "You na the only doctor, Dr. Em. You don finish already?"

"Very quiet today, Pa George."

"Hmmph. Chop not ready."

"No problem. Can I help?" Pa George looked horrified. "Okay, I'll read." I held up my book and Pa George grunted. He slammed the door behind him, and I half expected him to nail a 'No Trespassing' sign on my kitchen door. Smiling, I stuck my nose back in *Tess of the d'Urbervilles*, but my eye kept wandering to the jigsaw, hidden from Pa George under a piece of gara.

As soon as Pa George had dished up, I cast *Tess* aside and settled down to a tricky bit around the apples, listening to a re-run of *Hitch-hikers Guide to the Galaxy*. A rare forty minutes of pop tunes followed, and I sang along, popping piece after piece into place in time to the music, pausing only to spoon in mouthfuls of plassas. Just as I was thinking life was not so bad, Tom burst in.

"What is it?" I looked up, alarmed. "Rebels?"

"No, I think Joe is having a stroke."

"Not rebels then," I sighed, forgetting to hide the relief in my voice. Tom frowned and I cringed at my selfishness. "Right." I leapt to my feet. "I'm coming."

"Can you squeeze my hand?" I squatted in front of Joe. "Good. Now push me away."

"Yes. There's only a bit of tingling in my fingers now," Joe said with obvious relief. "I dropped my coffee cup you know, look, it's everywhere."

"I'll soon sort that." Tom touched the priest's arm.

"And I was slurring my words like some eejit, wasn't I Tom?"

"You sound real normal now."

"How's your vision?"

"That was the most frightening thing, everything blacked out down one side."

"Okay. Can you see my finger here? Good and here? Fine. And cover the left eye… and the right… Great." I smiled at the anxious middle-aged man. "I think you've just had a Transient Ishaemic Attack – a self-correcting mini-stroke. Nothing like it before?"

"No, no, thank the Lord. I've been well since I gave up the cigarettes last year. I do drink Star…"

"Well smoking's the worst thing for TIAs but a bit of beer might even be beneficial."

"That's mighty news."

"Alcohol opens up those blood vessels to the brain. Keeps everything flowing."

"So am I going to have a stroke?"

"No. Take this as a little warning. Your blood pressure is up a bit." His blood pressure was up quite a lot, none too surprisingly. "But half an aspirin is great at preventing strokes. Nice and simple and we even have it in stock! You'd better take things easy, though. Could you stay with Father Brendan in Mokanje?"

"Yeah," agreed Tom. "Things are getting real stressful round here."

"Oh no. I can't leave my people."

"Just for a few days' rest."

"Absolutely not, Tom. I must see Serabu through this unsettled time."

"Hmmm." A full-blown argument wasn't going to help anybody's blood pressure, so I got up to go and search our drug stores to see if we had any suitable, in date, anti-hypertensives. "I'll bring back the aspirin and redo your blood pressure once Tom's fed you a few cups of tea."

"Sure thing, Doc," said Tom. "The best cure for blood pressure!"

"Hmmm." I suspected I wasn't going to find anything much better in our limited supplies. Serabu was taking its siesta (the only sensible option for the middle of the day) as I wandered back home from the mission house. I had stopped under the shade of a palm tree to snack on some of Nurse's groundnuts when a roaring engine suddenly invaded the tranquillity. Coughing out a nut, I gaped at the truckful of soldiers bouncing over the hill, then screeching round the corner into the hospital compound.

"What on earth...?" I broke into a run, arriving in time to see ten soldiers jump out of the truck, brandishing their guns Rambo style, right outside Maternity. Screams suddenly filled the air as staff and patients flooded out of doors and windows to flee into the surrounding bushes. "Oh God."

Rooted to a spot behind TB Ward latrines, I stared at the suddenly deserted compound. What was this all about? What was I going to do? I looked frantically around for help and saw a lone figure striding towards the soldiers. It was MT.

"What do you think you are doing?" she exploded, a tiny seventy year-old woman against ten men with guns. Good Lord, she was magnificent.

"I done promise to protect you, Sista," a familiar soldier announced, pulling himself straight. It was our hitch-hiker, the 'rebel killer.' "We come to guard the hospital," he added proudly.

"Guard the hospital!" MT spluttered.

"Yes, Sista."

"You call terrifying my staff and patients guarding the hospital?"

"Sorry, Sista."

"None of you children should have a peashooter, never mind these monstrous weapons," MT continued, her passions more inflamed than I ever thought possible. "We don't want you here. Now stop playing soldiers and fok-off!"

"Yes Sista, sorry Sista," said the soldier. And that was that. They left.

213

Rebels This Way

"Sister Ignatius, you were fabulous!" I laughed, bravely showing my face now the danger had passed.

"Well, sweet Jesus, have you ever seen such a display?" MT was addressing me almost as an equal. "But more importantly, how is Joe?"

"Better. I suggested he take a break from Serabu."

"Oh, he won't be leaving us now."

"You're right, he won't."

"Dr. Emily, you will look after him very well, I'm sure."

Goodness, was that a compliment? But MT had already turned to call to the frightened faces in the bushes. "They have gone. Please come back. It was only soldiers, not the rebels. They have gone now. You are safe."

The next morning the sun streamed through my mosquito net. Nine o'clock! Where was Pa George? Not that it mattered if I were late – the hospital had been so quiet the past week.

Yawning, I admired my finished jigsaw, displayed in its full glory on the table in the morning sun. I ate some cold plassas for breakfast and ambled down to the wards. Tom was striding up the path towards me.

"Morning-oh Tom, come to drag me out of my bed?... what's up?"

"More problems, Emily."

"Oh no, now what?"

"Pa George has been arrested."

"Pa George arrested! What's he done?"

"Nothing. The soldiers are just arresting people," Tom told me. "Including my students."

"What? These same soldiers from yesterday?"

"I presume so."

"Why?"

"Because they've got guns."

"Does that mean they're in charge now? Nobody's going to argue with a gun?"

"Nobody except Pa George, who was last seen vanishing on the back of their truck shouting, 'You no able take me. I get for make chop for Dr. Em!'"

"Good old Pa George!" I smiled, despite the tightening in my chest.

"Anyway, the rescue party has gone storming after them."

"The rescue party?"

"Moses and Ignatius."

"Good Lord." Did the woman know no fear? "Should we, er…go and help?"

"Stay out of it, Emily. We need our only doctor." Tom squeezed my arm. "Bernadette and I will go if they haven't returned by ten."

"Oh dear," I said weakly, impressed by everyone else's bravery.

"The soldiers probably want the extra men as front-line rebel fodder."

"I hate to think. Anyway, to change the subject, Joe looked much better at Mass."

"He took Mass this morning?" I exclaimed.

"Six-thirty, as usual."

"Any more symptoms?"

"A bit more tingling in his fingers, but he told me not to tell you."

"I'll stick my nose in before rounds."

"Thought you might. See you later, Doc."

I tried to persuade Joe to seek some rest and relaxation somewhere far away from rebels and teenage soldiers with their lethal toys but the only thing gained from the encounter was a lunch invite and a three hour thrashing at cribbage. I was quite relieved to be called to an emergency Caesarean.

I was scrubbed and ready to start when a poomui appeared at the theatre window.

"Dr. Emily?" The white face peered uncertainly at my generous figure clad in theatre greens. "It's Preston."

"Preston?" I pulled my mask off. "From CARE? Goodness, what are you doing here?"

"I came to assess the rebel situation for CARE. We've got lots of projects in this area," he told me. "And Klaus asked me to check up on you. I sure don't like it. You should evacuate."

"Huh?"

"Klaus sent this." Preston handed me a letter. Klaus's writing covered two sides of an oil-stained page, which roughly translated to GET OUT.

I read it, a twinge of fear entwined with a surge of excitement. Klaus was worried about me! He cared! "Well, this is old news about Sumbuya," I said, in my most offhand manner. "The British High Commissioner and VSO will surely let us know if it's not safe."

"Don't rely on them," Preston snapped. "We think you should leave."

"I can't think about it now," I said. "I have emergency surgery."

"We can't force you," shrugged Preston. "Think about it."

"Thanks. Send Klaus my love." Gosh, I was getting to be a cool customer.

We delivered a particularly beautiful daughter (Dr-Em!) to Zainab, a refugee from Sumbuya, then cleared up theatre, joking about the rebels.

"Sesay don just put that new hospital sign," said Tiange, tossing her rubber gloves in the bucket for resterilisation. "Rebels this way."

"But Bernadette get for forbid the dirty rebels to attack the hospital because they will bring in germs," added Earnest. Serabu nurses were well drilled in cleanliness, godliness and the troubles caused by germs.

"After their baths, Bernadette would ask if they would mind attacking quietly, so as not to disturb the convalescing patients," I joined in.

"Please Mr. Rebel, I would be most grateful if you could kindly leave your guns at the entrance to the hospital. They are too noisy." Earnest gave a regal imitation of Bernadette. "But do come inside for a cup of tea."

"When Bernadette get all dem rebels in the convent, she get for lock the door," Tiange continued. "Then MT go thief their guns."

"Then what would MT do?" I asked, enjoying seeing Tiange in such a jovial mood.

"MT get for charge each rebel a thousand leones for their own gun."

My mood improved further on leaving theatre, for there was Moses coming into the compound with a familiar figure.

"Pa George! Kushe, Pa George!" I dashed towards them.

"What for chop today?"

"For heaven's sake, Pa George," I guffawed. "Have the day off!"

"Dem soldiers don arrest me!" Pa George sounded suitably outraged.

"I heard. How di body?"

"Look." He pointed at his forearm and I searched in vain for some slight graze or bruise beneath his finger. He was obviously going to play this for all it was worth.

"No harm done, Pa George."

"Hmmph."

"So what was it all about?"

"Dem soldiers want men to build a checkpoint at the Junction," Moses told me.

"So why not just ask nicely?"

"They get guns," Moses shrugged.

"So how did you get Pa George released?"

"MT say he is the only cook of the only doctor, and the only doctor get for eat."

"Hear hear!" I clapped. Pa George nodded gravely. "I'm surprised that the soldiers have such concern for my welfare."

"MT say they get for need a doctor if the rebels shoot them," Moses continued. "Dem soldiers are frightened."

"Of the rebels or of MT?"

"All two."

"Well plenty tenki, Moses. You were very brave."

"No problem."

"What for chop today?"

"Please, take the day off, Pa George," I insisted. "Father Joe has fed…" Pa George looked crestfallen.

"Dr. Em," Moses whispered. "The only cook of the only doctor no able take the day off."

"Of course not," I chastised myself silently. "Plassas please, Pa George."

God, I loved this job. The amazing realisation popped into my head as I was polishing off Pa Georges' plassas (my second dinner that day) with remarkable gusto.

"Dr. Em," a voice whispered from the darkness outside my mosquito mesh.

"Moses!" I jumped. "What are you doing here? It's eight o'clock."

"Dr. Em, Sister Bernadette and MT are at Mr. Tom's waiting for you."

"Oh?" It was most unusual for the sisters to come to the volunteers' houses. Moses knew it too. "Why?"

"I no know." He shrugged and waved good-bye without his usual smile. I didn't like the sound of this.

LAST ORDERS

MT was crying.

"What is it?" I clutched Tom's doorknob in alarm at this extraordinary sight.

"Have a seat, Emily." Tom stood up to make space for me. Bernadette and MT sat in silence opposite. The room was cramped and the thermometer must have been reading thirty-six degrees, but it still gave me the same shiver one gets when entering a morgue.

"We've had a radio message," sobbed Bernadette. "The Archbishop strongly advises Serabu Hospital to close and the British High Commissioner requests the immediate departure of all British citizens."

"Oh." I slumped down into Tom's seat. "More rebels?"

"No... well... I don't know." Bernadette shook her head.

"Perhaps they have news that we don't. We may be under threat." "Didn't they say?"

"Santano House only transmitted the message."

"You need to decide what to do, Emily, as Medical Superintendent," Bernadette continued.

"Decide what to do?" Me? My mind raced.

What did she mean decide what to do? Good Lord. Surely it wasn't up to me on my second day to decide whether or not to close the hospital. Hadn't we just been told what to do? We couldn't just disobey the British High Commissioner and the Archbishop, and why was Bernadette doing all the talking instead of MT, anyway?

"It might be useful to know whether or not there are actual rebels storming towards Serabu as we speak." My old friend flippancy put the words in my mouth.

"We don't know. We just don't know." MT shook her head, looking for the first time like the little old lady that she was.

"This is just a belated response to Sumbuya," Tom snorted. "Freetown's finger is hardly on the pulse where up country is concerned. I'm sure not accountable to the British High Commissioner. It's been quiet for three days now. I'm staying."

"Apart from the soldiers," I muttered.

"They're just little boys," said MT.

"With big guns."

"Oh Tom, I agree." MT ignored me. "We cannot abandon our hospital. After all the only Briton here is Emily, and she's a doctor."

What had being a doctor got to do with it? Did that mean I was expected to stay? MT was more upset at her beloved hospital being forced to close than the prospect of personal danger. It was the personal danger bit that bothered me. This wasn't a good time to get on the wrong side of the High Commissioner. On the other hand I didn't want to appear cowardly. I knew I'd stay if the others insisted.

"The Archbishop has also advised us to leave, and ultimately he is in charge of this hospital," Bernadette reminded us.

"And when did he last assist us in our recent difficult times? Or even pay a visit?" MT snapped.

We looked in amazement at the nun's blasphemy.

"Ignatius," Bernadette said gently. "It's about safety. I'm sorry, we must leave." I exhaled silently in relief. "We may actually be in danger," she continued. "We are the first sizeable target between the rebels and the rest of the country. We have equipment, vehicles, diesel, drugs, food and a couple of young Western volunteers."

"And why are we any more special than the rest of the staff?" Tom interjected.

"You and Emily would be worth a large ransom. And the rebels themselves may well be in need of medical attention."

"Poor Serabu." MT shook her head. Tom rubbed her bent shoulders.

"I'm sorry, Ignatius. You and I are responsible of these volunteers as well as for over a hundred and fifty staff and patients." Good old Bernadette. At least I wasn't supposed to be responsible for them.

"What does immediate departure mean?" I asked. "Tonight?"

"I think if we were in immediate danger we would know about it from the soldiers," Bernadette suggested.

"I wouldn't rely on the soldiers," said Tom with uncharacteristic cynicism.

"Well as long as they're here, we're safe. They'll be off at the first sniff of trouble," I snorted.

"That's as may be."

"I'm sorry, Bernadette," I sighed. Sarky comments were no help to anyone.

"We sure can't just sneak off in the dark and leave our friends," said Tom. "Not without an explanation."

"Tom's right," agreed Bernadette. "We can't be starting a mass panic in the middle of the night. I suggest we have a staff meeting first thing in the morning and try to do this awful thing in a controlled manner. Emily?"

"What?" They were right, of course they were right, but if we were going, couldn't we just go now? Why hang around to be embroiled in the chaos? I closed my eyes. "Of course, Bernadette. I'll arrange medication for all the patients for the next… I don't know." I stopped. "This isn't going to be forever, is it?"

"Let us pray it is not."

"How can we just walk out?" MT nearly howled.

"I don't think we have a choice, Ignatius." Bernadette put an arm round her colleague.

"Scrabu's doors haven't been closed for a single day in forty years," MT sobbed. "I never thought it would come to this."

"Neither did I, Ignatius. Neither did I." Bernadette shook her head. "I'd better go and tell Joe. Oh dear."

"I'll come too." I stood up.

"We'll all go," said Tom.

"Oh dear. Oh dear, oh dear." Joe sat down heavily. "I will stay of course."

"But you've just had a TIA," I exclaimed. "Braving it out alone is hardly going to bring your blood pressure down."

"I won't be alone. I have my God and my friends of twenty-five years."

"Joe, many villagers will flee when they hear the poomuis are pulling out," Tom suggested gently.

"Of course, but those that stay will need my support. My place is here."

"I know but…" I started.

"Oh Joe, you know Bernadette and I feel the same way," MT interrupted. "We will stay too."

"No. No, it's not the same for you at all. If the rebels did come, you couldn't safely evacuate everybody at a moment's notice, but I could just drive off in my truck."

"Not if you have a stroke, you couldn't!"

"Okay, Emily." Joe spread his hands on the table. "Here's the deal. My sabbatical's already booked next month. I will go home as arranged, and as soon as I get back to Ireland, I promise to see my doctor. Okay?"

"Let me stay with you until then," Tom offered.

"No Tom. You are young. You are just a volunteer. I am telling you, you will go to Freetown with the others. Who knows? It may only be for a few days."

"But…"

"No."

We all fell silent until Bernadette spoke calmly.

"We'll have an emergency staff meeting at eight. Tonight we should pack and try to get some sleep. Lord knows we will need it for what will be a most difficult day tomorrow."

"I'll do my bedtime rounds as usual," I said. "Let the patients sleep easy for their last night. They'll have long journeys in the morning."

"Tom, will you help us with the staff pay packages?" asked Bernadette. "I think we have enough for two months advance each. They're all going to need money."

"What about the students?" Tom asked. "Transport is expensive."

"And the patients," I added.

"There simply isn't enough," sighed MT. "All we can do is waive fees."

"At least most patients and staff are local, but my students have come from all over the country," Tom continued. "It's six hundred leones for a poda-poda to Freetown, but with demand so high they could charge anything."

"They can't go via Bo. The Junction is too close to the rebels."

"They'll have to go through Mokanje," said Tom. "Can't we give lifts in the hospital vehicles?"

"Forty students, seventy staff, eighty patients and Lord knows how many relatives? No Tom!" said Bernadette.

"Perhaps Moses could ferry the students as far as Mokanje," suggested MT. I gaped at her. "And if we could give each student a thousand leones, it would help. Please excuse me, I'll have to work out how much we can afford." She stood up and stumbled towards the door.

"Ignatius, wait for us," Bernadette said. "With Tom's help, we'll have all the money counted out in a couple of hours."

"I'll come too." Joe pushed himself out of his chair.

"No!" Tom and I chorused.

"You'll have a lot of distressed villagers seeking reassurance tomorrow. Tonight will be your last chance to relax." Tom pushed the older man's shoulders back into his seat.

"Oh dear. Well, would my doctor allow me a beer?"

"Good idea. I'll join you after my rounds."

An hour later we were drinking Joe's beer. "Here's to the shortest reign as Medical Superintendent in Serabu's history." Weak jokes were my only remaining weapon. "Two days!" I took a long drink.

"She's just drinking that to stop you yielding to temptation when we can't keep an eye on you," said Tom, an unlikely conspirator to my fake cheer.

"Thank you for your kind concern," said Joe, eyeing his empty beer crate as Bernadette reached for the last bottle. Tom drank his water. "Oh, I'm just remembering – I have a bottle of Bailey's!"

"Goodness, Father. How can you forget such a thing?" I teased.

"It was a present I've been saving for a rainy day. This, the Lord have mercy, must qualify as a rainy day." Joe stood up. "We can't be letting it fall to the rebels."

"Whatever you do, don't let them get the Bailey's," I exclaimed.

Joe returned three minutes later with a tea towel over his arm, two teacups, a tumbler, a chipped Charles and Di mug and a litre bottle of Bailey's poking seductively out of a brown paper bag.

I had never seen Joe so animated – danger obviously suited him. He poured out hefty measures into four of the inelegant but voluminous vessels and stopped, poised over the fifth.

"Tom?"

"You know I don't… oh what the heck!"

"Oh Joe, this is just heavenly." I smacked my lips.

"Hey, this is real nice."

"You've made an alcoholic out of him, Joe," Bernadette exclaimed.

"Tom that's 17%," I pointed out. "You're drinking it like a milkshake!"

"To you all – for all the hard work you have put into Serabu Hospital. Thank you." Bernadette raised her teacup. "Slainte."

"Slainte," I replied. "We'll be back!" Bernadette didn't respond, but gulped down half the sickly warm cream liqueur.

"I never thought I'd leave Serabu." MT was toying with her tumbler. She sat slumped into the chair with her skin folding into its greyness and tears riding over the ridges from her puffy red eyes. I instantly regretted all our clever-clever comments and could feel all the frivolity in the room dissolve as the others' eyes were drawn simultaneously to the old lady.

"Perhaps we all ought to try and get some sleep," Bernadette said gently, breaking the sudden awkward silence. "It's past midnight and tomorrow's going to be very stressful."

"I never thought I'd walk out of Serabu," MT repeated, struggling up from her chair.

"Come on Ignatius, we'll walk you home," Tom took her arm and gently guided her out of the door and into the warm, peaceful night.

DISCHARGED

"Dr. Em, come quick!" Laygby banged on my door.

"Laygby! Aren't you on maternity leave?"

"Yes, but there is nobody left. Mariama don already do a double shift."

"It's two in the morning and you're eight-months pregnant! Where's Almamy?"

"He don go," she shrugged. "Many are too much frightened and have run to the bush."

"Oh." Had they guessed that we were leaving? Was it the soldiers who had scared them? Or did they have more news of rebels approaching?

But there was no time to worry about rebels. "This doesn't look good," I whispered as we reached Maternity.

Zainab had started bleeding, her life pumping over the mattress, her face ashen and sweaty with Baby Dr-Em sleeping peacefully alongside. Zainab's mother sat quietly stroking her daughter's hand whilst Theresa tried to put up an IV.

"Run that saline in as fast as it will go, Theresa. Have you got another bag, Laygby? Laygby, are you okay? Sit down for a few minutes and get your breath. God, I can't get a blood pressure. Theresa, turn that on full and find another bag and syntocinon. Laygby can draw it up sitting down. We need blood NOW. Call Alamamy to fetch Latif."

"Almamy is not there," said Laygby.

"I forgot. Theresa, you'll have to find Latif, and Tiange too."

"No problem."

The blood just kept coming. The long delay getting to the hospital had disrupted Zainab's clotting mechanisms. "Another bag of saline, Laygby," I shouted. "And ergometrine. Come on Latif, where are you?

I need to transfuse her now." My orders dwindled to a mutter as I knew I could not realistically expect Latif for another fifteen minutes, and that was if he had not fled to the bush himself. "We are losing her. More saline, Laygby."

"Saline don don, Dr. Em."

"Then thief some from Surgical. Quick. We'll have to take her to theatre. I'll give some more ergometrine."

After two hours in theatre we finally stopped the bleeding, but she was slipping away. There was virtually no blood left circulating in her veins. Latif was knocking on doors in the village looking for a donor with the promise of double or treble pay, but the villagers had already fled, or said they needed their blood to fight the rebels.

"This is hopeless. She needs blood, not salty water."

"Latif is trying."

"I know Laygby, I know."

Zainab died at eight, just as the emergency staff meeting was starting. Her baby's cries rang in my ears as I hurried over to the convent. I opened the door to silence. Had the meeting been cancelled? But no, twenty people sat clustered in a circle, shoulders bowed and scarcely breathing. None of the swollen red eyes acknowledged my arrival. Why should they? Their Medical Superintendent hadn't even tried to save their hospital nor had she been present to deliver the bad news. I couldn't say I'd been delayed saving lives, because I'd just failed at that too.

"While the Poomuis stayed, we were safe." Patrick Kpukoma finally broke the silence. "But you must go to your own homes, and we must stay with our families."

"There will be a panic," said Mariama. "We get for keep calm ourselves and do the best for our patients."

"I'll, er…" I cleared my throat "… make sure everybody is discharged with plenty of medication." Big deal.

"We are waiving fees, but the dispensary nurses must fill in the charts," added Bernadette. "We'll need to do a stock take when we return."

"Are you coming back?" asked Patrick. He knew, like all the others, about July's financial review. If Serabu was already closed, then what better excuse for the Catholic Mission to send their funds elsewhere? The very act of evacuating, even if no rebel came a step closer, might be Serabu's death knell.

"We will return." MT's first contribution to the meeting was not a promise that she could make. The rebels and her superiors in Bo, Freetown and Ireland would determine Serabu's future.

"As soon as possible." Bernadette was vague.

"Days? Weeks? Months?" pressed Patrick. "We get for know. If Serabu don finish completely then we get for leave and look for other jobs. If Serabu go open back, we get for stay." Patrick looked around the room for the nods of confirmation.

"I can only pray that the rebels will come no further," Bernadette said. "And that Serabu's staff will come to reopen our hospital. But I cannot say when it will be safe."

"We understand," said Mariama kindly. "But we get plenti work today. The two nurses in dispensary go need help. We get for bring more drugs from the stores. Dauda, will you help me?"

"No problem."

"Tenki ya. The other charge nurses must stop palava on their wards," Mariama continued. She was being marvellous. I closed my eyes to shut out the thoughts of the chaos that was about to break out.

"What about the equipment?" asked Dauda very practically. "And the drugs? The rebels will thief it. If notto the rebels, the thief men go come."

"And the books and chairs and desks in the nursing school," added Tom.

"And the beds and mattresses – they will all be thiefed." Earnest directed his comments to Bernadette, rather than MT. Everyone sensed that Bernadette was now in charge. MT sat outside the circle of conversation, moist eyes gazing out of the window.

"You all make very good points," agreed Bernadette. "We must ensure that we have a hospital to come back to. Mr. East sent a message from the Mines this morning offering to help secure the buildings."

"Them theatre doors get metal frames," said Sesay. "And Surgical. Them Mines' people get for weld them shut."

"Excellent idea, Sesay," said Bernadette. "Then we'll have a safe store for our equipment. Moses can you get back on to Mr. East to ask if he has welding facilities?"

"No problem, Sister."

"Good. Sesay, you're in charge of moving beds and equipment to Surgical."

"And the birthing chair?" Sesay looked alarmed.

"No, let's leave that for the rebels." Bernadette managed a small smile.

"I'll start discharging patients from Surgical, to get it emptied," I suggested. "Then Maternity, Children's, Medical and finish on TB Ward."

"Why are my TB patients always last?" complained Patrick. "Many come from far. There will be plenti palava."

"Oh Patrick, I know," I sighed. "They're rebellious at the best of times. But they're on so many tablets they'll just jam up dispensary. Also they're fitter than most other patients."

"The two new ones are very weak," he retorted. Patrick was very paternal about his TB patients.

"Okay, bring me those two charts for discharge straight away."

"What about their daily injections?"

"You must teach them how to give their own injections, starting with today's dose. We'll supply the needles and syringes, if you can teach them how to sterilise them," I said. "That should fill some time until I arrive."

"No problem."

"Right, we must get started." Bernadette stood up after our brief plan was agreed. "I'll pay staff salaries at eleven in Admin and Tom will pay his students a travel allowance at the school. Everybody will be paid, so please be patient. I don't want a big palava outside Admin. Earnest, will you be responsible for getting the message to those currently off duty?"

"No problem, but they will know the news already, Sister."

"Probably yes," Bernadette sighed. The senior staff did not vanish into the convent at the busiest time of day for no reason. She took a breath and continued with a wavering voice. "Thank you. Thank-you for all the hard work you have given to Serabu over the years. We are very sorry." Bernadette hastily wiped her eyes with the back of her hand.

"We are very, very sorry."

All the heads turned to the tiny old figure shaking her head in the corner.

"Aw fo do, Sister Ignatius," said Patrick, gently. "Aw fo do."

We came out of the convent to a compound alive with sobs and screams. Within seconds I was in a whirlpool of patients and staff, grabbing my arm or my skirt and begging me not to leave. Tugging myself away from the distress, I ran over to Surgical to begin my role call of discharges. Mechanically, I signed off every patient, looking at their charts rather than their eyes, writing them up for as many dressings and tablets as might help them over the coming weeks. I discharged Rose, the young woman with terminal breast cancer, absolving myself from any further responsibility for her, before moving on to wash my hands of the next patient in line.

After only an hour's sleep, I walked from Surgical to Children's, from Children's to Maternity and from Maternity to Medical in an exhausted daze, only vaguely aware of the chaos surrounding me. There were relatives filing up to the dispensary, clutching their loved one's charts, nurses queuing up at Admin for their wages and people streaming out of the hospital with rolled up belongings on their heads. Even the unflappable Mariama was running backwards and forwards, between wards, stores and dispensary, stopping to shout instructions, point directions or hug patients and nurses. The only island of sanity was the "Kushe Dr. Em," shouted across the compound by Bockerie from TB ward, who was helping Sesay carry the mattresses over to Surgical.

My smile soon faded when a woman fell to her knees and threw her arms around my waist. It was Rose's mother.

"Dr. Em, don't go. You get for save my daughter!" she cried, tightening her grip on my middle. I froze. I couldn't cope with this mother's anguish and my impotence. Not today. There was no more I could do for Rose, just as there had been nothing I could do for her last week. I had to escape from her mother's grasp. The rest of my patients had to be sent home, and then there was Outpatients.

Prising Rose's chart from the elderly fingers that encircled my waist, I prescribed another type of different-coloured vitamin pill that would not save her daughter from cancer of the breast even if there had never been a single rebel in Sierra Leone.

At Outpatients, I closed the office door on Friday rush hour at Piccadilly tube station. Two hours later, once I had sorted out staff, students and their families who wanted medication for ongoing problems, or just-in-case supplies, the compound had become a Sunday morning Highland branchline. I shouldn't have been surprised; after all, I was the one to throw everybody out.

Serabu Hospital populated only by goats sent a shudder down my spine. Then, just as a reminder of how desperately I needed sleep, Zainab floated across the empty compound, a funny little smile across her deathly white face. "Stop it, stop it, stop it," I shouted, shaking the ominous vision out of my head.

Perhaps Zainab had taken the easier escape. What about everybody else? Her mother, for instance? Last week she had lived in peaceful Sumbuya with a beautiful daughter, happily awaiting her grandchild's arrival. Now she had no home, a newborn baby she could not feed, and her daughter's corpse which she could not carry or bury alone. Normally there would be plenty of people to help her, but not today, when everyone was so scared for their own family's lives. What would happen to Zainab's body?

I never found out.

Bed was not going to be on the agenda for a long, long time. Freetown was at least a seven-hour journey and I still had thirty-six TB patients to discharge. Working out a six-week supply of four or five different types of medicine apiece, each individually weight adjusted, would stretch my arithmetic skills at the best of times. But worse than forcing my sleep-deprived brain into number crunching was the prospect of facing the TB patients, who would surely be furious that I had left them till last. And they would have a point.

They already felt like second-class citizens, frequently cast out of their communities, certainly avoided by the rest of the patients and, since they were not acutely unwell, always left to the end of my priority list. Consequently they had bonded together against the common foe, the poomui doctors, who wouldn't trust them to take their tablets at home and forced them into an unwanted three-months admission away from their homes and farms. We didn't even feed them in return. Now here I was, blithely turning them out into the void. God, I wasn't going to be popular. I took a few deep breaths and forced myself to stride across the compound towards TB block.

I stood at their doorway and listened. Why was it so quiet? Had they decided I wasn't worth waiting for and fled already?

"Patrick?" I called tentatively. "Are you still here?"

"We de inside," he replied. And there was Patrick sitting crosslegged in the middle of the floor with two neat piles of charts piled on beside him. All the mattresses had gone, leaving only rusty bed frames and thirty-six TB patients sitting or squatting on the floor, with bundles of possessions at their feet.

"Kushe, Dr. Em," they chorused. My mind flashed back twenty years to primary school when two hundred little voices chanted 'Good mo-oorning, Mr. Stones' when the headmaster entered morning assembly.

"Er... yes... kushe." Flustered by this unexpectedly warm welcome, I hid my face behind the first of the charts and whispered to Patrick. "Where shall I start?"

"I don write one month's medication for all. Them nurses in dispensary are too much tired to do the sums so I write the totals at the bottom of the chart-self. You want check, Dr. Em?"

"Patrick, you are marvellous." I felt like hugging him. Oh what the hell, I did hug him. The patients cheered.

"The charts, Dr. Em," he chastised, blushing. I glanced at the first one, the drugs clearly marked with a little circle round each total.

"I can't do better than that. Why did you never go to medical school, Patrick?"

"There is no medical school," he shrugged. "Look at the charts."

"Okay." I dashed off thirty-six autographs and Patrick distributed the charts. Their patience exhausted, Serabu's last thirty-six patients welled out of the ward and headed towards dispensary.

"Well, Dr. Emily, you've earned your lunch." I stretched my neck in the doorway. "Oh, no. Now what?"

Bockerie was running back towards me, waving his chart. "Dr. Em,

Dr. Em, they have gone home."

"Who?" But I knew. I had sent over two hundred prescriptions to the dispensary nurses that morning. That was an awful lot of tablets to count and wrap and label in little paper packets. I couldn't really blame them, especially now that everybody else had long gone. They had families too.

"Them nurses in dispensary don go," wailed Bockerie. "The door is locked."

"Okay Bockerie, don't panic. Tell the others I'm coming. I'll try and find the key." Mariama would probably have it, if she was still here. I tried the wards first, but met only two Mines' security men wandering across the compound.

"Kushe. Have you seen our matron, Mariama?"

"Yes. She is collecting more drugs from stores before we seal it up."

Good old Mariama. Why had I doubted her? I ran over to the storeroom.

"Mariama?"

"Dr. Em?" Mariama turned round from the boxes of tablets. "You are finished? I just get them TB drugs to take to dispensary, but I no able carry all at once. This is my second trip. We need plenti, notto so?"

"Isn't there anybody helping you?"

"Everybody don go," she sighed. "I don forget about those TB drugs this morning."

"So did I, Mariama, it's been chaos. If only the dispensary nurses had stayed one more hour."

"They don stay longer than any others already. I will dispense the tablets myself."

"Mariama, there'll be hundreds. Come on, I'll help. The TB patients won't be able to control themselves for much longer."

We half-ran, half-walked with box loads of tablets and injections, past the two security men hovering at Pharmacy's doorway with their welders.

"We're lucky they didn't seal us in there forever," I joked.

"We get for give them rebels a big fright, notto so, if they tried to thief the drugs?"

We sneaked into the back of Dispensary, a windowless room little bigger than a public loo, and flicked the light switch. Nothing. Sesay had shut the generator down hours ago.

"I can't see a damned thing." I felt around on the table for a place to put my box of medication, but it was cluttered with empty containers and spilt tablets. "Oh, to hell with it." I cleared the surface with a sweep of my arm

"I put all the kerosene lamps in Theatre," shouted Mariama above the noise of fists banging on the wooden shutters outside. "The Mines' men don seal it already. Shall I fetch one from home?"

"Stay here, Mariama, they'll lynch you! They're terrified that the rebels are marching down the road. Dah! I can't open these damned shutters."

"Let me do it, Dr. Em." Shaking, Mariama released the catch and begging hands clamoured through the metal grille more suited to a Wild West bank than a hospital.

So we counted and counted and counted until tablets swam before our eyes and stuck to the sweat on our fingers. We had no water, so rubbed our hands on our skirts and counted some more. We took one chart at a time as it was thrust through the grille, concentrating only on Patrick's neatly circled numbers at the bottom, rather than the name at the top.

Mariama explained which tablet was which in the patient's little packages and how many should be taken each day, but whether the patients took any of it in, if indeed they could hear a word she was saying in the uproar, I'll never know. At least most of them had been on the ward for long enough to know their own daily dosages, so I was reasonably happy they wouldn't poison themselves.

We came to the last two charts. They belonged to Pa Ndanema and Bockerie, who had spent the past ninety minutes trying their best to control the unruly crowd as it surged forward onto Dispensary.

"There's no thiazina left, Dr. Em."

"Oh no, they've been so helpful, we can't leave them short."

"You get any of the children's thiazina on the shelves?"

"Mariama, you're a genius. We'll just have to triple the dose."

So Pa Ndanema and Bockerie left with 210 ethambutol, 168 rifampicin, 42 streptomycin injections, and 630 paediatric thiazina, plus a bagful of gauze for Pa Ndanema to dress his stump.

It was after five o'clock when Mariama and I emerged from our cave to the bright whitewashed walls of a silent hospital. "Poor Serabush," sighed Mariama.

"It's so sad." I was actually leaving Serabu, probably to return home forever. Was I sad or relieved? I didn't really know – all I could think of was that awful journey to Freetown, which was bound to be littered with military checkpoints. For a moment I envied Mariama staying. After thirty-five hours with no sleep and the most stressful day of my life, I just wanted my bed. Then I thought of the rebels. "I'm sorry Mariama."

"Aw fo do," she sighed. My stomach rumbled loudly. "Oh, Dr. Em, you get for chop!"

"Even Pa George' plassas will taste good tod…" I stopped, realising my blithe assumption that Pa George would make lunch was plain ridiculous. All the other staff had long gone, so why should he stay? It was now after five o'clock.

"You will be gladdi to sleep at Mokanje tonight, Dr. Em."

"Mokanje?" What was Mariama on about? Bernadette was going to drive us to Freetown in the truck in less than an hour.

"The Mines' MD don come with the security men this afternoon. Mr. East say you can stay at Mokanje."

"Really?" Electricity, air-conditioning, a pool, chocolate, SLEEP!

"Tom and the sisters want to go direct to Freetown, but Mr. East don insist you stay. Moses will take you at six."

"Well perhaps someone could give me a lift to Freetown tomorrow," I mused, feeling just a little less tired. There was always some expatriate going to the big city from Mokanje. "What about you?"

"We must wait for Ben." Mariama's smile faded.

"Have you heard from him?"

"No, he must still be near Kailahun, but the Catholic mission has gone, so there is no radio."

"Oh, Mariama." What else could I say?

"Aw fo do." Mariama folded her arms round herself. "We go see at the convent in one hour, Dr. Em."

Wandering back to my house with goats roaming where once there were nurses and patients, my legs felt quite wobbly with hunger. I nearly cried when I spotted Pa George sitting, chin in hands, on my doorstep.

"Oh, Pa George, you stayed!"

"You no chop yet, Dr. Em."

"I'm sorry to keep you from your family Pa George. You should have come to find me."

"You too bweezy. Chop bin ready four hours."

"Sorry."

"Hmmph." Pa George went to get my lunch that had been keeping warm on the embers of the three-stone-fire. I grabbed a plate, spoon and ladle from the kitchen and followed him eagerly.

"Aw fo do," said Pa George, stopping short of the fire.

"Aw fo do?" I asked. "Oh." The pan had been pulled off the stones and lay on its side in the dying embers with its lid lying two feet away.

The goats had eaten my lunch.

RUNNING AWAY!

MT left Serabu Hospital with tears flowing down her grey cheeks. For a moment, I wanted to hug her, but hung back and shuffled my feet instead. What could I say? Ultimately my posting in Sierra Leone was just an interlude. I would resume my job, my life, my family and my friends, but Serabu was Sister Ignatius' whole world and it had just collapsed.

"Er, goodbye." I limply raised my arm, but the old lady's eyes were fixed ahead. Next to MT sat Bernadette, dressed in veil and habit for ease of passage through the checkpoints. Tom sat in the back of the truck with six of his students.

"Good-bye, Emily," Bernadette waved. "Sleep well at Mokanje tonight, and we'll see you at the Venue on Saturday."

Oh to sleep... "Good-bye, safe journey." I managed a proper wave this time. Tom and his students all waved frantically from the back.

"God bless, Emily," said Bernadette. "Good-bye Mariama. Look after that young man of yours now."

"I will Sister Bernadette. We go see back. Look, Hindolu is waving."

"God bless him." Bernadette smiled at the baby, then turned the key in the ignition.

Only then did MT turn to face me. "Look after my hospital for me, Emily. Please."

And the sisters who had devoted their lives to Serabu were gone. What a sad contrast to the throngs of laughing and waving people that bade farewell to Philippe and his family only days previously. But how was I going to look after the hospital?

Before I could think further on MT's strange request, Moses pulled up. The Landrover was piled high with bags and bedrolls and filled with nurses and students hoping to get some transport from Mokanje to their homes across the country. Moses managed to strap my rucksacks on top of the mountain of luggage already bearing down on the vehicle, then opened the front door.

"We go see back, Dr. Em." Mariama hugged me before I climbed into the best seat.

"Very soon," I lied, squeezing her tight. The likelihood was that our Field Director would bundle me on the first flight home, leaving me free to continue my old life as if nothing had ever happened. Mariama would soon be just a memory. Ashamed, I released my grip and Mariama clicked the door shut behind me.

The Landrover strained into motion as Hindolu took his first steps holding tightly on to Mariama's thumb. Mariama waved, her face lit with her beautiful smile, and Hindolu copied his mummy, letting go of her thumb to wave his own little hand, and landed promptly on his bottom in the dust.

Hanging out of the Landrover window, I waved frantically at the two giggling figures we had left dwarfed beneath the large white convent building and whispered "Oh God, keep them safe."

Ten miles out of Serabu, I sat numbly in the front seat, secretly hoping that VSO would indeed order us all home. I had had enough. I did not want to witness any more suffering, nor take any more responsibility. I could board the plane and blame the Field Director for over-reacting, without having to feel guilty myself. Once in Gatwick, I would stock up at the nearest shop on chocolate and cheese and take it home to eat in bed. A bed that needed a cosy thick duvet rather than a mosquito net. A bed with a lamp beside it that would light up at the flick of a switch, and a socket that would power a cassette player that could blare out loud music. I could lie back, safe in the knowledge that nobody would come knocking at my door telling me that it was my job to stop someone from bleeding to death, or to kick a hospital full of patients out onto the street.

Staring vacantly out of the windscreen, I thought of Chicken Tikka. Pa George had taken her. Well, I suppose she would make a good chicken stew. Suddenly, I realised I was crying – not for the death of poor Zainab for the want of some blood, or the end of the hospital that had saved so many lives in its thirty years, or the fate of my friends left to face the rebels, but for a stupid hen. Oh Emily!

Wiping away the tears, I saw a lone bent figure, hobbling on one leg and a single crutch, chasing the evening haze as it met the horizon. It was Pa Ndanema, carrying two plastic bags filled with dressings and tablets, clearly oblivious to the straining engine behind him.

"Kushe, Pa!" I called out of the window. Pa Ndanema snapped out of his reverie and straightened his shoulders.

"Kushe, Dr. Em."

"How di body?"

"I tell God tenki."

"You only get one crutch, Pa?"

"That crutch don break," he snorted.

"Well, you have done very well. Nearly ten miles, notto so Moses?"

"Ten miles, Dr. Em."

"You better join us Pa," I offered, shuffling over, pushing Theresa, who sat with me at the front, into Moses' lap.

"Dr. Em, place not there," moaned Moses, trying to find his gear stick under Theresa's thigh. Theresa pulled her lappa protectively tighter round her waist and gave Moses the evil eye.

"I'll walk," came Dauda's voice from the back. "It's only twenty miles," he added virtuously.

"If Dauda walks, there will be space for two patients," teased Theresa, "And Dauda will lose his belly." Dauda was the least fit Salonean male I knew.

"Nobody need walk. Shove over Dauda." I pushed him playfully, and squeezed myself into the back like an extra elephant in a mini amidst shouts, giggles, arms and legs. Moses sighed and helped Pa Ndanema through the passenger door, feeding his remaining crutch into the melee behind. Lord Muck himself sat in the prime seat, surveying the dusty road ahead with a gummy grin. Theresa handed him an orange to suck.

Between juicy slurps of gum on pulp, Pa Ndanema alternately thanked us and complained about his crutch.

"Sorry Pa, but I doubt Sesay made them with long-haul journeys in mind."

241

On our way once more, the nurses were joking about like their old selves, despite the long uncertain journeys that lay ahead of them all. The brave old Pa had lifted everybody's mood. I had done what had to be done, and was now a mere thirty minutes away from twenty-four hour electricity. Electricity meant air-conditioning to clear up prickly heat and fridges that could keep things from melting. Things like chocolate. It was a Swiss-owned company after all. In fact, what was the rush to hurry back to Freetown? Back to the sweaty VSO rest house, stuffed with evacuated volunteers in limbo whilst our Field Director decided what to do with us? Perhaps I could stay at Mokanje for a few extra days?

"Moses." I leant forward. He grunted acknowledgement. Moses had spent the morning organising the rabble of staff into orderly queues to receive their wages, then the afternoon ferrying students to Mokanje. "What did Mr. East say about my staying at the Mines?"

"Mr. East say you can get your very own house."

"My own house for one night? Why would I need a whole house?"

"If you go, they get only Dr. Momoh, Dr. Em," answered Moses. "The house don empty. A very big house, Dr. Em."

"Moses, what are you saying?"

"Freetown is too far, Dr. Em. We gladdi if you stay at Mokanje."

"We? Who's we?"

"Oh Patrick, Tiange and Dauda. And MT."

Was that what MT meant? To stay at Mokanje to keep an eye on Serabu? "And where was I during this discussion?"

"You were bweezy. Sister Bernadette and Mariama don say you don tire too much. They say you get for stay na Mokanje this night, but you get for go see them VSO people in Freetown."

"I see. What did the others say?"

"The staff don aks me to aks you to stay."

"But you haven't, Moses. We're nearly at Mokanje. Why haven't you asked me to stay?"

"You don tire too much, Dr. Em." I looked at Moses' kindly face. It was drawn with fatigue and anxiety.

"We are all tired," I said through the lump in my throat, grateful that Moses had not actually asked the question. I steered the conversation away from myself. "I hear you will stay at the convent with your family."

"Yes. Sister Bernadette don give me the keys."

"To the convent?"

"To theatre, to pharmacy, to Admin…"

"That's an enormous bunch of keys, Moses."

"When the rebels come to thief Serabush, they look for me first to get them keys," he joked.

"I doubt that rebels bother with keys." I cringed as soon as the words were out. God, it was all very well for me, being driven off to safety. Fortunately Moses was as sanguine as ever.

"Aw fo do. The convent get plenty place to hide."

"What you need Emily, is a stiff gin and some fatherly solace," Rob East suggested late that evening. Michelle, his beautiful French wife, had led my weary body from the Landrover first to a hot bath, then to a laden dinner table. Thus revived, a gin did sound good, so I followed the Mines' MD to the bar in search of the promised solace.

Six priests sat at the bar, evidently several hours into a good session:

"Shouldn't have closed the hospital."

"A Sister's duty is to stay with her people."

"Father Joe knew his duty."

"You cannot be after running away and abandoning your mission."

"Sister Hilary would never have left…"

"Hilary should never have left in the first place…"

"… running away."

"We were told to leave!" I exploded behind them. "Ignatius was devastated."

"Ah, It's Dr. Emily, safe from the clutches of the rebels," Father Gregory turned to smile at me. "No dear, you were *strongly advised* to leave."

"Oh come on!"

"So where is this rebel army then?" asked Father Brendan. "You'd better sit down, Emily, while we sort this mess out."

"I don't know. Nobody knows." I flopped into the proffered seat.

"We're not criticising you Emily," said Gregor. "You have bravely decided to stay." Hang on a minute. Who said I was staying?

"Yes," agreed Brendan. "She can go back tomorrow, see a few outpatients and let's see what we can do to get the hospital reopened."

Go back tomorrow?! What about the rebels? What about the High Commissioner? What about my long lie in? What about the swimming pool? What about my lift back to Freetown? A large G and T appeared. I took a large slug. The sisters were the ones willing to stick it out, not me. I had been glad to pack and run.

"It broke the sisters' hearts," I said. "But they were told to go. Besides they had to think of the safety of their staff and patients."

"I suppose so," muttered Brendan.

"But all is not lost whilst we still have a doctor. And Father Joe has stayed of course."

"Joe isn't very well," I tried desperately to change the subject. "He's had a little stroke."

"Oh dear, I didn't know that now, did you Brendan?"

"I did not. It makes his stand more heroic altogether. Between such a mighty pair as Joe and Emily, we'll have Serabu back on its feet in no time."

But I want to go home!

Rob came to my rescue. "Brendan! All of you! Be realistic. We don't know the risks. You can't send a young girl back alone, even if she did have the High Commissioner's permission."

"Hear, hear," I thought, but then Rob revealed his own plans for my future. "We'll employ her here at Mokanje clinic. Full rates of course Emily, not just a paltry VSO allowance."

"But I don't want to be a Mines' employee!" I exclaimed, self-righteously. Good Lord! What would Klaus and Lindsey have to say about that? Selling out to a multinational company who stole the country's resources and reduced the landscape to dust.

"Steady on," laughed Rob. "I don't want you to abandon your principles, but listen. We are the only place that Serabu's patients can come to now. What if we agree to fund treatment for all who come, not just the Mines' employees?"

"But Serabu isn't dead yet!" Who was he to write off my hospital?

"No. So in the meantime I promise our security guards will give twenty-four hour protection from rebels or looters."

"Thank you." I suddenly remembered my middle class manners – the man was genuinely trying to help. "The Sisters will appreciate that."

"Well… Serabu does lie between us and the rebels, I'm not being entirely altruistic."

"So, we make a good outpost?" I raised an eyebrow.

"You know how heavily we rely on Serabu, Emily," Rob sighed. "We want you to reopen."

"Hmmm."

"But if it doesn't, why not continue Serabu's work here?"

Rob had argued me out of my excuse to go home. The problem with proclaiming principles was that then people expected you to stick to them. Bloody hell! I put my spectacles on the bar next to a third G and T and screwed my knuckles into the ridge between my eyebrows.

How had it all landed on my doorstep? Just because Philippe's contract had happened to end and Dan had just happened to be in Freetown. I sighed. Philippe had his family to think of and Dan had his wife. All I had was a touch of unrequited love. I picked up my drink – so nice after endless Star beers – and peered out from the bar to the pool, the surface ruffled by a little breeze, twinkling in the moonlight.

"Having Emily work here sounds like a grand idea now," said Brendan.

"Mighty," agreed Gregory.

"And you're just the person for the job, Emily," simpered Brendan. "You've got a mighty reputation you know. We'd hate to lose you."

"You can stay in the ex-Managing Director's house," Rob pressed on. "There's a gas oven, hot showers, air-conditioning of course, fridge, coffee percolator…"

"Chocolate?" I perked up.

Rob laughed. "Yes of course. An unlimited supply of Swiss chocolate."

"Well…"

"Think about it." Rob stood up and patted my back. "I'll see you back at the house."

Rob left me surrounded by his priestly accomplices, intent on claiming my soul with their conspiracy of luxury and ego stroking. Of course, that was exactly the way to go about it. I was too bloody exhausted to argue any further, and after a few more gins and Irish charmer compliments, my head was in the clouds, my brain was mush and my signature was on the dotted line.

QUEEN WITHOUT A THRONE

The chocolate fairy came in the night. I was sitting, tucked up in my duvet, tearing open the second bar of creamy Lindt when Michelle appeared with fresh coffee and croissants. "Bon appetite."

I set aside chocolate (temporarily) and stuffed in a croissant instead.

"Emily, I must say to you, everybody is talking about Serabu today. There is a little bad feeling that the hospital has closed."

"Have those priests been talking?"

"I don't know, but the staff, they think the evacuation was premature. It is easy to say now we know the rebels have not come." Michelle rubbed my shoulders.

"Not yet. Anyway, it's none of their business. Oh, these croissants are heaven. Are there any more?"

"You are very welcome, but it will be lunch in one hour."

After lunch, I decided to indulge in all the luxuries the Mines' Expatriate Compound had on offer and go for a swim. I dug my costume out of my hastily packed rucksack and skipped down the veranda steps. The Easts' houseboy called after me. "Quick quick, run, Dr. Em. Dem rebels de come."

"Hmmph!" I turned my back on him and marched down to the pool. Seconds later a ten-year-old ambushed me from behind a tree, pointing his finger-rifle.

"Look, dem rebels. Bang bang."

"Ah! You little…" I was about to practise my Krio expletives, but held my tongue. My giggling assailant looked just like Nurse. What had happened to Nurse and Maternity? But before I could dwell on how Nurse would survive without volunteers to steal eggs from, two expatriate wives drinking coffee on their shady balcony called out.

"It's the brave Dr. Emily from Serabu Hospital, off to the pool!"

"Don't worry, rebels probably can't swim."

"Kushe," I replied through gritted teeth and walked a little faster.

No normal person would venture under the sun mid-afternoon, so the pool offered sanctuary from snide remarks. Not for long. Within minutes I was parboiled and doubled over from a well-deserved stitch, so I retreated onto a lounger beneath a palm tree. I pulled out Thomas Hardy and tipped into recline. This was the life!

Ten minutes later, I cast the book aside. "Tess, you silly cow! Just tell Angel you love him and save us all a lot of trouble." I stretched to gaze at the lush green underbelly of the palm tree. Now what? Here I was, a cowardly intruder in Heaven, my hospital held in limbo and my love interest... uninterested. Hmmph. I was worse than Tess, lying around waiting for fate to squash me – it was time to take positive action. Serabu's fate wasn't really in my hands, but who said Klaus wasn't interested? I had never asked.

"Right then, Dr. Emily, just tell Klaus how you feel." Hmmm. It shouldn't be so difficult – Mokanje was halfway to Moyamba, and hadn't Klaus said CARE often collected supplies from the Mines? There was probably even a direct radio link! The boy had a motorbike, so all I had to do was invite him over.

Perked up by the simple plan, I dived back in the pool and swam an invigorating few lengths. A confident new woman, I was climbing up the steps when Rob appeared from under the palm trees by the empty bar.

"Gin, Doc?" offered Rob. "For courage to fight those rebels."

"Not you too!" I spluttered. "This whole damned compound has been haranguing me. It's all very well for you lot, locked behind these walls with security men on the gates."

"I'm sorry. We've only just realised how comforting it was to know that Serabu was there for us if we got sick and now... well, we really want you to stay."

"You could all try being kind to me and my Serabu friends."

"We're not doing very well, are we?" Rob sat on the lounger. "Actually, I came to apologise for pressing you so hard last night. Michelle says I'm an insensitive bastard."

"Well then," I sniffed. "A gin would be very nice."

"Good. Why don't you stay, as our guest only? You probably need a couple of weeks break before making any big decisions."

"Perhaps. Any chance of sending a message to CARE in Moyamba?"

"Moyamba? Why?"

"A friend."

"Ah." Rob smiled. "If we radio him this afternoon, then you'll stay?"

"Okay," I shrugged. Yes, yes, yes!

So with that, I moved into the ex-Managing Director's house, complete with flower-entwined veranda, gold-trimmed bathroom and fully stocked freezer. The CARE worker on radio duty told me Klaus was out in the villages and wasn't expected back for a few days, so I settled down to my new found opulence and waited.

By day, I drank coffee with the wives, swam and played tennis. There was even a squash court! Come on Klaus, get in touch. By night, I was plied with gin at the bar. Michelle took me on quietly as an addition to her three children, feeding me meals and chocolate whilst her five-year-old allowed me first lick of the cake-baking spoon and her baby gurgled as happily on my knee as he did on anyone else's. It was luxury. It was bliss. It was boring.

On the sixth night there was a knock at the door. A waif stood, motorcycle helmet in hand, scabs covering his face, forearms, legs, and presumably all the other bits in between.

"Klaus!" I squealed, throwing my arms around him. "Have you got AIDS or something?"

"Thanks, Doc, now I really feel better." He hugged back. "Hiding from the rebels in style, I see."

"Don't you bloody start! You told me to leave."

"Yes, and you didn't pay me the slightest bit of attention," he smiled. "Anyway, I was worried about you. I'm glad you're safe."

"How sweet!" My spine tingled. There it was again. He was worried about me!

"Will you allow a mere mechanic across your hallowed doorstep?"

"Do come in to my humble abode." I bowed and flung open the

249

patio doors. "I'd better feed you some real food."

"Yes please. Hey, not bad." Klaus looked round my palace and threw his arms open to the cool air. "Mmmm. Air-conditioning. Goodbye eczema! Oh, before I forget, I'm just back from Freetown. I've got a letter for you."

"Great!"

Kushe Em,

I'm so sorry about Serabu, are you okay? It's been chaos here. First the Canadians whisk Louise away, leaving us with only two doctors. The Sisters weren't leaving, so Sheilagh and I stayed. Then Sheilagh fell in a pothole and broke her arm. She didn't fancy the chicken treatment, so she's gone back to Ireland to have it plated. So that leaves me. There was supposed to be a Dr. Eelco coming from Holland, but I don't suppose anybody will be coming now. And then Segbwema Hospital closed, so I've got all their patients and, worse still, I've got nowhere to send my surgical cases. Help!

So if you're looking for another job, come and teach me some surgery. Wouldn't that be weird, you and me working together after all? Got to fly, there are still hundreds in Outpatients.

Love Morag

Poor Morag. I'd have to find a way up to Panguma to help out.

"... and to think all of this is only an hour from Moyamba," Klaus was saying.

"What? Only an hour?" My mind started buzzing. Suddenly Rob's East's job offer sounded very attractive indeed. After all, it was a way of being available to my Serabu patients, wasn't it? Perhaps I could even negotiate the use of a vehicle into my contract. Hell, I would even learn to ride a motorbike. In fact, Klaus could teach me himself. This was my big chance. I would smother him in luxury, take him for a swim in the pool, offer him a hot bath, drown him in gin (or beer, if he insisted), fatten him up with Western fare and then when he was mellow, I would oh so subtly slide in some comment about undying love.

Emily, Emily, Emily. What about Morag? And to think I always hated those girls who abandoned their friends for the sake of a man.

"Not a bad life," sighed Klaus. We were floating on our backs, side by side in the moonlight. So far, the 'plan' was going really well.

"Yes, I've adapted rapidly to refugee status."

"You and our esteemed leader."

"Huh? Where's our Field Director gone?"

"Home," said Klaus

"Home home?"

"On holiday! BA gave him two free flights!"

"But we're in the middle of a rebel invasion!" I spluttered.

"Yep, he's back in old smokey watching *Eastenders*. He dropped into VSO in London, and they thought we'd all been evacuated," Klaus laughed. "Now he's stuck in London coz the Foreign Office won't let anyone return to Salone until things settle down."

"So how's Nick?"

"He's thanking the higher powers for Jo."

"I'll bet. Any news on Sule?"

"No 'fraid not, but you won't recognise the office."

"Good for Jo."

"Yep, it was obviously crying out for a woman's touch. So what's for dinner, Doc?"

"Well, now It's a surprise!" What was the most delicious thing I could rustle up with my pantry full of ingredients? It would have to include cheese, of course, with chocolate for after.

"Dr, Em?" Sia, an impressively obese nurse from the clinic, suddenly obscured my view of the stars. I choked on a mouthful of water, flipped onto my front and swam to the side.

"What?"

"We get one patient for you."

No, no! Not tonight! I wasn't bored tonight. "What's wrong with Dr. Momoh?" I spluttered. So much for my big evening. So much for being a guest of the Mines. "Can't Dr. Momoh sort it out?" I repeated when Sia refused to reply. She folded her arms. "Sia?"

"Dr. Momoh say he need surgery."

"And does he?"

"Lamin very sick."

"But you've only got a treatment room! I know you're well stocked for drugs and dressings and things, but surely you don't keep theatre equipment?"

"We get a couch in that treatment room," shrugged Sia. "And two theatre packs-self."

"Okay." I hauled myself dripping from the pool. "Okay." I turned sadly to Klaus. "Sorry-oh."

"Oh don't worry about me, I'm quite happy."

"Keys." I rattled my keys and dropped them down on a lounger. "Look in the fridge and pantry for something to eat."

"No problem." Klaus flipped back onto his back and sculled down the pool. "I'll get dinner on, Doc."

"Thanks," I smiled. House-trained too! I dried myself off and pulled my dress over my swimsuit. "Let's go then, Sia."

Dr. Momoh had vanished, but he was right about Lamin. He would need surgery and very soon. Tears were streaming down Lamin's face as I touched the exquisitely tender grapefruit in his groin. It was a strangulated hernia, so called because it throttled loops of bowel until they died and rotted, killing the patient shortly thereafter. Strangulated hernias were tricky enough with top surgeons in the best of conditions, but here? And more to the point, without Tiange?

Our theatre for the evening was like any treatment room you might find in a GP's surgery, perfect for dressings, lancing boils and suturing small cuts, but a tad cosy for major abdominal surgery. Sia had sent a security guard from the front gate to find reinforcements and an hour later we had two more nurses, one from Dr. Momoh's clinic… and AJ!

"What are you doing here, AJ?"

"Person not there in Serabu to buy poyo. I get new job," he grinned. "Mines' clinic cleaner!"

The two Mines' nurses hadn't been in an operating theatre since they were students under Sister Hilary, so that left the new clinic cleaner as the most experienced scrub nurse. Urgh!

AJ sorted out the theatre pack and I eyed up the instruments cautiously. "Well I think that's probably all we need." Oh Tiange, where are you? "Right Sia, you're the anaesthetist."

"Dr. Em I no able!" she protested.

"Who else shall I ask, Sia? Mr. East?"

"Oh but Dr. Em…"

"Aw fo do, Sia. I'll put the spinal in, you just monitor the patient," I reassured her. "What are you looking out for?"

"Sister Hilary say the blood pressure get for go down. Maybe by too much because Lamin don dehydrate. I give plenty of fluid in the drip and check his blood pressure every five minutes. He awake, so I get for talk to him."

"Perfect." Gosh, Serabu had a bloody good nursing school. It would be criminal to lose it. "Okay, let's go."

I put the spinal in then scrubbed with some proper surgical scrubbing fluid under real running water and pulled on crisp new rubber gloves fresh from the packet. Unfortunately they were size eights. They may have fitted Dr. Momoh, but on me they flapped around like outsize Marigolds.

At least Lamin was thin and the hernia loosened a little as his muscles relaxed under the spinal anaesthetic. Being careful not to nick the excess glove, I made my incision and cut the ring of tissue that was starving the herniated bowel of oxygen.

So here it was. My second-ever bowel resection and anastomoses, but this time it wasn't Mr. Lord sheep's intestines, it was the real thing. Breathing deeply, I took a clamp from AJ.

"We've done it, Dr. Em," AJ exclaimed half an hour later. "Better than Sister Hilary-self!"

Wow. The best thing anyone had ever said to me. Look, look, Mr. Lord, the dead bowel has been removed and I have rejoined the ends with a fully patent anastomoses. No leaks!

"I couldn't have done it without you AJ." Well I couldn't.

"You na fine surgeon, Dr. Em!" The first-year student slapped me on the back.

"AJ!" I chastised. "Sterility! We've still got to close."

"Sorry-oh Dr. Em," giggled AJ. "I don forget. I go change my gloves."

"Fortunately there's no shortage here, but why such huge ones, Sia?"

"Dr. Momoh's size."

"So what do the nurses wear for dressings or delivering babies?"

"The same gloves."

"Size eights?" The babies are lucky not to be suffocated. "Does Dr. Momoh ever take blood, or suture wounds, or lance boils?"

"We do all that."

"Does Dr. Momoh ever actually need gloves?"

"He's the doctor."

Rather than asking Sia if that was a yes or a no, I bit my lip and got on with repairing the hernia, tucking the bowel safely back in the abdominal cavity.

"Don don. Thank you team!"

It was nearly midnight when I left the tiny operating theatre. Lamin still had to get through the next few days, but the early signs were good. Elated, I hurried back to my luxury quarters. What with another life saved and the miraculous appearance of Klaus, there was no way anyone could persuade me to go back to boring old Britain now.

EMERGENCY OPERATION:
PLEASE BRING
WELDING EQUIPMENT

Cheesy tomatoey smells greeted me as I opened the door. Hmmm, Klaus, what for chop tonight? Gentle snoring came from the spare bedroom. Rats! But his lasagne was excellent, if a little crunchy round the edges. My big confession would have to wait until breakfast.

And so it was that my undying love was garbled out over a bowl of Cornflakes.

"You'll get over it," was all Klaus had to say about that. "Wow! Real Cornflakes!"

"Oh, okay" I slurped my coffee.

"Oh, Emily look at you."

"Hoi, what do you mean?" I glared at him. "I get body?"

"Yes, lucky you. I wish I got body. My insides have vanished down the latrine and I'm shedding my outsides like a snake. There's nothing left of my body."

"You think I'm fat," I sulked.

"Nah. Voluptuous."

"Oh yeah? What's your problem, then? Scared of big strong girls?"

"Too right!" Klaus laughed. "And you're the biggest and strongest of the lot."

"Hmmph!"

"You're always so optimistic and so bloody healthy!"

"What?" Rejected because I was an optimist? Where had he been the last seven months?

"Aw fo do."

Aw fo do? Bloody hell! Aw fo do! So that was that. My grand passion. Fortunately there was still a bar of chocolate left in the fridge that I had been saving for Klaus. Forget that! I munched it down myself on the way to see Lamin.

Lamin wasn't great either. His temperature was up, his pulse rapid and his breathing shallow. Not too surprising really; after all, a rotten bowel had festered inside him for days. I knew strangulated hernias had a huge mortality rate, even when real surgeons operated on them with the help of real anaesthetists and real scrub nurses in real hospitals, but I wanted a miracle to cheer me up. "Cheer you up?" said the little voice on my shoulder. "What about Lamin? He's the one in trouble here. Do you only ever think of yourself?"

Yes.

Klaus had left a little note when I returned:

Kushe, Doc,
Sorry, had to get back to work, but how about that trip to see Morag?
Let's have that game of squash and go up first thing Saturday.
Love
Klaus xxxxx

"Hmmph, don't bother with the kisses, mate." I scrunched up the paper. Where would I put my hands on a six-hour journey on the back of Klaus' motorbike? I'd have to cling on to him else I'd fall off. No thank you. I was humiliated enough already. And Panguma was still in forbidden territory, so I was too scared to go without him. Now if our roles had been reversed, I was sure Morag would have come flying to help me. But that was Morag. Unfortunately Klaus had been right about me that very first week in Sierra Leone – I was not Heroic Doctor material.

I knew what I was. I was jealous of Morag for soldiering on through adversity whilst we had abandoned ship, I was scared of the rebels and I was scared of all that hard work. I would stay here at the Mines, where there wasn't too much work and plenty of food, drink and chocolate and perhaps a handsome Mines' engineer? How many deadly sins did that make? Pride, cowardice, greed, lust... Oh, who cared? I would radio CARE to tell Klaus not to bother. "Sorry Morag."

Deciding I might as well compound my misery with alcohol, I went down to the bar. It was scarcely eleven, but what the hell.

Father Brendan was already there, drinking Star.

"Hello, Brendan, you're indulging early," I sniped. At least I was not expected to be virtuous. I ordered a lemonade in a loud voice, just for spite. I would have that gin and tonic later.

"Hello, Emily. I'm after getting some bad news." I wasn't sure I wanted to hear Brendan's bad news.

"Oh?"

"Gregory says Serabu's closing for good. It's official."

"Oh," I repeated. "Oh."

"I'm sorry."

"So that's that, is it?" I asked bleakly.

"I'm afraid so. Joe's going home next week."

"Really?"

"Yes. We decided he'd better take his sabbatical and see his doctor back home. Joe is no use to anyone if he dies of a stroke."

"At last, someone's talking some sense but I'm surprised he agreed."

"Gregory wasn't after giving him a choice. Besides there's hardly anyone left in Serabu now." Brendan paused for a mouthful of beer. "Joe will come back in September. The church will not close."

"Hmmph." I was pleased that Joe would return, for the sake of the people of Serabu, but heathen that I was, I resented that the church would stay open at the expense of my hospital. "What about the others?"

"They took poor Ignatius back to Ireland, Tom and Dan will have been sent back to the States, and Bernadette's been redeployed to Freetown."

"But the Mines' security people went out Sumbuya way yesterday," I protested. "All clear on the south-eastern front, they said."

"So I hear," agreed Brendan. "But 'tis all about money, Emily. The Catholic mission isn't about free handouts. They feel the Saloneans have been passively accepting aid for too long now."

"But that's not true!" I howled. "Our staff are terrific. Admittedly our patients can't always pay their bills, but they just don't have the money. It's not their fault the economy's in free fall."

"Jaysus, Emily, it's not my decision!" Brendan threw his hands up. "But Serabu's been on a downward slope ever since Hilary left."

"No it hasn't! Our attendances have gone up by nearly half!"

"For a few months perhaps. But now you're closed."

"That's not fair. We were told to close!"

"Life's not fair." Brendan took a slug of his beer. "Salone must be after teaching you that?" He was right. Life was bloody unfair.

"Make that a gin and tonic please," I told the barman.

So here I was, Dr. Emily Joy, ex-optimist, chocoholic, sort-of-surgeon, with no man and no hospital. And I couldn't even call myself a big strong girl any more. Big strong girls would always help friends in need. Big strong girls weren't wimps.

So after several gin and tonics with Brendan, I returned to my three-bedroomed house to pack. I'd scrounge a lift to Freetown in the morning and get Nick to put me on the first flight home.

"Emily?" Michelle called from the patio doors. "You are there?"

"In here."

"Brendan told me about Serabu. I am very sorry." Michelle paused and looked at my things spread out on the bed. "Eh bien. You are leaving?"

"I'm sorry," I sobbed. Michelle took me in her arms.

"Do not be sorry. You have tried very hard for your hospital." She was assuming all my tears were for Serabu, when in reality they were for myself. I considered telling this kind woman about my thwarted love life, but it seemed all too pathetic in comparison to the end of Salone's best hospital – the region's lifeline for thirty years.

"You and Rob have been so good to me, it's just that…"

"Shhh. Shhh," Michelle interrupted. "I will tell Rob you are going, then we will say no more about it."

"Thank you. Sorry," I sniffed. Better they thought me a principled doctor, mourning her hospital than a frustrated spinster sulking because she could not attract her man.

"You will come for a big dinner tonight, yes?"

"Yes." I blew my nose.

Food could be relied upon to soothe most of my ills and Michelle's dinner gave sufficient fortification for me to assess Lamin's postoperative progress before bed. I crept into the clinic with the same dread that a borderline student opens exam results...

A+! Lamin had farted. Yes! Yes! Yes!

I could go home now, content in the knowledge that although I hadn't saved Serabu Hospital, I had saved lives. And those other goals? Well, any weight lost under Pa George had been replaced by Michelle, and you know about my love life. My soul was still up for grabs and I was still the same single, selfish, only child with no real commitments or beliefs, but at least I had seen some of the best that human nature had to offer. Meanwhile I was going to have a damned good night's sleep, free from worries or responsibilities.

My plans for a long lie in were interrupted by a seven o'clock knock at the door.

"Coming." I wrapped a lappa round me. "Kushe, Pa. What's the problem?" I yawned.

"I get radio message for you." The Mines' watchman handed me a piece of paper.

We get emergency operation but the theatre is sealed with arc weld. Laygby has started pains. Please bring welding machine and small generator for electrical purpose.
Moses

"Oh God! Laygby!" I had completely forgotten about Laygby. How could I? It would be fatal if she laboured for too long.

"I'm coming."

Without brushing my hair, I dashed up to the main Mines' compound and barged into the radio room. Men arriving for their day's duty looked at me in amazement.

"Kushe, Dr. Em," the radio-operator swung round on his barstool.

"Kushe. Can I speak to Serabu?"

"No problem." He put on his headphones, twiddled a few knobs and shouted into the mike. I danced from foot to foot. Oh why oh why, had I forgotten Laygby? Serabu was all welded up, and who would be left to help? Moses would have to bring her to Mokanje in the Landrover and somehow we'd have to manage a Caesarean in the treatment room. But there had hardly been room for a very thin Lamin, me and two nurses, never mind for pregnant lady, a baby and an extra nurse to look after it. Aw fo du.

"Sorry-oh, Dr. Em. No reply. This morning-self, the radio was too much faint. Moses say diesel don don and they no able to charge the radio."

"Damn." That meant no diesel for the Landrover either. I'd have to go to Serabu myself. And I supposed I would have to find a welder – at least Mining Companies had all that sort of stuff.

"Um, excuse me. Can you help?" I asked the first chap I met. "I need some welding equipment to do an emergency operation at Serabu."

"You no get scalpel, Dr. Em," he laughed. "See Mr. Kallon."

"Excuse me, Mr. Kallon. Do you have welding equipment? I need to do an operation?"

"You get for talk to Mr. Conteh."

"Mr. Conteh, I need the welding equipment to do an operation at Serabu. Can you help?"

Finally Rob East appeared. "What's all the commotion, Emily?"

"I need someone to unweld theatre so I can do an emergency Caesarean on one of our Nurses."

"I don't believe you," guffawed Rob, then saw my face. "Okay, let's go to Serabu."

The goats had seized the initiative from the rebels and were occupying the hospital grounds. They lay contentedly in the shade of the empty wards, undisturbed by our truck's engine as we pulled up outside Outpatients. It was so quiet. No voices raised to argue over bills, nor babies crying as Latif pricked their fingers to check for malaria, nor was Nurse Sankoh trying to sell oranges and groundnuts to those waiting patiently in snaking queues. There was just the gentle snoring of the two Mines' security men, stretched out on the long wooden benches that were usually filled with patients.

"Kushe, gentlemen," said Rob. "I can see who we have to thank for keeping Serabu free from rebels."

"No rebels, Mr. Rob." Mr. Yambasu, the first, sprang up with a military salute. The second smiled sweetly, sliding the yellow poyo container under the bench with his foot.

"I am most relieved," Rob replied.

"Dr. Em, you don come!" Mariama came flying out of nowhere and hugged me over and over, laughing and crying. "You are here, you are here! We thought you don go home!"

"Mariama, what a welcome!" I gasped, all the air hugged out of me. "How's Hindolu?"

"He is very fine. He can walk!"

"Great! And Layghy?" I asked anxiously.

"She is labouring too much. We have prepared her for theatre. Tiange is with her."

"Tiange is still here?"

"She came back yesterday."

"Any others to help us?"

"Earnest never left. He don arrange shifts to guard the hospital and the village."

"Our very own vigilante!" I clapped. "So with you and Earnest and Tiange, we're in business. Is the generator working?"

"Diesel, don don," apologised Mariama.

"Aw fo do," I sighed. "At least it's daylight, Let's go."

"Oh Dr. Em, I gladdi for see you," gasped Layghy, the only patient on the ward. It was weirder than seeing a single passenger on a poda-poda.

"Kushe, how di body, Laygby?" I took her hand.

"I tell God tenki," she smiled weakly. "Tenki-ya, Dr. Em. Plenti tenki." I squeezed her hand, embarrassed to receive such gratitude from one I had abandoned. Her contractions were very strong now, and her weakened womb wall would not hold for much longer.

"Kushe Dr. Em," beamed Tiange. "We are ready. Mr. Yambusa get for open dem doors jis now."

A small crowd of the remaining staff had gathered outside Theatre to watch the grand opening. Mr. Yambusa sizzled his way down the doors and flung them open. He strode into the theatre like John Wayne into a saloon bar. Earnest and Patrick Kpukoma carried Laygby, the star of the show, in on the stretcher behind him.

With Laygby installed centre stage, Earnest slipped in a spinal whilst we scrubbed to start the performance. The cast was triple the usual quorum, as everyone who had remained or returned to Serabu were in on the act. It was all Mariama could do to keep the dusty, oil-streaked Mr. Yambusa out of Theatre.

We celebrated our reunion with the best show in the business in the best Theatre in the country. I pulled a fine new man into the world and handed the ten pound bundle to a delighted Laygby. His furious cry was only matched in volume by the cheers of the audience.

"Serabush is back!" proclaimed Tiange.

How could I tell her that Serabu's death warrant had already been signed?

I changed the subject. "What happened to that bobo, Nurse?"

"Nurse and Maternity live with us, Dr. Em," said Patrick. "Ma Kpukoma missed Simone and Pierre too much."

"You are very kind, Patrick."

"Notto so, Dr. Em. Maternity is a beautiful girl and Nurse is a fine worker. My wife teaches him to dye gara. We were blessed with only one daughter and no son. Now we get three pickins."

"I'm so pleased." Trust Nurse to land on his feet. God helps those who help themselves.

"So no rebels?"

"Two rounds of gunfire no more," said Earnest.

"Gunfire? How awful!" I exclaimed. Tiange threaded a needle with a length of suture to sew up the first layer of Laygby's abdominal wall.

"No problem, Dr. Em," explained Tiange. "Only the soldiers who try shoot a pig."

"Are there wild boar round here?"

"No no, Dr. Em. One of Patrick's pigs."

"It took four soldiers two rounds of ammunition to kill an ordinary domestic pig?!"

"They don miss!" laughed Earnest. "Too much poyo."

"Just as well you set up your own vigilantes, Earnest. But how about the hospital? Did any patients come?"

"A few," said Mariama. "Patrick and I don treat some outpatients."

And the Catholic mission said there wasn't enough commitment from the local people? Why wasn't there someone here today, to see with their own eyes our staff's motivation? But our funders were in a land far away, trying to do their best with only so much money to distribute. MT had been right all along, Serabu's only way forward was self-sufficiency, charging reasonable fees and scrimping and saving. We couldn't stake our future on crumbs from the Western World's table, as there were other hospitals and schools and missions in other countries, all with their own stories to tell, all competing for those crumbs and their own survival.

Well, our staff had proved they would fight for survival, so I would fight too.

I was their Medical Superintendent, and I was going to set myself just one goal: Get my hospital back! Oh and the little matter of an unresolved squash match.

PANGUMA

Friday evening, Mokanje squash court.

I beat him, I beat him, I beat him! HA!

I must say Klaus was very sporting about it and I, well I hardly gloated at all! We shared a companionable beer at the bar and I decided I'd go to Panguma with him after all. For a few days, just for a token of moral support for Morag. I fell asleep contented. The Medical Superintendent of Serabu Hospital did not need a mere man. She had friends to visit and hospitals to open.

After six nerve-racking hours surfing Salonean potholes on Klaus' refurbished Honda, we finally arrived at Panguma Hospital. Where Serabu was the heavy rough that, at the best of times, could only be kept under control by a scythe, Panguma was all fairways and greens. But the bustle of patients and nurses running back and forth was reassuringly familiar.

Naturally Morag was out saving lives. So we knocked on the convent door instead. A nun greeted us.

"Hello, I'm a friend of Morag's, Emily Jo…"

"It's Dr. Emily!" she squealed. "Father, it's Dr. Emily!"

A smiling man in his late forties, looking very relaxed in shorts and a gara shirt appeared. "Ah, Dr. Emily. We are delighted to have you here. I'm Felim."

"Nice to meet you, Father."

"A new doctor, thank the lord!" said one of three sisters clustered at the doorway.

"The famous Dr. Emily." Father Felim pumped my hand, grinning.

"Isn't it nice to be wanted?" whispered Klaus behind me. "The *famous* Dr. Emily." Telling Klaus to fok-off didn't seem appropriate to the company, so I just smiled graciously.

"And this must be your young man?" Felim stretched out his hand to Klaus. My smile slipped a little. Klaus didn't flinch.

"Klaus. Von Hondabenda to my friends."

"Mighty! Stars all round!"

The next morning Klaus fixed the hospital Landrover and Felim's motorbike whilst Morag took me on her rounds. She floated from overcrowded ward to overcrowded ward and patient to patient with a sweet smile that put every frightened child and old man at ease. It was gratifying to see a doctor in action, running a hospital in full working order, assisted by smartly uniformed nurses. The only drawback were the queues and queues of patients.

"Good heavens, Harrods' sale eat your heart out. Is it always like this?" I asked when I had finally persuaded her to stop for a coffee and a banana.

"Panguma's catchment area is bigger than Serabu, but it's been chaos since the rebels closed Segbwema."

"Poor you." The sight of all those patients to see was giving me palpitations. Only Lamin and Laygby had interrupted my life of luxury in the past ten days. "Can't you nab Segbwema's doctors?"

"They've all gone, bar one who's in Freetown trying to re-open Segbwema for refugees."

"So perhaps we'll end up working together after all? Just in Salone instead of Zambia."

"Funny how things turn out," Morag laughed. "But you'll get Serabu back. Felim was really tickled by your antics with the welder!"

"How did he hear about that?"

"Catholic mission radio. Your Moses should be in PR!"

"Well we need as much help as we can get. Officially Serabu is don don."

"Can't Hilary help? From what I've heard, Hilary makes things happen."

"Trouble is, Philippe reckons Hilary believes Serabu's a bit of a white elephant. It's pretty inaccessible, now the roads and railways have crumbled. And I think she'd prefer the money to be spent on

Community Health."

"Fair enough, but you still need Serabu to train the nurses to do the outreach stuff."

"Good point. But it's not in your interest to provide all these good arguments, Morag. If Serabu does reopen, how will you cope alone? You can't go on at this rate."

"Our nurses are terrific – all Serabu trained, you'll be pleased to know."

"Really? We're the best you know." I fluffed up my feathers.

"But we can't sit chatting." Morag stood up. "TB ward next."

"Kushe, kushe, Dr. Em. How di body?"

"Good Lord, it's Pa Ndanema! And Bockerie! What are you two doing here?"

"We get for finish our treatment. Dr. Morag say one week to go."

"But how did you get here?"

"We de walka," Pa Ndanema shrugged.

"A hundred and fifty miles! On one leg!"

"No other hospital is open."

"No. Probably not. Are you causing trouble?"

"Oh, Dr. Em, we have been very good. Notto so, Dr. Morag?"

"Very good," she agreed.

"We get charity feeding," boasted Bockerie.

"All our TB patients get charity feeding," explained Morag.

"No wonder they all behave!"

Panguma was beginning to sound like a good place to work.

Morag vanished again that evening.

"Let me help," I offered. Her workload was making me feel guilty and what would I say to Klaus all evening?

"Don't worry, I'll put you to it tomorrow. There's a couple of beers in the fridge."

"Really, cold Star?" exclaimed Klaus.

"Twenty-four hour electricity here you know," boasted Morag.

Panguma was looking better by the minute. "Be good, you two."

I gaped at her. Had I hinted anything about Klaus? I didn't think so, but she was pretty perceptive. "Meaning?"

Klaus was sniggering. I kicked the bastard under the table.

"Well, you know. You'd make a good couple," she said cheerfully.

"He won't have me," I snapped.

"Why ever not?" joked Morag. "Look, I really better go. We go see back."

There was a knock at the door. "Dr. Em?"

"Yes?"

"Dr. Morag say you get for do Caesarean," puffed the nurse.

"I'm coming."

"Sorry Emily, but I've never done a Section," said Morag as we scrubbed in Panguma's little-used theatre.

"Well, I'm a lot better than I was."

"I'm going to have to start aren't I, with no Segbwema?"

"God, Morag, if I can do it, you'll have no trouble. Come on."

I assisted Morag while she completed the first Caesarean Section at Panguma Hospital for five years.

"Who needs Segbwema?" I said as Morag jiggled baby Dr-Morag.

"I do! Or I need you," she retorted, but there was a note of triumph in her voice. As anticipated, she was a natural.

Next day Morag did her rounds, whilst I made a start at Outpatients and Klaus serviced the generator. We all met back at Morag's for lunch.

Felim appeared at the door. "I'm after getting some mighty news."

"What?" we chorused.

"The new doctor's arriving tomorrow."

"Really?" Morag gasped, with a look of such pure relief that I couldn't stop myself hugging her.

"That's great!" said Klaus.

"Mighty news!" said Felim. "Mighty."

Dr. Eelco Krijn arrived the next day, fired with schoolboy enthusiasm. He was a tousle-headed Dutchman, who put me in mind of how Philippe must have been when he arrived, before the flesh had fallen off his bones and MT's purse strings had strangled his idealism. But food was more plentiful in Panguma and its funding more generous than Serabu's. Even the broken legged chickens were fatter. Eelco would do well.

That evening we helped him unpack case loads of medical and surgical books, various bits of equipment, syringes, needles and rubber gloves, plus seeds for carrots, onions and flowers. And a teddy bear.

"For Zietje." Eelco straightened the lapels on the bear's stripy waistcoat. "Karin's bringing her next month. Look, here they are." He pulled out a photo frame, and sat his beautiful smiling wife and dimple-cheeked baby with her dad's curly hair and endearing grin, in the middle of the dining-room table.

"Wow! You're one lucky guy, mate," sighed Klaus.

"I know," blushed Eelco.

"Isn't she just adorable?" enthused Morag. Hell's Bells, that gorgeous little girl even made me feel broody.

"Ah, but I have forgotten something." Eelco pulled a letter from his trouser pocket. "They gave me this at the Freetown convent."

The letter was from Bernadette, asking me to return to Freetown to discuss their decision on Serabu. I frowned.

"Bad news?" asked Klaus.

"I don't know." I showed him the letter.

"Well you'd better get down there ASAP. I'll take you on the Honda tomorrow."

"All the way to Freetown?" I exclaimed. "Would you really, Klaus?"

"Anything for you, Doc. The sooner you get down there, the sooner you can get that hospital up and running again."

"Yes, you can do it, Emily," beamed Eelco.

For a moment, I almost believed them.

"Here we are madam, the Freetown convent," announced my pal Klaus.

"Aren't you coming in?" I extracted my head from the helmet - glad to be free of the overheated goldfish bowl.

"Nah. Better get back to CARE."

"Sweet Jesus, it's Emily already!" Bernadette burst through the convent's mesh door to greet me.

"We heard all about the welding equipment; oh, you're a mighty woman!"

"It's lovely to see you." I hugged her.

"So how's Laygby? And the baby? A little boy wasn't it?"

"Yes. A grand fellow." I smiled at the precious memory. "They're both just fine."

"I'm being very rude now. Enough questions. Come inside and sit down." Bernadette took my hand. "And your young man?" She held out her other hand to Klaus. I cringed again. Klaus was unperturbed.

"Thanks, Sister, but Preston's expecting me at CARE," he smiled and put his helmet back on. "See you, Doc."

"We go see back," I called as he kicked his motorbike back into action. "Thanks Klaus."

Three revs of his engine and he was gone as the sun set on Freetown.

"What a nice young man. Tea?" Bernadette lifted a teapot on the tray that sat in permanent readiness for visitors. "I think it's still hot."

"Thank you." I flopped into the flowery patterned armchair in the airy sitting-room and lifted the gold-rimmed china teacup off its saucer. "Father Brendan said Serabu is closed." I came straight to the point.

"Oh, these are terrible times." Bernadette averted her eyes and toyed with her plain white cup.

"Well? Is it true?"

"My superiors rely on funding from the Catholic Mission you know." She looked up at me. "They've been threatening us with closure for years."

"And the rebels were the perfect excuse. Was that why we were told to close the hospital?"

"Oh no! Oh, please believe me that was genuine concern over the safety of staff and patients." Bernadette looked horrified. "It's just… I mean… oh, I really don't know."

"Bernadette, I'm sorry. I didn't mean it." I touched her arm. "But do the superiors know how marvellous the staff have been? What with Earnest's vigilantes protecting the hospital, Mariama and Patrick treating Outpatients and all those who came to help save Laygby. We deserve another chance."

"We do, we do," agreed Bernadette. "Hilary and I wrote when we closed, pleading for a reprieve."

"So even Sister Hilary couldn't persuade the superiors?"

"They are worried about Serabu's long term sustainability. Hilary just can't leave her work in Bo to come and be our doctor again. Especially now there are all the refugees."

"But the staff can do all sorts without a doctor," I protested. "And besides, don't I count as a doctor?"

"Of course, but Hilary assumed you would go home. Now if we can tell them we have a doctor who is willing to stay after all..."

"What about funding?"

"She did suggest that Serabu could take in refugees until we build up our numbers."

"But refugees won't make us any money."

"My dear Emily, you're beginning to sound like Ignatius."

"I'm sorry, but isn't money the problem?"

"Yes indeed," agreed Bernadette. "But the Catholic Mission has special funds for refugees. It is a cause that people will donate to."

"Ah. The politics of charity," I sighed, "Still, you're right. We might as well play whatever game will bring in the funds."

"You are learning," Bernadette smiled wryly. "Meanwhile there's a mighty fellow who will fight our corner. He is flying out to Ireland to turn his charms on the Superiors."

"Oh yes?"

"In fact I can hear him coming now, with another grand fellow. They are both dying to see you." Bernadette was drowned out by tyres, brakes, slammed doors and laughter outside. The door burst open.

"Well now, would I be hearing the musical voice of our very own Dr. Emily?"

"Nat!" I was too busy throwing my arms round the old rogue to notice a thin pale figure hobble in on crutches behind him.

"Hey girl, what about me?"

"Dan? Did the rebels get you? You look bloody awful."

"Gee thanks."

"They said you'd gone."

"Are you trying to get rid of me?"

"No. It's great to see you." I hugged him too. "But you should be tucked up in bed at home convalescing with that beautiful wife of yours. Seriously, what happened?"

"Nothing as exciting as you and your rebels, I'm afraid," moaned Dan. "A sting ray."

"A sting ray?" I repeated.

"You know, one of those big fish with wings and teeth," Nat prompted helpfully.

"Yes and believe me, this boy had my name written all over it." Dan pointed to a two-penny sized hole punched in his foot, with a sinister red line of infection tracking up to his thigh.

"What a mess!"

"Hey, it's heaps better. I stood on the sonofabitch having farewell drinks with Philippe and Nicole at the Venue."

"Ouch!" I sympathised.

"Philippe felt real bad that he'd abandoned you."

"But he had a family to think of..."

"And our embassy threw Tom out for working in a banned area with no permit, so the guys made me promise to hang around to check you were okay."

"Your knight on shining crutches," Nat winked.

"So why didn't you get slapped on the first plane home?"

"No flights 'til Friday," Dan said sheepishly.

"And I hear the Ex-Assistant-Administrator of Serabu Hospital is going to Ireland to beg for our survival."

"Tomorrow. I thought a personal account of Serabush would help: its rising attendances, the lives saved, the increasing staff morale, and the heroic young lady doctor..." Nat sighed melodramatically.

"Nat!" I punched him in the arm.

"Worth a try," he shrugged.

"And I promise to come back with Cyndi if Nat gets the go ahead from Ireland," said Dan. "I'd hate to miss any more excitement."

"We'd better go to the Venue, then. Cyndi's never going to let you come back unless we feed you up a bit."

"... so apart from the soldiers manfully trying to shoot a twenty stone pig it's all peace and quiet," I concluded to a very harassed Nick. The Field Director was still in Britain on his unscheduled holiday.

"Serabu may well be a haven of peace and tranquillity but you're not allowed back," Nick said, thrusting his forefinger at my chest.

"What's up? Where's our cool, carefree Nick?"

"Aaagh." Nick put his head briefly in his hands then looked up, flicking back his designer fringe. "Thank God for Jo."

"How is she? Any word from Sule?"

"No, not yet."

"Poor Jo. How awful."

"I should send you home," said Nick irritably. "One less person for me to worry about."

"I don't want to go home!"

"Sister Bernadette told me you were hiding in Mokanje. I even heard that you and Klaus had eloped to Panguma."

"Shouldn't listen to rumour, Nick."

"Pah! Panguma is more dangerous than Serabu." Nick gave a Gallic shrug. "And Klaus? I thought he at least was sensible."

"Mokanje isn't off limits, is it? Even the wives and children are still there and they need another doctor."

"You are thinking of defecting from VSO to work for the Mines?" Working for the Mines did not fit into Nick's code of ethics at all.

"Then I'll go back to Serabu."

"This is the blackmail! And if the thumbs are down for Serabu?"

"Then I'll work at Panguma, but Nat won't let them close Serabu."

"Jaysus!" Nat choked on his Star. "When did you become such an optimist?"

Bernadette put Nat on the plane next day, and Dan the day after. I spent the next six days waiting: mornings at the Crown Cafe and afternoons at the Venue. On the seventh day, I wandered into the Crown to find Lindsey, sitting with an older lady.

"Dr. Emily. Over here!" the lady called.

"Er, kushe. Hi Lindsey." My eyes begged an introduction to her mystery companion.

"This is your biggest fan, Em."

"Oh?" I smiled tentatively. My fan? Had Lindsey's granny come on holiday in the middle of a rebel invasion? I looked at the petite lady dressed in gara that Nat would have killed for.

"Hello, pleased to meet you, Mrs. Er..."

"The mighty Dr. Emily. We meet at last. I'm Hilary."

"Sorry?" Lindsey's granny wasn't called Hilary, was she? No. Good Lord it was her! "Sister Hilary?!"

"Hilary, please."

"'The' Sister Hilary. The great Hilary Lyons?"

"Jaysus, will you sit down. Coffee?" I nodded dumbly at the iron angel. "So, have you heard the news?" she asked. I shook my head. "Serabu is to reopen."

My eyes widened.

"Partly thanks to you running around with welding equipment. Apparently Nat told the story, with great flourish altogether."

"He would. Did he sing too?"

"I'm sure he did," laughed Hilary. "But seriously, Bernadette has to stay in Freetown for several weeks to clear some red tape, so you must be willing to go back on your own. Well?"

"Can't you come?"

"I'm afraid not. We have many refugees of our own in Bo."

"Okay," I nodded. "Yes, of course."

"Serabu has a year's grace from refugee funds, then we'll review it."

"Okay."

"It's so good to meet you, Emily. You're a mighty girl."

"You're very sweet, Sister Hil..."

"Hilary. We've been given another chance to do things right. For twenty-five years I ran that hospital, treating every patient that walked through the door. Then I would go back to that dreadful big convent, often alone, whilst the people lived twelve to a hut. They assigned me mystical powers, not really human, you see. I was... I was..."

"The legendary Sister Hilary!" I added.

"Hmmm. Whereas you, Emily..."

"I am full of human weakness," I suggested.

"No, no. Well, yes, of course you are, like the rest of us, but you played football with the villagers!"

"I only touched the ball four times!"

"But you were on the field with them! Don't you see? Serabu has no future unless the people run it themselves. There are so few Sisters left these days, and even if there were, a hierarchy is no way to run a hospital in someone else's country. You volunteers can facilitate the hand-over. Why can't Tiange do the Caesareans and Mariama and Patrick run Outpatients? You see what I'm saying? I did it all wrong."

"Oh, no!" I protested.

"Yes. I was almost… a graven image." Hillary gave a wry smile.

"But, now Serabu really can have a future. The Saloneans have proved it to themselves."

"Let's drink to Serabu Hospital." Lindsey stood up.

"To Serabush!" Hillary lifted her coffee cup. "Pity this isn't something a bit stronger."

"Aw fo du," I giggled at my heroine, who was getting marvellously less angelic by the minute. "Serabush!"

The rains were due again. The storm clouds hovered, ready to ambush the streets of Freetown and someone had jammed the sauna doors shut. Hilary, Bernadette and I drew up contingency plans A to Z and headed out to the VSO office on Monday morning, ready to do battle with the Field Director.

The Field Director was back at his desk under his broken fan, with sweat patches creeping out from his oxters, apparently entirely unrefreshed by his little holiday. He was a good man in the wrong job. His heart was golden where any Salonean child was concerned, but decidedly leaden when it came to we volunteers.

The heavy atmosphere dampened any expression of surprise that Serabu had been closed in the first place, never mind any lust for battle to prevent me from returning. I was rather disappointed, nay alarmed, that I would not be saved from my foolish bravado by a Directorial veto.

Two days later a kindly Mines' engineer I met at the Venue (not uncoincidentally – we VSOs could all spot a potential lift from a hundred paces) offered to take me back as far as Mokanje. I tried to contact Serabu, but news of my triumphant return was lost in the static.

"See ya, Emily." Lindsey hugged me. "I'll come visit. Perhaps Klaus will bring me?"

"Klaus would take you anywhere you wanted, Lindsey."

"Meaning?" Lindsey put her hands on her hips.

"Nothing. It'd be great to see you. I'll need all the company I can get."

"Are you sure you'll be alright?" said Bernadette. "A young girl like you alone, even without rebels?"

"No problem. Earnest and his vigilantes will look after me."

"I'm sure they will, but there are so few staff left…"

"Don't worry Sister, Klaus will keep an eye on her," smiled Lindsey. I shot her a glance but something told me she was right. He probably would.

Moses had left the hospital truck in the Easts' drive, polished out of all recognition and with a tank full of Mines' diesel. Since I was to be the only expatriate in Serabu, Bernadette said I should have my own transport. For emergencies. After nine months of scrounged lifts and poda-podas, I was as excited as I had been on unveiling my first bicycle. Just wait till I told Klaus.

Unfortunately I was about as adept at driving it as I had been the first time on that bicycle. This time I did not have my Dad puffing behind, hanging reassuringly onto the back. There were several false starts as I tried to remember what to do with a clutch, but finally I was hiccoughing out of the Mines' compound.

Heading down the road, watching the speedometer hit thirty miles an hour, I yelped with glee. This was it. I was going back, the last remaining poomui, the conquering heroine, returning to her mission to save the world (or at least a couple of patients). With four bars of Swiss chocolate, a jar of jam, a pound of cheese and a jigsaw puzzle given to me by the Easts' seven-year-old, I was ready for anything.

Coming down the hill into Serabu, I had to turn on my lights as the skies were clogging up with black cloud. By the time I jumped out of the truck outside the convent, God was emptying buckets of water over the compound.

My drumming fists on the convent doors were no competition for the pounding rain – little wonder there was no reply from Moses. I took refuge back behind the wheel and watched the rain splash into the dust and gradually become puddles.

Forty minutes passed and nobody came to meet me. Admittedly they didn't know when I was coming, but I had still rather hoped for fanfares and fireworks. The only cascade was water, rushing off the lean-to's corrugated roof. Even the goats had taken shelter. Only the jungle grass was thriving, drinking up the rain and seeming to grow even higher before my very eyes. Panguma's neatly clipped lawns seemed a long way away.

My enthusiasm of the past few days washed away with the rain into the ditch outside Medical Ward.

"Well, Dr. Emily, you'll sit here forever if you wait for a lull in the rain." I threw open the truck door, jumped down into a puddle and heaved my rucksack on my back. The rain bounced off my glasses and my feet slid in their flip-flops as water streamed over the parched ground that led to my house. The path was now lined with shoulder-high grass that damply fingered my neck as I made my way home.

Home!

Why hadn't I flown home when I'd had the offer, the several offers, from the Field Director? I could have gone with Susan, or Tim, or Philippe and Tom, or Dan. What had made me so keen to come back? To show off to Klaus, Morag and Lindsey's granny? To prove that I was equal to Hilary's challenge? Why couldn't I make my mind up about anything? Why had nobody come to meet me and tell me how marvellous I was for returning? Hmmph.

This was not the grand reopening I had imagined. Aw fo do. I sniffed, tears of self-pity mingling with the raindrops on my face. I had offered to take the baby, and now here it was screaming for food, needing new clothes and lots of love that I was just too tired to give. What was I thinking of? I had been in Africa for nine months. Surely I should now be a more rounded and mature person with a firm grasp on the meaning of life. Whims rather than morals had formed the basis of every decision I had made; *Tess of the d'Urbervilles* remained unfinished and I hadn't even lost weight!

Emily! Honestly! Never mind death, disease, malnutrition or civil war, all this silly spoilt Western woman was worrying about was that she get body. Come on! Yes, I was fat. Yes I get body! A big healthy body. Just what Salonean men liked. I started walking more quickly, squaring my shoulders against the rain, closing my eyes briefly to enjoy the cool water against my face. I had been in the perfect place all along – a place where the big strong girl was Queen. Ha!

My house appeared from behind the vegetation, and there, on my doorstep, was a bedraggled figure.

"Pa George? Kushe! Kushe, Pa George." I squealed with delight. He looked up.

"What for chop today?"

"Plassas."

I quite fancied a nice plate of plassas.

EPILOGUE 2003

On 12th March 1994, Father Felim, the sisters and volunteers were ambushed as they evacuated Panguma Hospital. The sisters' vehicle escaped, but Felim, Karin and Zietje were killed outright.

Dr. Anne (Morag's replacement) was in the same vehicle and broke her back. There was nothing she could do but comfort a fatally wounded Eelco who knew his wife and daughter had been killed. After Eelco passed away, Anne crawled to a hiding place behind some rocks. She was later rescued by soldiers and taken to Sister Hilary in Bo.

This book was written in their memory and for all the other unnamed people who lost their lives in Sierra Leone's unspeakably brutal civil war. Foday Sankoh's rebels, funded by President Charles Taylor of Liberia, burnt Serabu Hospital down in 1995, killing over thirty mothers and children taking refuge in TB ward.

The rebels attacked the Mokanje Mines in 1995. Foday Sankoh fuelled his propaganda machine by holding the Managing Director and sixteen others (including two VSOs) hostage for three months. The 1999 Lomé Peace Agreement rewarded Mr. Sankoh with a cabinet position – senior government minister for mineral resources (the Mines he effectively destroyed... and the gold and diamonds). The British High Commission really stepped up to the mark in the nineties, especially the new Commissioner Peter Penfold, who showed remarkable bravery in face to face negotiations with the rebels.

Peace was short lived. Rebels attacked peace-keepers outside Freetown and abducted several hundred UN troops. Finally the

United Nations Mission in Sierra Leone trained the Salonean Army and disarmed 45,000 rebels. Peace was declared in 2002 and Foday Sankoh imprisoned. In 2003, he died the peaceful death he had denied so many. Meanwhile Charles Taylor was indicted for crimes against humanity but fled to Nigeria.

I spent another eighteen months in Sierra Leone. Dan did come back with his wife, but they were sent home 5 months later during the 1992 coup. We British took delight in teasing the Americans for their 'over-reaction'. The reality was less heroic – the British High Commissioner was on holiday and by the time the Deputy worked out the radio system, it was all over. Captain Valentine Strasser hadn't been planning a coup. He just wanted more rice for his men, but President Momoh took fright and fled. The 27-year-old Captain Valentine shrugged, adjusted his sunglasses and decided he might as well run the country. Posters declared him Sierra Leone's savior. Sales of sunglasses boomed. When I left in December 1992, Serabu was thriving and the country was filled with optimism.

I returned to York, became a partner in a small General Practice and met a handsome man. Danny and I married and Nat sang beautifully at our wedding, with Klaus, Morag, Lindsey and six other ex-Salonean VSOs donning their kilts and finery to celebrate with us. We are now parents to two energetic little boys, Art and Frankie, a bossy little girl called Ella, and a very hungry dog called Bo.

Nat finished his theology and philosophy degree, but decided against the Priesthood. He now works with the homeless. Nat and Hilary invited me to the Sierra Leone/Ireland Partnership dinner in 2002. Aminatta Forna was the guest speaker. Three quite different books were piled together on the front table, all featuring quite different doctors in Sierra Leone: *The Devil Who Danced on the Water*, Aminatta's biography of her father, who was a doctor before he locked political horns with Siaka Stevens; *Old Wateringholes*, Sister Hilary's autobiography; and *Green Oranges*.

On the Sunday, I took Sister Hilary for afternoon tea at the Royal Dublin Hotel and in the evening, Nat took me to Drag Queen Bingo at The George. Ah Dublin!

After 103 years in Sierra Leone, the Holy Rosary Sisters were pulled out in 1995. Hilary had been there for 42 years. They returned in 1999 to run refugee camps and Sister Hilary visited Serabu in 2000 (what a lady, she was nearly eighty!) I was sent photos of what was left of Serabu. One featured the birthing chair, rising unscathed like a phoenix from the burnt out walls of the hospital.

Klaus built up a very successful motorcycle business in Fife, and after a short relationship with Lindsey, he married Jenny, one of my best friends from school. A very successful bit of matchmaking by Yours Truly!

Morag married her childhood sweetheart and is now a GP and mum to three little girls. Anne started a family back in New Zealand, finding happiness after her horrifying ordeal. Tom lives in an eco-house in a remote forest in the States, with his doctor wife and young family. Rob East took his family to grow grapes in France. Phillippe and Nicole went on to have two (or maybe three?) more children and have worked in Public Health in Namibia and Nicaragua. Dan is back in the Emergency Room in Virginia with Cyndi and their three children. Jo and Sule were finally reunited and are now married, regardless of the opinion of High Commissioners, and now have a baby boy. Even Father Brendan got married.

With no postal service or telephones, and with everyone scattered, I lost touch with most of my Salonean friends. I did hear that Mariama and Tiange were safe in Freetown with their families.

Despite the atrocities that I can scarcely bear to read about, Sierra Leone has taught me to believe in the power of the human spirit, even in the most appalling circumstances. One day I shall return with my children.

RETURN OF THE PRODIGAL DAUGHTER: EPILOGUE 2008

"One day I shall return to Sierra Leone with my children." A nice finish to a book, perhaps, but not the sort of thing you actually do with three small children and an unstable country. But Peace was declared in 2002, and this time it lasted.

"Kushe, Doc!"

"Klaus! Good to hear you. How di body?"

"A tell God tenki. Guess where I'm taking the wife on holiday?"

"You aren't! Wow…"

"I'm exporting some spares. Thought we might mix a bit of business and pleasure."

"Will Jenny think it's pleasure?"

"You know she'll love it."

"Hmm. I don't suppose you can pop into Serabu and find out what's going on? Sister Hilary says the EU are rebuilding it."

"Pop in?! Serabu's in the middle of bloody nowhere!"

"Remember your lovely bridegroom speech? When you declared your eternal gratitude to me for fixing you up with Jenny….?"

"Danny…?" I asked, flicking through Klaus' photos.

"Hmm?"

"How would you feel about going to Sierra Leone?"

"What, all of us?"

"Well … yes."

"Keeping up with the Von Hondabendas?"

"Well, no. Just call Klaus and Jenny the, er, advance party."

Danny frowned. Perhaps renting *Blood Diamond* last month was a mistake – very harrowing for a Hollywood film, despite Leonardo DiCaprio, and unlikely to boost the Salonean tourist industry.

"Is it safe? What did Klaus say?"

"That you'd scarcely know the rebels had been," I said airily.

"Okay. Let's do it."

"Oh!" I hadn't meant him to agree so readily. "Really? There's still malaria, diarrhoea, vomiting, schistosomiasis, rabies, crashing helicopters..."

"So, we'll take anti-malarials, boil the water and avoid dogs and helicopters."

"Okay." Okay? Really? "They're having elections... Art has a school trip... work's very busy... the dog's not well..."

"For heaven's sake Em, just book the flights."

"Maybe we should wait until Serabu is actually open for business?"

"It may never happen. Book the flights."

"But I'd want to be useful. Save the world, save lives and all that."

"You said Kambia Appeal were desperate for doctors."

We'd done some fundraising for Kambia Appeal, a small charity running a link from Cheltenham Hospital in the UK to support maternal health across Kambia District. Normally they sent obstetricians and midwives on training visits, but since Médecins Sans Frontièrs had pulled out (a good sign really – MSF only work in disaster zones) any old doctor would do.

Ella, my six year old, pulled her sleeve up. She scarcely flinched, forcing her brothers into similar acts of bravery. We decided not to bother with the rabies vaccine (three more jabs and a few hundred more pounds). This was only a six-week trip, not two years, and last time the only dogs I saw were Scooby, the dying fourteen year old, and a dead dog in a storm drain.

"Just stay away from dogs."

We had booked the flights, renewed the passports, paid for the Visas and wangled six weeks off work and school when the Kambia Appeal emailed: "Kambia's been without a doctor for three months so the Government has declared the hospital closed. The community is not happy. You may prefer to cancel."

Cancel?

I replied: "Don't worry! I am uniquely qualified at re-opening Sierra Leonean hospitals!" As soon as I hit 'send', I started to panic. This would be different, I had my family. What if they were sick, what if the rebels came back, what if they got rabies, what if... And I hadn't done a Caesarean Section for sixteen years. I phoned up a local obstetrician. "Help!"

THE JOURNEY

"Just a random check, madam."

So why was I the only passenger in Inverness airport at the baggage handling area? And out of our eight bags, why choose the one filled with tablets, ampoules, syringes and needles? Fortunately I had decided against bringing any Class A drugs. I smiled sweetly.

By evening we were manhandling our bags into a family room at Gatwick, knocking my only pair of glasses under the suitcase full of books and footballs. The frames snapped across the brow. Great! I was going to be really good at those Caesarean Sections now. Then Ella started vomiting. For heaven's sake – we hadn't even left the country yet! What was I thinking, taking my children to Sierra Leone?

Four days ago we had been sledging in the Scottish Highlands: now we stepped off the plane into the dark at 30 degrees and 99% humidity.

"What is your mission in Sierra Leone?" asked the man at Arrivals Save the world, save lives, save my soul and lose weight? I had a man now (and children – Pa George would have been proud of me!) but as for those other goals ...

"We'll be working at Kambia Hospital."

A quick consultation on a sore knee excused us from more random checks and we left the relative calm of the terminal building to look for Moses from the Kambia Appeal. He could scarcely have missed us – we stood out like a handful of pink thumbs. Our intercontinental communication must have broken down, and we were dismayed to find our mobiles were both blocked. Looking lost was a bad idea, inviting a swarm of people: men waving tickets for the helicopter to Freetown, taxi drivers and lads fighting over our luggage. We bought our escape with fistfuls of leones.

The Lungi Hotel didn't have our booking. Sorry-oh! Thirty Americans in yellow T shirts declaring their love for Jesus had just arrived.

"Maybe the God Squad will pity the little children and give up a room?" whispered Danny. I felt a pang of nostalgia for the priests and nuns who spent their entire lives working in Sierra Leone, not just a couple of weeks in matching T-shirts taking the last rooms at the Inn. But who was I to be so hypocritical? We were only there for six weeks.

"Is this our hotel, Mum?"

"Sorry, darling. It's full."

"So where are we going to sleep?" asked Frankie, perfectly reasonably. "I'm so tired."

"I know a better place," the taxi driver declared. Danny rolled his eyes. I shrugged. We had no choice but to trust him. It was eleven at night.

On the third attempt we found a 'better place' with a vacancy. The air-conditioning hadn't worked for years, there were no mosquito nets and the locks were dodgy, but it did serve Star Beer and lemonade and we could hear the sea and see the moon between the palm trees. I felt ridiculously happy.

We borrowed a mobile and phoned Moses. Sierra Leone might still be third from bottom on the human development index, the under-five mortality still 20% and life expectancy still only 42, but mobile phones had come to Salone!

The next morning, Marray, the Kambia Appeal driver, drove us onto the Freetown ferry, a floating junk yard of dilapidated taxis, lorries and shiny Aid Organisation Landrovers.

FREETOWN

Freetown was a boiling jam pot of traffic, humanity and wares. Cigarettes, fruit and veg and entire three-piece suites were laid out in the dust. Freetown was ghastly enough in the nineties with a population of half a million, but the war had brought an influx of refugees who had never returned to their villages, and now there were one-and-a-half million people jostling for space. How Marray managed to avoid knocking down any pedestrians, bikes or stalls, was a miracle.

We gasped for air. Opening the Landrover windows made no

difference at all. Thank goodness for Moses' fiancée, who sat us down on a wooden bench in her pharmacy and handed out frozen water bags from the drug freezer. Meanwhile Moses went off to buy us two mobile phones and replace my frames. It took him less than an hour. I could see again! We could even text our parents back home!

Moses said that given the difficult situation at Kambia, it would be politic to meet the Health Minister. After three visits to the Yu Yu building (seven floors of concrete offices built by the Chinese) we gave up and headed North.

Every time we slowed down, something was thrust through our window.

"How much the bananas?" I asked.

"One thousand."

"A thousand leones! Marray, that can't be right?" Marray said it was. Bloody hell, last time a bunch cost twenty! We were hungry, so bought bananas and boiled eggs, but politely refused the live chickens and tortoises.

After an hour, the tarmac ran out and we were on laterite. Ah yes, this I remembered. And the potholes. And the ravines running down the middle of the road. The boys loved it, squealing as Marray lurched from one side of the road to the other, over humps and into ditches I clung onto our suitcases and Ella hid under a towel, cushioned by a multipack water bed of plastic bags of drinking water.

Five hours later, we arrived at the compound - pretty little huts, overhanging trees and the drive lined with painted white stones. It was a veritable oasis. The fiercesome guard dogs, Isatu and Wilson (both with a bite out of their left ear, covered with flies) bounded over, smothered us with licks and rolled on their backs for their tummies to be tickled. So much for avoiding canines.

Marray said he had to go, so Charles and Alhaji, two of the compound lads, helped us unload our bags. Later Moses told us that Marray had a text whilst he was driving us round Freetown to say his newborn baby had died.

KAMBIA

M oses took us to greet everyone: the paramount chief; the police chief; the hospital staff and the local councillor, Samuel Sankoh. Samuel gave us a history lesson on the roller-coaster relationship between Britain and Sierra Leone: the slave trade and William Wilberforce's heroic interventions; colonialism and the chaos at Independence; the missionaries (good and bad); the Aid workers; the sense of abandonment when everyone pulled out at the start of the war and finally how grateful the Saloneans were when the British Army finally came. Samuel was thrilled to hear that Danny came from Hull, twinned with Freetown and home of the great William Wilberforce.

Then it was the children's new school. Well!!! David Beckham had been in Sierra Leone just a few months previously, and even he could not have been given such a reception. Children poured out of the classrooms shouting "Aporto! Aporto!" We were in the North now, Temne-land, so instead of being called 'Poomuis' we were now 'Aportos', a derivation from the first Portuguese settlers. They clamoured to touch Art, Frankie and Ella's clothes, or stroke their hair, or shake their hands. We were only saved from the mob by teachers thwacking their pupils across the backs of their legs. Good Lord, how were our children going to survive six weeks of this?

A teacher took us to the market to buy material, then on to the tailor. He ran up two green dresses, four green shirts and four khaki shorts overnight on his pedal-powered Singer sewing machine.

Next morning, apparently unfazed, our children trotted off to school in their new uniforms. Assembly was at eight with over seven hundred children singing the National Anthem. By the end of the week, our children were word perfect in all three verses of *High We Exalt Thee*. None of them can get past the second line of *God Save the Queen*.

School finished at two, allowing local children to go to work on the farms or sell groundnuts or bananas, or whatever else was needed to keep their family afloat. We saw one schoolboy eat dust at the side of the football pitch to stave off hunger. In comparison, we had a cook who had lunch ready for our children when they got back from school. What an improvement in the food!

No criticism intended of Pa George, but Kambia was a much bigger place than Serabu (more ingredients) on a big river (fish and prawns) and only eight miles from the Guinea border, home of the Fullahs, the travelling tribe (often with cows!)

The Fullahs also made great baguettes. Our neighbours made bread in a stone oven in their back yard, ready at two o'clock – not that I was ever home in time. My family would all sit in the outdoor hut, eating hot fresh baguettes and drinking water from little plastic bags. Later, when it cooled down a little, they might play badminton or football. Our children had a head start with the badminton (since we brought the set) but they didn't stand a chance at football! Danny did his best down on the local dust pitch, considering he was a middle-aged Aporto amongst twenty ripped young men. The first time poor Danny was puce after ten minutes and glugged down a whole litre of water. The children ran back to the compound to fill six more bottles. They caused a near riot as the players fought over the Aporto water.

KAMBIA HOSPITAL

Kambia Hospital was just as empty as Serabu Hospital had been when I returned after the rebels. Only this time as well as goats, there were dogs everywhere – one with no nose, one with no eye, and every one with the Kambian canine badge of honour, a bite out of the left ear. Why hadn't we had those rabies vaccinated?

Mohamed, the rotund and enthusiastic Community Health Officer, was in his office seeing the second of two outpatients. The CHO is the lifeblood of a Salonean hospital, acting as a Paramedic/ Nurse Practitioner, very often with no doctor on site.

"Kushe, kushe, Dr. Em!" Mohamed greeted me delightedly. "Can you do small small surgery?"

I'd heard that before. "Well, not for sixteen years, but ... "

That was enough. Mohamed announced he was taking a fortnight to graduate from Bo Paramedic School. Fair enough, it wasn't exactly busy.

Ha! You can't hide a family of five Aportos in a town that hasn't seen white children for twenty years. And I hadn't bargained on the local radio station announcing the arrival of a new Aporto doctor.

I was expecting war injuries, longstanding untreated infections, HIV and TB, but most of the queue that stretched outside Outpatients that first Monday morning were women with infertility – perhaps as tragic for a Salonean woman as any of the above. Sadly I could only treat any underlying anaemia, worms or syphilis. This may have helped their general health, but wasn't the miracle they wanted from the Aporto.

The women seemed to wear an extraordinary amount of undergarments.

"Why all the clothes?" I asked my nurse translator after my fifth patient peeled off two pairs of pants, a pair of shorts, trousers and a lappa. "It's so hot!"

"Awareness," said Mariatu.

The rebels had now gone and the raping had stopped, but the women kept their 'awareness.' That was the first indication I had had that there had been any rebel trouble at all. So far everything had been, almost shockingly, business as usual.

On the sixth day a cavalcade of Landrovers with motorbike escorts drove into the compound.

"What the….?"

"The Ministry of Health have come," said Mariatu. "To see if the hospital is open. If we are open then we will get a District Medical Officer. Then we will be open."

"Huh?"

I hadn't realised how crucial this was: if the hospital was not officially 'open', the Government wouldn't pay staff or supply drugs. The Minister wanted facts, figures and reports, so Danny showed the Administrator how to do some simple spreadsheets. First he had to debug the computers, loaded with a mishmash of incompatible donated/acquired/pirated software packages. The computers needed electricity, so the generator was turned on. A strange noise started up in the far upper corner of my office. An air conditioner! Fab! What a pity there was no sink or running water.

"Can you do a Section in half-an-hour, Dr. Em?" asked Sister Conteh, the nurse anaesthetist. "We only get very small diesel."

Help, I'd only just remembered how to do a Section at all. Thank goodness for Alhusan and Bobson, who filled Tiange's role as scrub nurse and tutor.

"Diesel don don," announced Sister Conteh the next night.

"But Admin had light this morning."

"Theatre has its own emergency generator."

"This *is* an emergency, why don't we have fuel?"

"There is no money, the hospital is closed."

"Can we get Matron to supply some? This lady needs a Section now."

"Matron is not around. The hospital is closed."

I sighed. Why couldn't the Minister have his reports in a squared jotter? "Okay, how much diesel do we need for a Section?"

"A gallon. Fifteen thousand. Bobson will get it."

I pulled out the leones from my little backpack.

"But diesel is not there at Kambia na night," Bobson complained, not considering this a nurse's job. "Only at the Checkpoint."

"Okay? Is that far?"

"Three miles. Bobson can take the Hospital motorbike," said Sister Conteh.

"But petrol don don."

This was sounding a bit too 'hole in my bucket' for me.

"Now what?" I pleaded.

"I go ask if petrol there," Bobson nodded to the stalls behind the hospital gates. I knew you could buy oranges, little bags of sugar, triangles of processed cheese and even plastic bags of water, but petrol? And at midnight?

"Petrol five thousand," he added. I just had enough left.

Five minutes later, Bobson poured a Star beer bottle filled with petrol into the bike, then strapped on a yellow gallon rubber for the diesel. I lay down on the wooden bench outside theatre, looked at the stars and prayed that the mother's womb wouldn't rupture.

"Dr. Em, I am most sorry, but we have used the last drapes." Sister Conteh nodded to a week's worth of bloody drapes sitting at theatre's entrance. Sister was an excellent anaesthetist (midwife and lay preacher too!) but what could she do? No money, no diesel. No diesel, no pump, no water. No money, no pay. No pay, no cleaner. Sister sent a couple of lads off to the river slipway to wash the bloody drapes alongside the rest of the village doing their laundry, bathing and swimming. Aaargh! Next morning Alhusan and Bobson were squatting by the charcoal fire, sterilising the drapes in a pressure cooker.

There were some improvements since the nineties. We could now send obstetric fistulae to the Mercy Ships in Freetown for repair, a life-changing procedure for these women, who were otherwise condemned to a lifetime of continual urinary leakage. The hospital admission fee was a flat five thousand leones that included a daily meal of rice and sauce, so no more fights over Charity Feeding (fantastic!) The Government also paid for certain basic drugs for children and pregnant women on 'cost recovery'. This only worked if those drugs were in stock, but at least it was a start. However intravenous fluids, cannulae and lab tests weren't included in the scheme, so I would end up in the ridiculous situation of having a child with cerebral malaria who would get the ampoule of quinine on 'cost recovery' but not the two thousand leones (25p) for the cannula to give it. A new Government 'free treatment' program for maternal and child health is due next year, so there is hope. And as we left Kambia they were installing a large water tank and solar panelling.

SERABU

At the end of week three, Mohamed returned and Marray drove us to Serabu. Father Jabati met us at the hospital entrance. We quickly established that Nat had taught him at the Seminary.

"Ah Mr. Nat! He was a great teacher. And he knew how to laugh-oh! Mr. Nat will be Father Nat now?"

"No. He changed his mind. He's working with the homeless."

"Homeless?" Father looked disappointed, or perhaps he was just struggling with the concept of homelessness in the unimaginably wealthy West. "So when did you last see Mr. Nat?"

"In Ireland, for a Sierra Leone/Ireland Partnership dinner." I didn't mention the drag queen bingo. "And Sister Hilary was there too!"

"Ah, Mama Hilary!"

Name dropping Sister Hilary in Serabu will get you far. Father beamed and unlocked the gates.

"It's the birthing chair!" I squealed. The monstrous beast was standing guard at the entrance.

"So it is. In pretty good nick too," said Danny, who had been subjected to my talks and photo collection several times over. "Frankie, get down!"

"I can't, Dad!" Yep, that was about right. Art took a photo of his brother, spread-eagled in the chair.

We continued into the parallel universe that was the New Serabu Hospital. It was like an alien spaceship, crash landed in the middle of the West African bush and abandoned by its crew (possibly in search of fuel and water, or perhaps just unable to tolerate the heat, humidity and isolation?) The only inhabitants were the goats. There were always goats.

The shiny-tiled wards were unsullied, not even by a single bed. The engines lay quiet in a triple-sized generator room for the brand new triple-sized generator. The water tank was the size of a swimming pool. It could only be filled if there was power to pump it, but the host land could not provide fuel. The old Convent stood behind the water tank – the only building that remained; a charred carbuncle amongst all the gleaming white.

"Why didn't they rebuild the convent?" asked Danny.

Father shrugged. "There are no more nuns."

"Or at least knock it down?"

"There is no more money."

"Frankie…"

Frankie jumped down from the crumbling convent walls and found a tree instead. Art was busy taking photos of lizards, goats and butterflies, whilst Ella plonked herself on a concrete veranda of the nursing school buildings and complained that her feet were sore. We ignored her, distracted by another life form coming to greet us.

"Kushe, kushe, Dr. Em!" It was an ex-patient, my first amputee some nineteen years ago after he trapped his fingers in a boat propeller. He pumped my hand with delight. I was very pleased with his grip. We visited the Southern Eye Clinic, a gleaming beacon of American excellence, almost as out of place as the hospital, but fully equipped and functioning. An American ophthalmologist, Cathy, and her husband, Tom, came twice a year and blitzed thousands of eye operations. In between their visits, the highly motivated local staff had been trained up to fit glasses and do minor operations (like cataract removals!) A really excellent example of what can be achieved with the funds and commitment.

Then Danny piggy backed Ella, with her horribly blistered flip-flop toes, through the village to the Compound. No one else recognized me; I had become a stranger. So much for my triumphant return.

John Ganda, the Archbishop's brother, gave us two cool and airy rooms for the night, fed us fried spam and lemonade and to top it all, put the generator on so the children could watch Superman II – a rather unexpected find in the Archbishop's video collection. We submerged Ella's gungy feet in a bowl of salty water and went to speak to the man himself.

The rebuilding of Serabu had been Archbishop Ganda's swansong. The now quite elderly man painted his undimmed dream of returning Serabu to its former glory. It was clear how he had managed to persuade the EU to invest in the first place.

"But who will run it?"

"God will provide."

KAMBIA

Marray took a short cut back through the Mines. Sierra Rutile had resumed operations, but the Mokanje Compound, where once I had drunk G&T, was gone. Just a bare hill. Two hours later, we stopped for beef and onion baguettes from the streetstalls at Moyamba Junction, then it was another four hours to Kambia. Marray had barely parked the Landrover when Mohamed arrived.

"We have a lady who needs a Section."

Right. I was rather hoping for a Star Beer.

Seeing a desolate Serabu had left us all feeling down. Art was doing fine as his friends were a little older and had better English, and

Ella was at the stage where language didn't matter so much. Frankie found it the hardest. Not helped by his mother who was either absent or exhausted.

One day he handed out some bread through the compound fence-line and within minutes, there were queues of children. Frankie went to buy more bread, but could only afford four baguettes. He tried to break it into pieces, but could not manage a loaves and fishes miracle. He was quite upset that he didn't have enough. That night he had obviously been stewing it over.

"Do they only want to be my friend because I might give them things, Mummy?"

Oh, how to answer that one? As a volunteer it was easy, we were broke, and so were the sisters, so we gave our time and rarely did people ask for our money. In Kambia, the Aporto visitors came for weeks or months rather than years. It's really hard not to hand out money when you are surrounded by so much need, but the more you give, the more is expected. However, away from the town, where the need was greater, people gave *us* gifts of oranges, bananas or chickens.

My own low point was the boy with 'rabies'. A dog had bitten him on the foot five months ago. Just a tiny scar now, but he was wide-eyed and feverish, glugging down a bottle of water like he had been days in the desert. His malaria blood film was positive.

"That boy has rabies!" cried the student nurse. "Look how he drinks!"

The mother started howling, the nurses, relatives and patients gathered and everyone started shouting in a combination of Temne, Sosso, Limbu, Krio and English. I was lost. There were so many tribes in Kambia.

"You no get for touch am! You will get rabies too."

I tried to explain how rabies was spread. A bite five months ago was unlikely to give rabies, and that rabies gave you hydrophobia, not overwhelming thirst. The boy was probably just scared, feverish and dehydrated with malaria.

"A dog bite does not give malaria."

"No, of course not," I sighed. "But children get malaria all the time."

Then I was accused of refusing to give the vaccine. I didn't even know if we had it in stock. As the shouting continued, I started to doubt myself. The Saloneans estimated time by the season, not the calendar, and maybe you could get late onset rabies if the bite was on a peripheral part of the body?

The student's conviction won out. After all she was my translator. They took the child away to Freetown. Five hours on that dreadful road, then through the Freetown traffic to four different clinics to find one that stocked rabies vaccine. It cost the family nearly half a million leones for the transport and the ultimately useless vaccine. The boy died. No one treated his malaria.

PARENTS & FATHERS

My parents had always promised to come and visit me during my two years in Sierra Leone, but of course the rebel business messed that one up. So I jokingly suggested they come along this time. And they did! It was a huge psychological boost for all of us and the Saloneans loved it. Sierra Leone has a great respect for elders and my Mum and Dad were treated like royalty.

While the Landrover had gone to collect them and Dr. Tom, my replacement, Ella started with a high fever. We took her to the lab to check for malaria, sandwiched between Charles and I on the motorbike. The test was negative, but her temperature hit 40, so I had to treat her anyway. The anti-malarials made her sick, and when Tom and my parents arrived, she had been vomiting all day. So before he even unpacked, Dr. Tom put up an IV on Ella, hanging the infusion bag on a nail in the hut. Call me a hypocrite (again) but I wasn't sending my daughter to that hospital! Why had I taken my children to Sierra Leone?

The next day we left my Dad (a confirmed agnostic) to look after Ella, now thankfully just sleeping it off, so we could go to the Palm Sunday procession. We all met at the Central Mosque (!) carrying our real palm fronds. My Mum was persuaded that going to church in Sierra Leone was a must-do activity. Where else would you get singing, drumming, dancing, a huge mural of an African last supper and hilarious sermons delivered in Krio with an Italian accent?

Father Franco asked us back to the Mission House for a glass of cold water. He also produced a bar of chocolate for the children that he had been saving for months in his fridge. Sierra Leone had been his home for thirty-four years, and he had stayed throughout the war.

At first Kambia was quite safe as the rebels were in the South, but by the late nineties they wanted to expand from Liberia, through Sierra Leone and onward North to Guinea and Mali. Capturing Kambia's bridge, only eight miles from Guinea, would open up the West African coastal corridor.

Some rebels genuinely considered themselves Freedom Fighters, releasing Sierra Leone from years of corrupt leadership. The rebel Colonel in Kambia was such a man, telling his eleven and twelve year old bodyguards that there was to be no killing or looting.

One day, the twelve-year old demanded fish from an old man on the river, and shot him in both legs when he refused. He bled to death. The Colonel was furious. The boys turned on him, and he retaliated by attacking one of the boys.

A line had been crossed. The next day a gang of boys with petrol torched the town's houses. We saw more burnt out houses in Kambia than anywhere else. Some of them had been quite grand.

Father Franco was kidnapped. The rebel battalion voted eight to four to kill him, but the Colonel had a great respect for the Father and talked them out of it. Finally some parishioners mounted a rescue and canoed the Father across the river and into Guinea. He broke his hip during the escape and was flown back to Italy.

You'd think that being medi-vacced at sixty-five from a country in the middle of civil war, would convince you it was time to retire, but Father Franco had made a life long vow, and returned six weeks later. He was kidnapped for a further three months, before escaping again.

Father Franco is now in his seventies and due to move parish to a more remote part of Sierra Leone, as Kambia is too well established. Not enough of a challenge!

My paltry two years as a VSO could scarcely compare with the bravery of the priests like Father Franco and Father Felim. Both were determined to stay with their people come what may. Back then I'd been cross with the priests for expecting similar levels of bravery from us! Now I could see just how much courage and hope these priests gave the people by their presence through Salone's darkest years when all the other expatriates had abandoned them.

Father Franco worked with the rebels to promote peace, helping them write out their part of the peace agreement. He continues his dialogue to this day and still takes confession from the Colonel.

I am not a Catholic, and my relationship with a God who could allow such wars to happen in the first place can be a bit wobbly, but I would never have believed how much forgiveness and redemption we saw on returning to Sierra Leone. They truly do seem to have moved on, with ex-rebels and ex-child soldiers living in the community amongst many who must have been their victims. The people have retained their sense of optimism and fun, and don't seem to be ground down by the atrocities they had suffered during the war. Sierra Leone was just as frustrating, chaotic and heartbreaking as it ever was, but for all that, a place that somehow gladdens the heart.

There will be thousands more stories of courage and humanity that we will never hear about. Mariama for instance. We met her in Freetown, where she works for an organisation that supports all the mission hospitals and clinics in Sierra Leone. At the height of the war, whilst her husband worked upcountry with the Red Cross in the rebel-held areas, Mariama worked as a midwife.

One expectant mother had seen her family killed and had her hands amputated by the rebels. Her physical wounds healed, and Mariama delivered her baby, but her post-traumatic stress was so great, she just lost the will to live. Mariama took the newborn baby and the woman's twelve year old daughter into her own family. That twelve year old is now twenty and has a baby of her own – both still live as part of Mariama's family.

On our last day, the seven of us, my parents, my husband and my children, sat on the beach at Banana Island, watching the sunset through the palm trees over the Atlantic. "It was just like your book," Danny said, washing down a forkful of fresh lobster with Star Beer. "But the food's better!"

EPILOGUE 2009

"Serabu is fully functioning," I read out the email.

"Really?" Danny raised an eyebrow. "Who pays the running costs?" Once an accountant…

"The EU have given them three years to get on their feet."

"So, you want to go back."

"We can't afford to go en masse … but I don't want to go on my own."

"What about your practice nurse? Didn't Izzy say she'd go with you if you ever went again?"

"Yes, but I think she was joking."

"Kushe, Dr. Em and Elizobel!" The hospital security guard grinned and levered his way out of the birthing chair. "I will get Matron."

Matron (Theresa!) took us on a guided tour of Serabu Hospital. 'Fully functioning' is rather an overstatement, but it did have nurses, beds, one (exhausted) doctor, drugs and equipment.

In church the next morning, Izzy accused me of staring at a lady two rows in front.

"Do you know her?"

"It's … Tiange!"

At the end of the service Tiange threw her arms round me.

"Tiange! How di body?"

"I tell God tenki, Dr. Em. I gladdi to see you. Who is your friend?"

"Isobel. This is my first time in Sierra Leone."

"Welcome, welcome, Elizobel. How do you find our country?"

"It's very…. Interesting."

A queue of old nurses had appeared. "Kushe, kushe, Dr. Em."

"Aisha? Aisha, kushe!"

"Do you remember me?"

"What about me?"

"Who am I, Dr. Em?"

"What's my name, Dr. Em?"

Help! It was easy for them, even seventeen years on, as everyone soon knows the only poomuis town, but I was happy. I was no longer a stranger. We heard that Earnest was working with MSF in Bo, Moses was a big man in Freetown, Dauda was at World Vision, and Patrick Kpukumo and Latif had jobs at the Sierra Rutile Clinic.

"And what happened to Pa George?"

"He done die."

"Oh. I'm sorry. The rebels?"

"No, no. He was old."

Ah, Pa George. So he was old after all.

At the time of publication there is a permanent resident Sierra Leonean doctor in Serabu. The German committee Ärzte für die Dritte Welt (Doctors for Developing Countries) are sending specialist and generalist doctors to support the work of Serabu Hospital.

www.german-doctors.de

SCHOOL IN AFRICA
BY ART (11)

The jeep pulled over into an empty, dusty playground surrounded by three buildings. Mum and Dad got out first and walked over to the head teacher with Me, Frankie and Ella following behind.

"APORTO! APORTO! APORTO!"

The three of us gawped as children swarmed out of every classroom and ran towards us in the centre of the playground. In about twenty seconds we were surrounded by hundreds of children screaming in our ears and shaking our hands or trying desperately to get a grasp on our clothing. Ella looked round for our parents but we had completely lost sight of them. For a second Frankie was pulled by his collar into the crowd and disappeared. My hands started to ache as they were shook ferociously and then seemingly given to someone else. It was like pass the parcel. A teacher came forward and started whacking everyone in her sight with a cane and making them run back into their classes. Dad and Moses battled through the crowd to get the jeep doors open. As I got back in the jeep I felt a pair of prying hands on my back and then the doors shut. I slumped back in the seat and started laughing.

Every morning at 5am the cockerel jumped onto my window and started wailing loudly for 15 minutes. When I finally got back to sleep the mosque would play a prayer over the loud speakers so the whole of Kambia could hear which sounded like a distressed donkey calling for help. The sun would start to shine through the mosquito net like a 200 watt lamp so I could not get back to sleep.

On our first day at school, Mum insisted on taking photos of us in our wafer thin school uniforms. We were led to the school by a group of kids I had met on the first day through what was basically lots of people's houses. A teacher came up to me and put me in a line. Apparently this was assembly.

The head teacher came forward and suddenly everybody went quiet. He said something and suddenly everybody was singing and dancing. I asked the boy in front of me what was going on but he just kept on singing. Every so often I heard some words and realised that they were singing in English.

"Can you not sing?"

"I don't know the songs."

He started laughing at this.

If you arrived early you had to pick up litter, including leaves, round the school.

"Pick up the papers Art!" I would bend over and then they would laugh at me and the head boy would say, "Don't pick them up."

"Pick them up Art."

"Don't Art!"

If you were late you were flogged. Some kids helped their parents in the morning and were beaten every day for arriving late. There were no excuses. One woman who sat outside one of the houses stopped us every single morning to talk and talk.

We didn't want to be late. A little girl the same age as Ella was late and tried to run away but was caught. The teacher brought her into our classroom and picked the tallest person in our class to give her a piggy back so his cane would reach her back and legs. He was so mad that he also hit the boy holding the little girl.

Assembly would be four songs, the national anthem and the Lord's prayer which started, "Papa God who de in heaven" and changed from, "and forgive us our debts as we forgive our debtors" to, "forgive us our forgivenesses and we forgiving us". We had a Muslim prayer at the end of the day.

After assembly our line marched round all the school buildings singing, "John BUUUULL!" Ella was in class one and had to walk round her desk five times. Frankie was in class five and had to march round his classroom twice.

Every year was split into two classes. I had 94 people in my class with two people next to me on a desk only really fit for one person. There were 18 boys called Alhaji. Normally we would do Maths, Geography then English and a big bit of agriculture.

Every so often the teacher would leave the class and one boy to my right called Mustapha (nick named Hot Stuff) would do his trick where he could spit across the classroom from both sides of his mouth at once and Alhaji no.17 would fall asleep on my shoulder. And it wouldn't be long before: "Art do you love dis girl?" "No Art! Dis girl is hot yes?"

When the teacher came back the head boy gave him a list of all the loud people and they would be taken out and flogged in front of my desk. I found out later the head boy had put my name on the list 5 times. This was the same boy who sent me a letter saying he was my best friend and how he needed me to send him money for a pair of trainers, a camera and a bicycle.

One time Alhaji fell asleep when the teacher was there and the teacher grabbed a thousand paged deep dictionary and whacked it over his head making a loud "crack!" noise that echoed round the class. I was never flogged but Frankie got a question wrong on purpose to see what it was like. They called Frankie the troublesome boy.

One day when we were doing BODMAS, which was some very confusing way of solving equations, I got my pen and my jotters out without looking at them. Suddenly I felt something crawling up my arm. I looked down and saw thousands of ants teeming inside my bag. There was a giant brown smudge in my pen lid and a long line walking up my arm and onto my face. Urgently I started sweeping them off my desk. I then looked in my bag and saw a brown ball of ants covering the cashew nuts that had been given to me by my mum on the first day for a snack. I tried to save my jotters before they were engulfed by the ants. Mustapha set upon turning my bag inside out, some dropping off into his short hair while Alhaji no. 17 set upon laughing his head off. That night I found more ants under my shirt clinging to my back like limpets.

Then came the tests. I got 20% in agriculture, 40% in geography, 60% in maths and 19 out of twenty in English. The question I got wrong was this:

What goes in the gap?
The radio has _____ working.
a) stopping b) stopped c) had stopped d) stops e) stop

Apparently the answer is d) stops and not b) stopped.

Four girls got 100% and were rubbing it in my face for the whole day. In one of the tests there was a question about a shnil and I didn't know what it was.

"Have you no shnils in UK?"

The teacher asked someone to find a shnil and bring one in. The next day a guy brought in a huge snail shell the size of a rugby ball.

"That's a snail," I said.

"No, it's a shnil," the teacher said.

Later Mum said that maybe the big ones have a special name. When we came home, we went to see my grandparents in Hull and went to The Deep and there was a big shnil! The sign said 'West African Snail.'

At the end of term our class had a football match for girls versus boys. The boys had their hands tied behind their backs to make it even. One fell over and broke his arm. They untied my arms as I was so rubbish at football.

At least I could beat them at badminton. We had a tournament with Big Alhaji who worked at the compound, Santos, Alhaji in Frankie's class and another Alhaji who didn't go to our school at all.

Then there was a big party called the Jump. Our whole family went and the teachers made us say a speech and do a dance in front of everyone. Ella got too scared but Frankie, Dad and I said something and did a dance.

"You a good dancer Art," said Alhaji no 17. They just laughed at Dad.

On the way home a woman was trying to give us a baby and the woman who always stopped us tried to make Frankie marry her daughter. I never knew when the Africans were being serious as they joked a lot.

The school was one of the weirdest experiences I have ever had.

Sierra Leone – A Potted History

Sierra Leone was probably colonised by the Sherbro and Buloma people along the coastal areas. The Mende and Themne tribes moved in waves, setting up chiefdoms. The Fullah peoples followed from Guinea in the North.

1460: Pedra da Cinta names it Serra Lyoa, Lion Mountains, from the shape of the Freetown Peninsula. Some say it looks like a lion's head, others, lion's teeth.

1495: Portuguese fort built on today's Freetown site.

15th/16th century: Slave trade.

1787: First settlement for rescued slave fails.

1791: Sierra Leone Company created by Act of Parliament to repatriate slaves to Freetown.

1807: Slavery abolished.

1808: Freetown becomes Crown Colony. 50,000 'recaptives' returned over next 50 years.

1896: Freetown hinterland becomes British Protectorate.

1954: Sir Milton Margai becomes chief minister of the Sierra Leone Peoples Party.

1961: Independence.

1967: Military coup.

1968: Siaka Stevens, chief of All Peoples Congress, gains power.

1971: Siaka Stevens declares Sierra Leone a Republic and himself President.

1978: Stevens' new constitution declares Sierra Leone a one party state.

1985: Stevens resigns, hand picking Major-General Joseph Momoh as his successor.

1990: West African peacekeepers attack National Patriot Front of Liberia (NPFL) using Lungi Airport as a base. In retaliation Liberia's President, Charles Taylor, rounds up Sierra Leoneans. Foday Sankoh recruits these jailed Saloneans and forces them to train for the Revolutionary United Front (RUF).

1991: Start of civil war. Foday Sankoh's RUF 'recruits' and fighters from the NPFL capture towns on the Liberian border.

1992: 27 year old Captain Valentine Strasser ousts President Momoh in a military coup.

1994: Panguma ambush.

1995: Serabu Hospital burnt down.

1996: Strasser ousted by his defence minister Brigadier Julius Maclai Bio. First multi-party elections since 1967 elect President Ahmad Tajan Kabbah. Kabbah sings peace accord with Sankoh's RUF.

1997: Kabbah ousted by Major-General Paul Koroma of the Armed Forces Revolutionary Council (AFRC) supported by RUF rebels. Kabbah exiled to Guinea where he tries to mobilize international support. Koroma abolishes political parties. The Commonwealth suspends Sierra Leone and the UN Secretary Council imposes sanctions. Meanwhile Sandline, a British Company of mercenaries, supplies weapons to President Kabbah's allies.

1998: ECOMOG (West African peace keeping force) storms Freetown, deposing the AFRC and allowing President Kabbah to return.

1999: AFRC rebels seize part of Freetown in January. ECOMOG drive them out again (at a cost of 50,000 lives). Lomé Peace Agreement signed in July. Sankoh gets immunity from prosecution of war crimes and made Senior Government Minister responsible for mineral resources in return for peace but ECOMOG troops attacked outside Freetown in December. UN troops arrive.

2000: Several hundred UN troops abducted and rebels close on Freetown. British paratroopers mount a rescue, evacuate British citizens and secure the airport. In August 11 British soldiers captured by the renegrade, drug crazed teenage gang 'The West Side Boys'. They are eventually rescued by British Paratroopers.

2001: UNAMSIL (United Nations Mission in Sierra Leone) train Sierra Leone army and deploy them in rebel held areas. 45,000 rebels disarmed. 14th May Cessation of Hostilities signed.

2002: War over. Kabbah landslide in elections with his Sierra Leone People's Party holding the majority.

2003: Foday Sankoh dies of natural causes awaiting war crimes trial. President Charles Taylor of Liberia indicted by Special Court for Sierra Leone for crimes against humanity and escapes to exile in

Nigeria. Moses Blah becomes President of Liberia.

2005: UN Peacekeepers pull out.

2006: Charles Taylor arrested for 11 counts of war crimes and crimes against humanity. Liberia has its first female president in Ellen Johnson-Sirleaf.

2007: Charles Taylor's UN war crimes trial starts in the Hague. It continues to date, after many postponements, boycotts, and probable murder of key witnesses.

2009: Sierra Leone contributes its own soldiers (trained by International Military Advisory and Training Team) to the UN peacekeeping force in Sudan.

LINKS

Serabu Hospital is always desperate for doctors, so if there are any medics out there who fancy a trip to Serabu, even if only for a few weeks, contact me via my website www.emilyjoy.co.uk.

Publisher's note: website addresses are particularly susceptible to change. For up-to-date details for the organizations below, and for more about what they do, we suggest that you visit our site at: www.eye-books.com/greenoranges.

For those of you (and not just those in the medical field) who want a longer overseas adventure with some funding, then VSO in the UK, or Peace Corps in the US, are good places to start. They need all sorts of professions.

Peace Corps: Established in 1961 by President John F. Kennedy to promote world peace and friendship. www.peacecorps.gov

Voluntary Service Overseas VSO works through volunteers to fight poverty in developing countries.
www.vso.org.uk or the North American branch www.cuso-vso.org

See below for some other organisations you could contact below for work, and a bit of tourist info for anyone just fancying a holiday in Sierra Leone. And why not? It's a beautiful country, only about 7 hours flight from the UK. Start with the *Bradt Travel Guide* for Sierra Leone by Katrina Manson and James Knight.

SIERRA LEONE LINKS

The Kambia Appeal started a link to foster improved maternity and child health via Cheltenham Hospital in the UK.
www.kambia.org.uk

The Southern Eye Clinic of Serabu was established in 2006. All medical and surgical services are provided to all patients free of charge. For more information and some lovely photos of Serabu have a look at: www.southerneyeinstitute.org

The Welbodi Partnership is a small charity that has been supporting The Ola During Children's Hospital since 2007.
www.welbodipartnership.org

Other medical volunteers working in Sierra Leone are:
Sandra Lako sandralako.blogspot.com
Kate Meehan katemeehan.wordpress.com

For almost everything you need to know about Sierra Leone, our ex-Field Director's son has a great site www.visitsierraleone.org

Sierra Leone has its own travel agent in the UK in the form of Kevin McPhilllips Travel and this seems to be the cheapest way to go (certainly from the UK)
www.sierraleonetravel.com

Another excellent site by an ex-Peace Corps, now a native
www.sierra-leone.org

Ex Peace Corps started a site back in the US for ex-volunteers, Sierra Leoneans, and anyone who would call themselves Friends of Salone
www.fosalone.org

For current news: www.allafrica.com/sierraleone

Mercy Ships brings hope and healing to the poor, mobilizing people and resources worldwide. They set up the West African Fistula Centre in Freetown in 2005 to provide obstetric fistula repair, improve maternal health and reduce childbirth injuries. Now known as the Aberdeen Women's centre, the work is being continued by the Freedom from Fistula Foundation, offering free surgery, a maternity unit and children's clinic.
www.mercyships.org
www.freedomfromfistula.org.uk

SOME OTHER ORGANISATIONS WORKING OVERSEAS

American Field Service www.afs.org

Australia www.ausaid.org

BUNAC working adventure holidays worldwide. www.bunac.org

Children in Crisis, founded by Sarah Duchess of York
www.childrenincrisis.org.uk

A great site for medics' elective & overseas work opportunities
www.medicstravel.org

CARE and Concern Worldwide are humanitarian organizations fighting global poverty www.care.org and www.concern.net

Christian Medical Fellowship www.cmf.org.uk

Concordia International Volunteers www.concordiavolunteers.org.uk

Coral Cay Conservation are specialists in coral reef and tropical forest conservation www.coralcay.org

International volunteering with www.crossculturalsolutions.org

www.doctorsoftheworld.org.uk

Earthwatch is an international environmental charity
www.earthwatch.org

German Development Agency www.gtz.de/english

Geekcorps promotes stability & prosperity in the developing world
www.geekcorps.org

www.globalservicecorps.org

www.globalvolunteers.org

Japan send volunteers via Go MAD (make a difference)
www.go-mad.org

Worldwide conservation volunteering www.greenvol.com

www.internationalservice.org.uk

Lattitude Global Volunteering is a charity specialising in volunteering
for 17-25 year olds' gap years www.lattitude.org.uk

Mission Finder Database for worldwide mission run organizations
www.missionfinder.org

Medicins Sans Frontiers www.msf.org

www.projects-abroad.co.uk

Raleigh International encourages people to be all they can be through
adventure, challenge www.raleighinternational.org

The tearfund works in partnership with churches in communities to
fight poverty. www.tearfund.org

UN Volunteers. www.unv.org

www.unites.org

www.volunteerabroad.com

International Volunteer Programs Association (NY)
www.volunteerinternational.org

eyeSight

Our greatest fear is not that we are inadequate, our greatest fear is that we are powerful beyond measure. By shining your light, you subconsciously give permission to others to shine theirs.
Nelson Mandela

Travel can be a liberating experience, as it was for me in 1990, when I was just one hundred yards from Nelson Mandela as he was released from prison. I watched this monumental occasion from on top of a traffic light, amidst a sea of enthralled onlookers.

This was the 'green light' moment that inspired the creation of Eye Books. From the chaos of that day arose an appreciation of the opportunities that the world around us offers, and the desire within me to shine a light for those whose reaction to opportunity is 'can't and don't'.

Our world has been built on dreams, but the drive is often diluted by the corporate and commercial interests offering to live those dreams for us, through celebrity culture and the increasing mechanisation and automation of our lives. Inspiration comes now from those who live outside our daily routines, from those who *challenge the way we see things*.

Eye Books was born to tell the stories of *'ordinary' people doing 'extraordinary' things*. With no experience of publishing, or the constraints that the book 'industry' imposes, Eye Books created a genre of publishing to champion those who live out their dreams.

Twelve years on, and sixty stories later, Eye Books has the same ethos. We believe that ethical publishing matters. It is not about just trying to make a quick hit, it is about publishing the stories that affect our lives and the lives of others positively. We publish the books we believe will shine a light on the lives of some and enlighten the lives of many for years to come.

Join us in the Eye Books community, and share the power these stories evoke.

Dan Hiscocks
Founder and Publisher
Eye Books

www.eye-books.com

eyeCommunity

At Eye Books we are constantly challenging the way we see things and do things. But we cannot do this alone. To that end we have created an online club, a community, where members can inspire and be inspired, share knowledge and exchange ideas. Membership is free, and you can join by visiting www.eye-books.com, where you will be able to find:

What we publish
Books that truly inspire, by people who have given their all, triumphed over adversity, lived their lives to the full. Visit the dedicated microsites we have for each of our books online.

Why we publish
To champion those 'ordinary' people doing extraordinary things. The real celebrities of our world who tell stories that celebrate life to the full, not just for 15 minutes. Books where fact is more compelling than fiction.

How we publish
Eye Books is committed to ethical publishing. Many of our books feature and campaign for various good causes and charities. We try to minimise our carbon footprint in the manufacturing and distribution of our books.

Who we publish
Many, indeed most of our authors have never written a book before. Many start as readers and club members. If you feel strongly that you have a book in you, and it is a book that is experience driven, inspirational and life affirming, visit the 'How to Become an Author' page on our website. We are always open to new authors.

Eye-Books.com Club is an ever-evolving community, as it should be, and benefits from all that our members contribute, with invitations to book launches, signings and author talks, plus special offers and discounts on the books we publish.

Eye Books membership is free, and it's easy to sign up. Visit our website. Registration takes less than a minute.

www.eye-books.com

eyeBookshelf

THE AMERICAS / ASIA

	Thunder & Sunshine (Alastair Humphreys)	The Good Life (Dorian Amos)	The Good Life Gets Better (Dorian Amos)	Cry From the Highest Mountain (Tess Burrows)	Riding the Outlaw Trail (Simon Casson & Richard Adamson)	Trail of Visions Route 2 (Vicki Couchman)	Riding with Ghosts (Gwen Maka)	Riding with Ghosts – South of the Border (Gwen Maka)	Lost Lands Forgotten Stories (Alexandra Pratt)	Frigid Women (Sue & Victoria Riches)	Touching Tibet (Niema Ash)	First Contact (Mark Anstice)	Tea for Two (Polly Benge)	Baghdad Business School (Heyrick Bond Gunning)
eyeThinker		•	•		•		•				•	•	•	•
eyeAdventurer	•	•	•		•		•	•	•	•		•	•	•
eyeQuirky					•									
eyeCyclist	•						•	•					•	
eyeRambler														
eyeGift	•					•								
eyeSpiritual														

THE AMERICAS											**ASIA**		

AFRICA / EUROPE

	Moods of Future Joys (Alastair Humphreys)	Green Oranges on Lion Mountain (Emily Joy)	Zohra's Ladder (Pamela Windo)	Walking Away (Charlotte Metcalf)	Changing the World from the inside out (Michael Meegan)	All Will Be Well (Michael Meegan)	Seeking Sanctuary (Hilda Reilly)	Crap Cycle Lanes (Captain Crunchynutz)	50 Quirky Bike Rides...in England and Wales (Rob Ainsley)	On the Wall with Hadrian (Bob Bibby)	Special Offa (Bob Bibby)	The European Job (Jonathan Booth)	Fateful Beauty (Natalie Hodgson)	Slow Winter (Alex Hickman)
eyeThinker		•	•	•	•	•	•							•
eyeAdventurer	•	•				•						•	•	•
eyeQuirky	•							•	•			•	•	
eyeCyclist	•							•	•					
eyeRambler										•	•			
eyeGift	•								•					
eyeSpiritual					•	•								

AFRICA							**EUROPE**						

eyeBookshelf

ASIA / AUS

	Jungle Janes · Peter Burden	Trail of Visions · Vicki Couchman	Desert Governess · Phyllis Ellis	Fever Tress of Borneo · Mark Eveleigh	My Journey with a Remarkable Tree · Ken Finn	The Jungle Beat · Roy Follows	Siberian Dreams · Andy Home	Behind the Veil · Lydia Laube	Good Morning Afghanistan · Waseem Mahmood	Jasmine and Arnica · Nicola Naylor	Prickly Pears of Palestine · Hilda Reilly	Last of the Nomads · W J Peasley	Travels in Outback Australia · Andrew Stevenson
eyeThinker		•	•		•	•	•		•	•	•	•	•
eyeAdventurer	•	•		•		•	•	•	•			•	
eyeQuirky			•										
eyeCyclist													
eyeRambler													
eyeGift		•											
eyeSpiritual													

Region: ASIA (Jungle Janes – Last of the Nomads), AUS (Travels in Outback Australia)

EUROPE / CROSS CONTINENT

	The Accidental Optimist's Guide to Life · Emily Joy	Con Artist Handbook · Joel Levy	Forensics Handbook · Pete Moore	Travels with my Daughter · Niema Ash	Around the World with 1000 Birds · Russell Boyman	Death · Herbie Brennan	Discovery Road · Tim Garratt & Andy Brown	Great Sects · Adam Hume Kelly	Triumph Around the World · Robbie Marshall	Blood Sweat and Charity · Nick Stanhope	Traveller's Tales from Heaven and Hell · Various	Further Traveller's Tales from Heaven and Hell · Various	More Traveller's Tales from Heaven and Hell · Various
eyeThinker	•	•	•	•		•	•	•					
eyeAdventurer				•		•	•		•	•			
eyeQuirky	•	•	•	•		•					•	•	•
eyeCyclist					•								
eyeRambler													
eyeGift	•	•		•		•		•	•	•	•		•
eyeSpiritual													

Region: EUROPE (The Accidental Optimist's Guide to Life – Con Artist Handbook), CROSS CONTINENT (Forensics Handbook – More Traveller's Tales from Heaven and Hell)

Riding with Ghosts
Gwen Maka
£7.99

Gwen Maka, a forty-something Englishwoman, was told by everyone that her dream of cycling from Seattle to Costa Rica, across the deserts, over the Rocky Mountains, and into the sub-tropics of Central America, was impossible.

Riding with Ghosts is Gwen's frank but never too serious account of her epic 7,500 mile cycling tour. She handles exhaustion, climatic extremes, lechers and a permanently saddle-sore bum in a gutsy, hilarious way. Her journey, intertwined with the legends of past events, is a testimony to the power of determination.

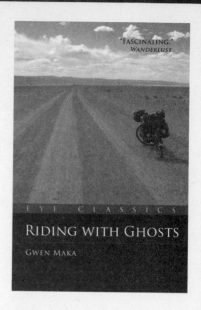

Frigid Women
Sue & Victoria Riches
£7.99

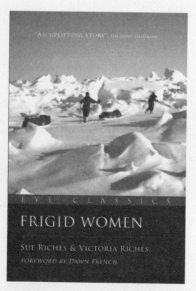

Women wanted to walk to North Pole, the advert read. Sue & Victoria Riches, mother and daughter, never imagined how much one small article in a newspaper would change their lives.... Within two years, they were trekking across the frozen wilderness that is the Arctic Ocean, as part of the first all women's expedition to the North Pole. At times totally terrifying and at times indescribably beautiful, it was a trip of a lifetime. Having survived cancer treatment and a mastectomy it was an opportunity to discover that *anything* is possible if you put your mind to it.

www.eye-books.com

Riding the Outlaw Trail
Simon Casson
£7.99

A dramatic account of what it was like following the trail of the most elusive and successful bandits of the Wild West: Butch Cassidy and the Sundance Kid. An obsessive trouble-shooter and a cool-thinking, ex-Special Forces Marine Commando, with nothing in common but mutual suspicion, join forces for a gruelling, hazardous 5-month horseback journey across 2,000 miles of desert, mountain, canyon & high-plains wilderness through the 'Old West'.

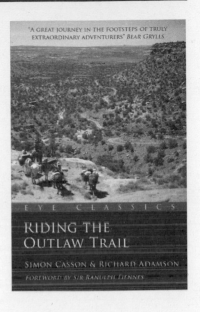

"A GREAT JOURNEY IN THE FOOTSTEPS OF TRULY EXTRAORDINARY ADVENTURERS" *BEAR GRYLLS*

EYE CLASSICS

RIDING THE OUTLAW TRAIL

SIMON CASSON & RICHARD ADAMSON

FOREWORD BY SIR RANULPH FIENNES

Triumph Around the World
Robbie Marshall
£7.99

At 45 Robbie Marshall had it all, or so it seemed. So what on earth made him trade his suit for leathers, his office for the saddle of a great British motorcycle, and his bulging appointments diary for an out-of-date world atlas?

The prospect of a new challenge held such overwhelming appeal that he was prepared to risk it all – his hard-won career, wealth and the love of a good woman – for life on the road, and a life-style completely removed from anything he had known before.

EYE CLASSICS

TRIUMPH AROUND THE WORLD

ROBBIE MARSHALL

www.eye-books.com

Jasmine & Arnica
Nicola Naylor
£7.99

Nicola Naylor had always been enthralled by India, but her travel fantasies dissolved when she lost her sight. Overcoming her own private fears and disregarding the warnings, Naylor set out to experience India alone.

This is the inspiring account of her unique journey. Told with a vivid and evocative insight, *Jasmine & Arnica* is a story of a young woman's determination, a celebration of the power of vision, beyond sight, to reveal what's closest to the heart, and to uncover life's most precious, unseen joys.

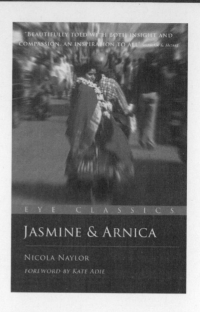

Touching Tibet
Niema Ash
£7.99

Niema Ash was one of the first people to enter Tibet when its borders were briefly opened to Westerners in 1986. In this highly absorbing and personal account, she relates with wit, compassion and sensitivity her encounters with people whose humour, spirituality and sheer enthusiasm for life have carried them through years of oppression and suffering.

Touching Tibet takes the reader on a unique journey into the heart of this intriguing forbidden kingdom.

www.eye-books.com

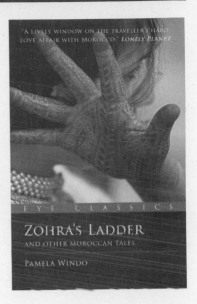

eyeAuthor
Emily Joy

Emily Joy was born in the Outer Hebrides, educated at St John's Primary School in Stockton-on-Tees, Dunblane High and Edinburgh Medical School. Once qualified she spent eighteen months working in New Zealand, eight years as a GP in York and two years with Voluntary Service Overseas as first Medical Officer then Acting Medical Superintendant at Serabu Hospital. She has now landed as a GP in the Highlands of Scotland. Dr. Em finally kept her promise to return to Sierra Leone for six weeks in 2008 with her husband and three children, and again for three weeks in 2009 with a colleague. She is currently working on *The Accidental Optimist's Guide to Gluttony*. Emily Joy is a pseudonym.

Also by Emily Joy:

Green Oranges on Lion Mountain: Audio CD

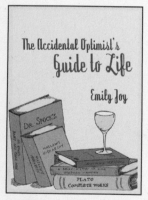

The Accidental Optimist's Guide to Life

So what happens when you find your man? Emily thought she was kind, considerate, good-natured with a great sense of humour, but that was before she had a husband. She thought being the only doctor on call for a whole hospital in Sierra Leone in the middle of civil war was hard, but that was before children. She thought she loved chocolate. Hmmm... she still loves chocolate. If 42 is the meaning of life, then why is it at 42 years of age the Accidental Optimist is still searching? *The Accidental Optimist's Guide to Life* explores Emily's inimitable philosophy of hope and humour through the example of her own ups and downs.

To find out more, or to contact Dr. Emily Joy, visit www.emilyjoy.co.uk

www.eye-books.com

THE JUNKIE

"D r. Em, I no well!" moaned Ibrahim. The monkey had got the last laugh but I bit my tongue. I bent to palpate Ibrahim's abdomen but the pressure of my fingers was obviously too much and he vomited all over me. I tried to catch the worst of it with his chart.

"Theresa, I need a bucket of water," I cried, holding the young man on his side and clutching the vomit-soaked chart with the others.

"Water don don, Dr. Em."

"What! Why is there no water?"

"Sorry-oh. I don only use one bucket all shift."

"Then send Almamy for more." I was beginning to understand Patrick's stance that afternoon.

"Almamy no go fetch water, Dr. Em. He say he here for emergencies."

I pictured him, snoozing peacefully under his woolly bonnet.

"This IS an emergency!" Vomit dripped over the side of the bed onto my foot. Only three days to Freetown, Emily. Theresa threatened Almamy with MT and he trotted off, returning with a full bucket in minutes.

"Well done, Almamy. That was very quick." I gave praise where praise was due and set about washing my hands.

"Very quick. Really very quick." Theresa shook her head and started to wipe the floor.

"Yes, you're right, too quick..."

Laygby burst into the room. "Where is Almamy?" she thundered. "He don thief my water. Now there is none on Maternity."

Theresa shrugged and carried on mopping the floor. I made a diplomatic exit to bed. One day to Freetown, I hummed as I sauntered down to Surgical.

"Urgh!" An overpowering smell of rotting flesh enveloped me as soon as I opened the door.

"Kushe, Dr. Em, this is Gasimu," said Dauda. "His leg don rot."

"Kushe, Gasimu," I forced myself to say. The man lay directly on the brown mattress, surrounded by sodden, stinking, gauze swabs. I didn't add 'How di body?' The answer was blatantly clear.

The infection had eaten down to the bone of Gasimu's foot, and the flesh from his calf was sloughing off in black and green strips.

Mariama had put a plastic sheet under his leg, which seemed to be turning to liquid before my eyes.

"Gasimu get diabetes," explained Mariama. I nodded.

"Tiange is setting up theatre," said Dauda. I nodded again.

"Latif say his blood sugar is forty. Too much high. Dr. Fleep gone look for insulin." Dauda slipped in an IV. "Will I give the antibiotics?"

I carried on nodding dumbly and concentrated on writing up the medication.

"Ah Emily, tu es arrive. We are ready for you." Philippe breezed in and slapped me on the back. "You will have to amputate."

"What do you mean, ready for *me*?" My vocal cords jolted back into action.

"Well you are the expert on amputations now, yes?"

"What? NO!" Last week I had amputated three fingers crushed in a boat propeller.

"Oui. You have amputated three fingers more than myself."

"Hell's bells!" I looked at Philippe in horror. He shrugged and handed a bottle of insulin to Mariama. "Thirty units. Latif will check his sugar in an hour."

"No problem, Dr. Fleep."

"Merci, Mariama. We take him to theatre as soon as his sugar is stable." Philippe briskly wrote his instructions on Gasimu's chart. I gazed at him in disbelief. He couldn't be serious?

"Eh bien, Emily. Shall we find your big book of surgery?"

"Oh hell, oh hell, oh hell." We were reading the three paragraphs that claimed to cover everything one needed to know about amputating a leg. "Let's just clean it up and leave well alone."

"If we take away all the necrotic tissue, we will leave only bare bones. Amputation is his only hope," said Philippe.